THE **EPISODIC CAREER**

THE EPISODIC CAREER

How to Thrive at Work in the Age of Disruption

FARAI CHIDEYA

ATRIA BOOKS

NEW YORK   LONDON   TORONTO   SYDNEY   NEW DELHI

ATRIA BOOKS

An Imprint of Simon & Schuster, Inc.
1230 Avenue of the Americas
New York, NY 10020

Copyright © 2016 by Farai Chideya

First Atria Books hardcover edition January 2016

ATRIA BOOKS and colophon are trademarks of Simon & Schuster, Inc.

For information about special discounts for bulk purchases, please
contact Simon & Schuster Special Sales at 1-866-506-1949 or
business@simonandschuster.com.

The Simon & Schuster Speakers Bureau can bring authors to your
live event. For more information, or to book an event, contact the
Simon & Schuster Speakers Bureau at 1-866-248-3049 or visit our website
at www.simonspeakers.com.

Interior design by Dana Sloan

Manufactured in the United States of America

10 9 8 7 6 5 4 3 2 1

Library of Congress Cataloging-in-Publication Data has been applied for.

ISBN 978-1-4767-5150-4
ISBN 978-1-4767-5152-8 (ebook)

To all of my family past and present, on my American and Zimbabwean sides—the farmers, public servants, military, teachers, and writers, stretching back generation after generation—who worked hard and led me to my own path.

Contents

The way you support yourself can be an expression of your deepest self, or it can be a source of suffering for you and others.

—*Thich Nhat Hanh, Buddhist teacher*

Introduction

The Future of Work Is You

J UST AS I was finishing this book on careers, I ended up at the cross-roads myself, with an apples-and-oranges set of job choices. On the one hand, I know I'm lucky, especially in a volatile economy. On the other hand, I'm terrified of making the wrong decision. One opportunity would lead me to be (at least temporarily) bicoastal, while the other would allow me to remain mainly in New York. I'm also considering adopting a child as a single woman, and my "workstyle"—the place where job meets personal life—has to align with that goal. I could list all the ways in which my choices differ, but suffice it to say that while I write, I am weighing the scales *right now*.

You'd think that writing a book on the future of work in America—specifically on how to find your best and most fulfilling options—would enable me to make a snap decision. Well, not so much. I'm not some kind of job oracle, speaking from the mountaintop. I'm here, right here with *you*, as we both make important choices. Years of reporting and researching this book have exposed me to the many different ways that people think about life and careers, and have given me a big-picture vision of jobs and the economy; they've also helped me understand better my own heart and my own choices.

1

How do the most successful people in America do so much? How do people recover from devastating employment disasters, whether that's getting laid off, fired, or cleaning up the mess left by your own on-the-job mistake? How do we choose ethical ways of earning over unethical ways, if we know we will have to work harder and earn less? And how do we make smart decisions about whether and when to change jobs, when industries change so quickly?

We live in a globalized economy where not just jobs but also entire career tracks are created and destroyed in front of our eyes. Technological innovation is creating immense wealth but, in many cases, eroding jobs. Many people have more flexibility in how, when, and for whom they work; but less stability when it comes to planning budgets, the future, and retirement.

Whether the unemployment rate goes up or down in the short term, we are living in an age of rapid disruption. We can barely adjust to a new reality before a *new* new reality comes along. What we learned about work from our parents and family, or even from our own past careers, might not work for us anymore. Make no mistake: some aspects of work are tangibly getting harder. So how do we evolve?

This book is not about pounding square pegs into round holes—meaning, you should *not* leave work you love just because another field is creating more jobs. It is about figuring out how to navigate the inevitable changes in the job market and making the best decisions for you. I believe real-life stories help connect us to information in a powerful way—a gut-level, soul-level way. So even though this book is filled with data and research, I want you to feel like you're at an incredible gathering full of the most surprising people, and that you can relate to something about all of them.

You'll hear from Justin Dangel, who started three companies before the age of forty, including an auto insurance brokerage with a market capitalization in the hundreds of millions of dollars. Betty Reid Soskin went from working as a clerk in a union hall in the 1920s to becoming an entrepreneur, as she had to create her own opportunity in the face of racial segregation. Now in her nineties, she still works, doing community outreach and conducting historical tours for the National Parks Service. There's Kristine Danielle, who went from being a drug-addicted prostitute to a sober and skilled shipboard welder. Michon Lartigue had to keep her career as a fund-raising strategist going while helping to care for parents ill with cancer. Adam Freed was a reporter who lost his job but then used his language skills to gain entree to a career as a tech executive, starting with Google. Aaron Keough went from being an armored guard transporting money to working in the energy industry by burning the candle at both ends, working and going to school at the same time. Elaine Chen trained to be a lawyer at the urging of her family; but after losing her job during the 1990s recession, she pivoted into tech writing, and then advertising and marketing, taking a practical approach to the constant need to upgrade her skills and build new teams. Each of them has faced different challenges and risen to them, finding new opportunities and gaining wisdom and experience along the way.

Perhaps just one of their stories stands out to you and seems a bit more like your own. But you may be surprised at how much you will identify with the challenges and opportunities facing each of them, and the hundreds of others I interviewed. I also include wisdom from the thousands of people I surveyed. Our lives can be real-life parables, and here you'll be able to access what I've learned from meeting some of the most fascinating people in the world—rich, poor, and everywhere in between—and distilling their wisdom.

This book provides a new map of the job landscape and economy, with hard facts to help you plan your journey. But it's also important to realize that whatever exists *out there* in the broader world of job creation and elimination, *you* have the ability to transform your life right *here and now*. The people I've spoken with, no matter how privileged or challenged, share many traits. One of them is resilience: the ability to recover and grow from what many people would see as setbacks or even shocking reversals of fortune. The victors in today's job market are people who know the landscape, adapt to change, and are willing to reboot and give *of* themselves in order to get *for* themselves. In order to thrive in today's job market, you have to know not only which job sectors are going gangbusters but also what you are truly willing to do—as well as what employers are willing to pay for your particular set of skills, values, and work ethic.

That match between doing and receiving isn't just about your salary, whether you work in an office, on a construction site, or in your pajamas at home, and for how many hours per week. Lifestyle, family, health, and ethical questions are some of the thorniest ones we face.

That leads us to the emerging reality of the "episodic career." In the past, the model (if not always the reality) of a career resembled an escalator. You got on a certain track at a low level when you were young, and as the job "escalator" moved up, you gained seniority and increases in salary—all in the same field. Decades later, you reached the top, where you stepped off the escalator, received a gold watch (or at least a retirement party), and went off to enjoy your sunset years.

But in today's episodic career, you might have to tap into different skill sets at different times in your life. You might not travel on only one career track. You might not be on a traditional track at all. Some people work at two or more similar or drastically different "microcareers" at the same time. Others have several jobs in sequence that seem unrelated, but each ties closely to a different skill or interest.

My mother is a perfect example of the episodic career. When I was a child, she worked at a hospital, which later shut down. Although my mother was a skilled medical technologist, a weak job market meant that her best offer was working the overnight shift at a lab a long drive away. Some nights, my sister and I stayed with my grandparents while she worked. It was exhausting, but my mom found her way into new employment and eventually a new career (her third) as a public school science teacher, which she excelled at for sixteen years before retiring.

Mom's career illustrates the increasingly common model of moving among very different disciplines and using different skill sets. She was a journalist, and then a medical technologist, and then a teacher. Now, in retirement, she is a certified master gardener who leads tours at a local arboretum and also volunteers doing intensive tutoring for children at high risk of falling behind in school, often ones with some instability in their homes. She's used skills she learned in undergraduate education, the Peace Corps, graduate education, and even her childhood 4-H Club to build her career and postretirement pursuits. But, going back to that critical moment when the hospital closed, if my mother hadn't had the family support in order to work the overnight shift, she might have faced even tougher job choices.

None of us has the same exact set of skills or options or attitudes or aptitudes. That's why, as you read on, you'll explore the Work/Life Matrix, a self-evaluation tool backed up by national research that will help you find your sweet spot in this hectic job world of ours.

Your path to a better job—and a successful episodic career—stands on three pillars:

- Self-knowledge. Start with your heart, and you will find which kinds of workplaces and workstyles give you the best shot at success.
- Understanding the job market. Know your field(s) and how the market is locally, nationally, and globally—as well as how it's evolving.
- Emotional resilience. No one, not even billionaires or centi-millionaires, has lived a life without setbacks. And no one, not even the long-term unemployed or people with life, family, or health challenges, is shut out of meaningful work.

There are still traditional linear careers in America: for example, a person who studies science in undergraduate and graduate school, and works as a scientist for her entire career. But the three pillars critical to a successful episodic career also apply to linear careers. It's simply that in episodic careers, there is often more of a need to be self-directed, a more frequent need to make job decisions and evaluate options, and more of a need to evaluate how today's decisions will affect not just today's earnings but also tomorrow's earnings and savings.

The stories and economic analysis in this book can help you focus on the ways that career decision making has changed in the modern era. You'll learn how not to paint yourself into a corner, waiting for a dying industry to recover or deluding yourself that having a higher education alone guarantees security. The tools and stories in this book will help you cultivate the winning spirit within you—and *you* get to define what "winning" is. So many people think success in the career space has to be done on someone else's terms, schedule, or salary level. In the first chapter, we'll explore the ways that the myth of keeping up with the career Joneses actually keeps us from finding happiness. The solution, as you'll see, is as easy—and hard—as embracing your ideal workstyle, and realizing it is yours and yours alone.

I'm thrilled you're joining me on this journey. As you can see, I'm very much on the path with you. So let's get going.

PART ONE

The *New* New
Realities of America
at Work

Understanding how America is working (and not working) is a critical first step to finding your best place in the world of work. Since the Great Recession of 2007–09, America's work landscape has changed dramatically. Many people experienced long-term unemployment that eroded their savings, as did the mortgage crisis. (The average length of unemployment as of this writing is twenty-eight weeks, or more than a half year. But most Americans are living paycheck to paycheck, making unemployment potentially devastating.)

On the corporate side, even companies with big cash reserves have not been hiring at high rates. Overall hiring has picked up since the recession, but labor force participation is not as high as it was before. At the same time, the federal Affordable Care Act (referred to by some as Obamacare), signed into law in 2010, ensured that freelancers—and there are more Americans every day who fit that bill—have new options for purchasing health insurance. People in the workplace are facing increasingly complex choices about how to navigate their short- and long-term options. Understanding the forces on the economy, as well as the role played by our culture and personal desires, can help us frame the issues.

1

Work and the Pursuit of Happiness

WORK IS THE linchpin of American life. We work the longest hours among the biggest developed economies in the world, having outstripped most European nations and Japan, among others. Sure, we complain about not getting enough time off—yet collectively we left 577 *million* earned vacation days unused in 2013.[1] Many of us are anxious, worried that if we don't work those extra hours, someone else at our job will and win favor for doing so. We also worry that we won't have enough to make ends meet. That's *real*. But there's also an emotional and even national component to what some people call a strong work ethic and others call the rat race. In America, work is not just a means of earning a living but also a form of self-definition and a cultural obsession.

If you were to walk into a cocktail party in Paris and, right after being introduced to a stranger, ask, *"Qu'est-ce que vous faites comme travail?"*—"What do you do for work?"—it would be considered *très désagréable*. Yet in many parts of America, that's our opening gambit.

Why? We see jobs as the human equivalent of computer data meta tags; ways to neatly sort people and decide if they're valuable or desirable to us. If you're single, hearing *doctor* might make you think "Good catch!" If you're a job seeker, you might be focused on meeting someone in your field and head to the other corner of the room to see who else is more useful. That's natural, at least in our culture. Still, after my own career ups and downs, as well as our nation's job crises, I've become less likely to judge someone based on current or past employment. I definitely don't presume to know whether he or she is happy or not.

"The pursuit of happiness" is written into the founding documents of our nation. Yet our society puts so much emphasis on work and money as the cornerstones of our dreams that many people imagine that happiness is a luxury they can't afford. (Think of those millions of unused vacation days.) A focus on success by the numbers can undermine the satisfaction that we might gain from a more balanced workstyle.

This book is divided into four parts. In the first, I lay out the landscape of American jobs present, past, and future. You might find this edifying, terrifying, or tedious (if the latter, bear with me—this is crucial). There's no way we can figure out how to plot and navigate our course without good landmarks. In the second section, you get to explore your own desires with a self-diagnostic tool, the Work/Life Matrix. It will give you greater insights into how you want to use your skills and how you want to position yourself within a corporate or independent work structure. You'll take a simple quiz about your desired workstyle and then get to see how people who fit different patterns and archetypes based on the answers succeed. This storytelling-rich center of the book allows you to learn from others' hard-won wisdom. You'll see how different people have navigated their careers; overcome family and cultural programming that no longer suited them; or forged their own paths even in times of hardship. Part three looks at some of the hard decisions that require us to blend head and heart. How do we connect our intellectual knowledge with our intuitive, soulful knowledge? (The Work/Life Matrix will help.) This section covers issues such as the critical role of emotional resilience—that is, how to bounce back from hard times—a skill that you can learn and cultivate. We'll also look at questions such as when job retraining or additional higher education is worthwhile and when it's a potential waste of money and time. Finally, part four examines success, both on your own individual terms and how we can build healthy employment options for America as a whole.

Throughout this book, I'll also speak frankly of the challenges that different demographics face, including employment discrimination. The idea of a modern labor market, with a reasonable degree of protection for people of all races and sexes (though not yet for gay and lesbian Americans on the federal level) is only a few decades old. America's roots include inspiration as well as exploitation. "The pursuit of happiness" wasn't designed for all.

One of the big questions facing this country is whether, in a time of rising income inequality, we can sustain the American Dream. While we focus on the ways that you can maximize your position in the US workforce, we also have to acknowledge frankly the systemic challenges and look at ways that individuals as well as groups can confront them.

Let's start, though, with that vast territory held within our minds and memories. We each bring to any situation a set of expectations about how things *should* be and how things *could* be. Those expectations can cloud our ability to see clearly, evaluate our options, and make the best decisions. Even jobs we love—perhaps *especially* jobs we love—can break our hearts. So let me share one of my own stories from a career that has taken me to Nelson Mandela's house and onto Air Force One but has also tested my limits of endurance and sometimes my finances. I share here for a reason—because I want you to see that I approach the topic of careers and society not just from an intellectual perspective but also from a human perspective.

A few years ago, I was totally ambushed and sabotaged on the job by someone who should have been my strongest ally. She worked me senseless, burned me out, and knew every button to push to make me feel angry or sad or defeated. Yet today I feel nothing but compassion for her. Of course, that woman was me.

September 2006: I had just become the host of the NPR show *News and Notes*, a daily live program encompassing African American issues as well as digital community, national politics, arts, and culture. It was such an honor, and the connection I felt to the audience is still one of the highlights of my career. *News and Notes* had been hosted from the East Coast originally, but since I was out west, taking the host seat initially required waking up at three in the morning Pacific time. Then, after writing and reading through scripts and adding the latest news to the rundown, I had to be lucid at six to talk to hundreds of thousands of public radio listeners. It was the second time in my career that I had unexpectedly gone from reporter to host. Although I was thrilled, I didn't anticipate how profoundly the sleep deprivation and pressure of daily production would affect my body, down to what foods I craved.

My routine changed entirely. Instead of going to see a band or cooking dinner with friends in the evening, I ended my weekdays mindlessly shoving food into my mouth. I remember standing late one night outside Ralphs supermarket in Culver City, a municipal peninsula surrounded by the vast sprawl of LA. It was dark, and the cool night air was a good forty degrees warmer than winter back east where I'd grown up. I was clutching a plastic bag filled with red velvet cupcakes, my drug of choice. And I didn't even like sugar—or so I thought, until my crazy work schedule upended my life.

My first seven months as a host, I worked from four in the morning until one in the afternoon. I'd been dating a guy. I'd be lying if I said we were serious, but he was great: a creative professional and loving dad whom I'd met at a conference. Heck, my mother, visiting from Baltimore, had even met him and his daughter. My regular shift had bonus midafternoon pretapes plus "homework": hours of daily interview prep (including reading up to three books a week). Now catch this: the man I was seeing worked from three to eleven at night at a film production company. And he had his daughter on weekends. So with our schedule mismatch, it's no surprise the wheels fell off that bus, which left me dating Red—Red Velvet, that is.

Red was as seductive as a bad college boyfriend; the kind you know is lifting you up just to watch you fall down. I'd been a stress-driven eater since childhood, but the sleep deprivation changed my patterns from salty-fatty (like mixed nuts or cheese) to sugars. I used the sugar rush as fuel for doing my radio homework, but I had to be in bed by nine. Early bedtime was *so* not my style. I started working at *Newsweek* magazine full-time the summer after graduation, right before I turned twenty-one. I became a fact-checker by day, club kid by night, and went to bed at three in the morning. So going to bed at nine o'clock in LA made me bitter.

Another part of the job I had a hard time accepting was not being in the field—that is, traveling to interview real people with amazing, fresh stories. After joining NPR, my first job as chief correspondent and backup host at *News and Notes* gave me some great opportunities to see the country and tell our stories. In 2005 I covered Hurricane Katrina and its heartbreaking aftermath, and also filed a series of feature stories while driving cross-country. The downside of becoming host was not just the hours (which after several months shifted to a more reasonable start time) but also being lashed to my desk. Instead of making peace with the pros and cons of my job, or leaving, I literally swallowed my resentments in sugar form.

I gained forty pounds in the four years I worked at NPR, which I am still working off. That certainly wasn't the company's fault. I haven't heard of a job yet that doesn't have potential for stress. In my case, I had to help lead coworkers through editorial and emotional changes, as we lost staff positions and worked for more than a year under rumors that the show might be canceled. In 2009 it ultimately became part of a

Great Recession wave of cancelations that took out three NPR shows and dozens of staffers. After the cancelation, I knew I needed to spend some time getting healthier. Yet I didn't understand until I began researching this book how harmful on-the-job stress is to your physical and mental health. Stress even explained the biological basis of my food cravings.

Once I moved back to New York in 2009, I found a new physician, Dr. Roberta Lee, who'd authored *The SuperStress Solution.* In it, she wrote of the recent emergence in many developing countries of the same stress- and diet-related illnesses that Westerners have long experienced, such as obesity, diabetes, insomnia, and heart disease.

"Chronic job stress is as bad for you as smoking a pack of cigarettes a day," Dr. Lee told me. "Your cortisol level rises, and your body goes into fight-or-flight mode." Cortisol is a steroid hormone that our bodies produce in reaction to stress. It's a normal part of our physiology, and when we need it as a "spot treatment," it can be beneficial, giving us energy. But prolonged stress and cortisol production can weaken our immune system, making it harder to recover from illness and injury. Excess, prolonged cortisol also increases our chances of developing osteoporosis, or bone loss, and it can even impair memory.

Sometimes job stress is inevitable, but we can always change how we deal with it. According to Dr. Lee, just taking a five-minute break in the middle of your day—"a walk, or quiet time with *no devices*" (no smartphone, television, or computer)—can reset your entire system and allow you to be more productive. Stress can cause the body to crave sugars, which exacerbates inflammation and generates layers of belly fat. That's exactly what happened to me, and because both my mother and grandmother had double knee replacements due to hereditary arthritis (not from their weight), I knew I was headed for joint complications that could greatly diminish my quality of life. This alarming realization pushed me to lose weight and follow Dr. Lee's advice. I'm certainly no triathlete, but I use my bicycle now for both exercise and transportation, and take time to do high-intensity workouts with a local boot camp. At the height of my job stress, I could have used the calm that follows an intense workout, but I'd convinced myself, quite wrongly, that a cupcake was better for me than a hike. Exercise also produces endorphins, natural pain and stress relievers; and other research shows even a slow, meditative walk in nature without high calorie-burning value is good for our mental health and mood.[2]

To investigate stress-related issues further, I interviewed Dr. Elizabeth Blackburn, a Nobel Prize winner in medicine whose research has centered on cellular aging and *telomeres*. Telomeres are parts of our DNA that protect our constantly dividing and renewing cells from becoming corrupted copies of themselves, which can lead to diseases including cancer. She compares telomeres to the little plastic pieces at the ends of shoelaces that keep them from being frayed. In this case, telomeres keep our DNA from fraying as our cells divide. Telomeres naturally get shorter and less protective as we age, but stress accelerates the process. Studies of caregivers, for example—mothers caring for seriously ill children or spouses caring for a partner with dementia—found that meditation can reduce stress-based damage to the cells.[3]

Sadly, people under extreme job stress sometimes make irrational decisions. Unemployment and job stress are linked to depression, substance abuse, marital problems, and many other difficulties that can destroy lives and families. In July 2015 I ran into a friend at a Maryland arts festival. He told me that a man he knew had just killed his two sons and then committed suicide, despondent after losing his temporary job after years of unemployment. The next day, I read about the incident in the newspaper, and saw photographs of the heartbroken friends and relatives grieving the tragedy. Thankfully, incidents like this are extremely rare, but depression and health problems are common.

In a 2015 nationally weighted survey for this book that I conducted, 61 percent of respondents agreed with the statement "At times I have sacrificed my health and wellness for my job." In truth, stress is always

gunning for us. We have to decide how we can mitigate it, or if we simply need to choose a different job or workplace. I thought about searching for a new job when the strain of hosting a show that was clearly on
the chopping block proved more than I could handle gracefully. But a
voice in the back of my head said, "Good employees fight for their team!
Leaving would be a betrayal of everyone on the show! And it would
show you're not tough enough to mount a proper fight!" Some of that
was my own ego and pride, and some was my family programming.
With parents and elders who were independent African Americans on
my maternal side, and strivers raised in apartheid-like Rhodesia (now
Zimbabwe) on the other, we as a family are not quitters. I was able to go
to Harvard University and have a career because I was supported by my
ancestors—the ones still alive, the ones I knew as a child, and the ones
who fought for freedom and independence before I was born. I believed at the time that leaving my job would betray my family's values.

Once the show was actually canceled, however, I learned that our
team's loss was part of a much bigger fiscal picture, both for the company and for the nation in its Great Recession. Three shows ultimately
were canceled as part of the overall budget readjustments, all of them
based in locations other than the DC headquarters. Like so many people do, I overpersonalized the systemic issues at my company and made
the mistake of thinking that championing my own well-being was somehow disloyal to others.

One of the people I admire deeply both for his work and for embody-
ing a positive approach to work/life travails is Barry Johnson. Barry
worked in the music industry as an executive, did international business
development in President Barack Obama's administration, and now is in
the private sector *and* runs a nonprofit. He grew up in the 1960s in Birmingham, Alabama, a deeply segregated city where in 1963 four little
girls were murdered when racial segregationists bombed the 16th Street
Baptist Church during Sunday services. His family was middle class, but
circumstances still could have limited his opportunities. Yet he kept

growing through adversity. As one of his friends put it, "You were pushed into mud and came up dipped in chocolate." That resilience is key to succeeding—and finding happiness—in today's economy.

Barry uses a daily practice to keep himself focused and his career growing. Every single day, he writes down on a note card a vision of what his life will be like in the near future. Then he sets it aside with other cards in a dedicated space in his home. "There's something profound when you put it on paper, and it gives you something to interact with outside of your own head on a daily basis," he says. "I write in the present tense. It's short, but I actually describe the details of the scene—like reading from a script." He paraphrases: "'I'm working in this space. There are many people around me. They're thrilled about working on the projects around us.'

"Sometimes I will put a date by something," he continues. "I wrote: 'I work for President Obama in this kind of role . . . I start no later than October 19.' I wrote that on August 9. I started work on October 13."

Not everyone will experience the same direct linkages between vision and action as Barry Johnson does, but writing exercises are a powerful way to explore your own heart and desires. Scripting what you envision for your life can be a powerful—and sometimes surprising— way of tapping into your most deeply held feelings. You might not want to write a page or a note card every day, but consider taking a week to write this type of envisioning-the-future every day. Are you writing more about the details of a job you want to have, or do you find yourself drawn to broad ideas about moving into a new field or even a new work-style? For example:"I work doing commercial gardening four hours a day, which keeps me in great physical shape even though it's hard; and two days a week, I work for the catering company. This gives me enough time to spend with my family most of the week." When you look at your note cards, do your dreams seem too small? Too unrealistic? If the latter, what can you do to envision a series of steps between what you're doing now and your desired workstyle?

Learning to focus not just on work but also on workstyle—how work and pay and time spent on the job integrate into your life—is something you can do with a variety of tools, including ones found both in traditional job search guides and in creativity programs such as the book *The Artist's Way: A Spiritual Path to Higher Creativity*, by Julia Cameron. Some people plan through calendars and spreadsheets, knowing the timetables will inevitably change. Others use artwork as a way of visualizing the life they want. Whether you are methodical and have a five-year plan or you want to see where the winds of change take you, it's important to stay in touch with what you envision as well as the realities of day-to-day life. In the resource section of this book, you'll find lists of works that lead you through visioning-as-planning, and how that can help you identify true happiness and fulfillment.

The pursuit of happiness and life/work synergy is vulnerable to your hidden agendas—particularly internal clashes of values, such as "Obey thy parents" versus "To thine own self be true." Elaine Chen works in corporate marketing communications, which requires learning new digital technology platforms and having managerial skills. She also earned a law degree primarily to please her parents, scientists who immigrated to the United States from China. Like her older sister, she was admitted to Harvard. Her mother and father made it clear that their support of her education was based on her pursuing a traditional high-status, high-skill trade. Liberal arts alone would not cut it.

"My parents told me they would take me out of Harvard if I did not basically have a major and have a career path they approved of, which is a lot of pressure to put on a seventeen- or eighteen-year-old who's been killing herself to get into this kind of school," Chen reflects. "As I grew older, I came to understand that that was pretty typical" in Chinese and other Asian immigrant families, "and that they didn't understand why I was so resistant to their demands. I picked law with the full understanding that I was being told, 'If you have interests, and you enjoy music or art, you can do that in your spare time, but work is for making money.

Law is a stable career and it's a profitable career and that's what you're going to do.' So I entered law with the belief that I was here for the money, and I wasn't going to enjoy it."

Eight months after Chen got her first job as a lawyer, the firm downsized due to economic pressure and let her go. She had entered a field that promised security; but the economy after the 1990–91 recession proved that promise false. Today there is an even greater oversupply of lawyers. As *Forbes* contributor Paul B. Brown wrote:

Let me go back up 30 years.

I went to Rutgers Law School at night and it was ridiculously hard to get into back then . . .

There were 60 of us who started. Some 40 graduated and 30 of us passed the bar on the first try.

Of those 30 kids, only three of us should have been lawyers . . .

A random survey shows they think it is an okay way to make a living, but with the exception of Rob, Karen and Bill, no one seems emotionally fulfilled.

So, why then did they (and I) go to law school? Well, then—like now I believe—the majority of students went because they didn't know what else to do.[4]

There are many reasons for what's now being called the "lawyer glut," including that law schools ramped up enrollment and the number of lawyers in America tripled in the past forty years.[5] Consequently, law school enrollment has been dropping. Elaine learned early on in her career what our nation is learning collectively now: that relative job security, even in long-respected fields, changes constantly. Elaine went through many understandable moments of fear and anger—after all, she and her family spent tens of thousands of dollars paying for that law degree, and yet she had not reaped the expected high-status, high-paying career.

Ultimately, she turned an experience that could have left her bitter into a launching pad for new careers: first as a reporter covering the mobile technology industry; and then in marketing/digital strategy. In a sequence common to episodic careers, Elaine used skills she had already to gain new skills and find new career directions. Improving her writing as an undergraduate and during her brief time as a lawyer positioned her well to become a writer-reporter. The tech insights she learned from reporting on mobile technology allowed her to shift into marketing for companies with a strong technology base. Her current field offers her a good chance of remaining well employed as long as she continues to update her skills. And if or when that is no longer the case, she remains the kind of practical and self-analytical employee who is willing to seek out new skills and opportunities in different fields. (We'll hear more of Elaine's story later on.)

Happiness is certainly not the only goal of work. Some people would argue that it is trivial compared with the financial aspects of earning a living. But of course, the two are related. The Gallup organization estimates that worker disengagement—or people being mentally and emotionally "checked out" of their jobs—costs $300 billion per year in lost productivity. Harvard Business School professor Teresa Amabile and researcher Steven Kramer looked at that finding as they ran a study of thousands of daily diary entries by a cohort of workers. As they wrote in the *New York Times*, "The results [of our research] were sobering. In one-third of the 12,000 diary entries, the diarist was unhappy, unmotivated or both. In fact, workers often expressed frustration, disdain or disgust . . . Conventional wisdom suggests that pressure enhances performance; our real-time data, however, shows that workers perform better when they are happily engaged in what they do."[6]

"The pursuit of happiness" on the job can be frustrating when we feel consumed by external pressure from peers, partners, or family; financial constraints; or internal pressure about what constitutes success. And episodic careers—where many of us switch fields or jobs more

often than in the past—place more responsibility on us to be flexible
and resilient, and also to champion our health and happiness. But just
because we sometimes find ourselves mercilessly teased by this elusive
thing called happiness does not mean that we shouldn't pursue it. True
happiness, as the Gallup study and many more indicate, is a key factor
in productivity and creativity. This is not the trivial form of happiness,
but the deep pride that comes from a job well done and fairly compensated, whether that job is minding small children, serving customers in
a deli, or running a research lab.

Employers have to take responsibility for their side of the bargain.
As Kramer and Amabile wrote, "Unfortunately, many companies now
keep head count and resources to a minimum, and this makes progress
a struggle for employees. Most managers don't understand the negative
consequences of this struggle. When we asked 669 managers from
companies around the world to rank five employee motivators in terms
of importance, they ranked 'supporting progress' dead last. Fully 95
percent of these managers failed to recognize that progress in meaningful work is the primary motivator, well ahead of traditional incentives
like raises and bonuses." They concluded, "Working adults spend more
of their waking hours at work than anywhere else. Work should enno-
ble, not kill, the human spirit. Promoting workers' well-being isn't just
ethical; it makes economic sense."

I think of the "the right work" as work that suits you. It's ethical, and
you're fairly compensated for it. The phrase is inspired by the Buddhist
tradition of "right livelihood," a version of which is found in every major
religion and secular humanist tradition. For example, the Bible's Book
of Proverbs includes the statements "Better is a poor man who walks in
his integrity than he who is perverse in speech and is a fool" and "Wealth
obtained by fraud dwindles, but the one who gathers by labor increases
it." In a time of repeated financial scandals—from negligent lenders
who took people qualified for traditional loans and pushed them into
subprime mortgages to gain higher fees, to banks that hid money be-

longing to dictators and terrorists—it's easy to be cynical about money and ethics. But most of us have the opportunity to shape the ethical environment of our workplaces in ways big and small, and we shouldn't take that lightly.

Of course, paid work is, fundamentally, a transaction between employee and employer. We are living through times where workers are increasingly productive, but employers are not raising wages. And in many cases, they are also shrinking benefit packages—sometimes even changing pension and retirement health care benefits retroactively. For example, shortly after buying the venerable but financially vulnerable newspaper the *Washington Post*, billionaire Amazon founder Jeff Bezos ended the pension system that older employees had relied on for their retirement years. Yes, he offered them a fund in exchange, but it was not expected to have the same stability or dollar yield as the pensions. Employees who usually covered the news made news by picketing in the streets.[7] Without Bezos's purchase, the paper as a whole might have faced a less promising future, but with these retirement changes, certain employees felt they personally faced a less promising future.

Professor Carl Van Horn directs Rutgers University's John J. Heldrich Center for Workforce Development. In his 2013 book *Working Scared (Or Not at All): The Lost Decade, Great Recession, and Restoring the Shattered American Dream*, Van Horn wrote, "[Most] American workers want more than just a good day's pay for a good day's work. Rather, they expect their steadfast contributions to a company to be rewarded with a 'permanent job' that enables them to retire with dignity. Naturally, employees hope for reciprocity from their employers. If they are loyal and work hard for the firm, they expect loyalty and honest dealings from their employer." But according to data from the Heldrich Center's surveys, which tracked twenty-five thousand people between 1998 and 2012, "More than eight in ten (85 percent) workers said that they were loyal to the organization where they work, but only 63 percent said that their employers were loyal to them." The news is even worse when it comes to overall job satisfaction, which according to its data dropped from 59 percent in 1999 to 25 percent in 2009. (Admittedly, 2009 was during the worst of the shock of the Great Recession.)

Research such as Professor Van Horn's raises plenty of questions for anyone seeking satisfaction through work. First of all, the concept of the "permanent job" is yielding to new realities of episodic employment. That can be sequential: one job or career path following the other, as in my mother's case. Or, as is my case right now, episodic careers can also involve doing different types of work simultaneously. I am currently a journalism professor, an author, a media consultant, and a freelance broadcaster. I get paychecks, and I write paychecks. I worry, quite often, about matching the ambitions of my ideas with the realities of my budgets. I have flexibility and freedom but constantly have to ride herd over demanding projects and give each of them its due. And, of course, all of this affects my own personal finances. For now I am a writer at FiveThirtyEight.com and a visiting professor at New York University. The job decision I had to make that I mentioned in the introduction would not take me from academia but complement it, although it would require constant long-haul travel for me to do both. Nothing is perfect, and certainly it never will be, for me or for anyone.

But "happy" doesn't rely on "perfect." It's a paradox. Happiness, in work and life, is a state of being that comes ultimately from within, yet most of us (except the most highly emotionally trained) need certain minimum external requirements to sustain our inner glow. That can include a minimum income. For example, research by economist Angus Deaton and psychologist Daniel Kahneman suggests that there is little difference in happiness between people who earn $75,000 a year and those who earn more. (Of course, the spending power of $75,000 in Canton, Ohio, is very different from $75,000 in Los Angeles.)[8] It can also include feeling respected or feeling a part of something (an employee peer group, a local community, a family, or a circle of friends as "chosen family") as opposed to apart *from* something.

Elaine Chen, for example, says one of the things she loves most about work is feeling part of a community of peers and, as she becomes a more senior manager, being a fair manager and mentor to younger employees. She enjoys organizing social and holiday outings for her company, and employees tell her regularly how much it means to them that she treats them as a community. Yet she switches jobs every few years, usually remaining friends with some but not all of her former colleagues. Her attitude toward "work community" is that you create a collegial environment wherever you go, but she doesn't expect that environment to remain the same. It changes through attrition and addition even as she remains at a company. She has a permanent attitude toward work and employment, but not a permanent job.

So: Do *you* feel as if you have a "permanent job"? If so, what would it mean to you, financially and psychologically, if that job disappeared or changed radically? Do you have sufficient savings to weather a period of transition? How would it affect you to change how you describe yourself to people? (Think again about how often we ask, "What do you do?")

When I got laid off from my radio hosting job, I felt at a loss for how to describe who I was and what I was doing. I threw myself frenetically into multiple projects in an effort to reclaim some sense not just of what I did but also of who I was. In the intervening years, I found out something delightful: even though I faced financial challenges by not working full-time for one employer, I began to see more clearly what happiness actually meant to me, on and off the job. I returned to old personal pursuits, like visual art. I took up some new ones, like Cuban salsa. I visited several more countries and began doing travel writing. I got serious about examining my options for adopting a child.

When it came to work, I realized how much mentoring of young journalists I'd done and how much it meant to me. I applied to teach at Harvard's Institute of Politics for a semester, an honor I was thrilled to receive. Being back at my alma mater and teaching the current crop of young leaders—who took me to an improv show by a troupe I'd belonged to two decades before—filled my soul. And so I began to search for a faculty position and was delighted to get one at New York University.

This is where my life can start to sound charmed and magical and privileged. It's certainly privileged, but not easy. Even given the happy "ending" to my still-unfolding story, I've had to accept a level of uncertainty about my work and career path that seemed unthinkable when I was a cub journalist in the early 1990s. I've never faced life-altering financial distress, but I've drifted into and out of credit card debt when I made bad bets on how I would earn a living. Journalism, a vocation I fell in love with—and that allowed me to see the world and grow as a person—has lost thousands of jobs since I started my career. *Newsweek* magazine, the first place I worked and where I was trained by a series of extraordinary journalists, passed through a series of owners and redesigns, ending up with a much smaller audience and circle of influence. Journalism turned out to be even more volatile than the labor market at large. Academia fulfills my calling to teach and mentor—and, unlike my current journalistic work—offers direct deposit. I appreciate both.

If I had to sum up the job market today in one word, it would be *volatile*, the result of technological and economic disruptions. Disruptive innovation changes entire markets, which can provide new jobs and means of growth but often displaces workers in existing industries. We humans have a tendency to romanticize or demonize the past as the "good old days" or the bad old days. As we'll explore in the next chapter, the American workplace has simultaneously become more diverse and legally fair, *and* also more divided by income and wealth. How well we understand work today shapes our choices and options profoundly. After all, unless you know the current state of play—both the challenges and the opportunities—you can't effectively pursue happiness on the job, or off.

2

The *New* New Realities of Work

CHANGE ISN'T ALWAYS good, but it is inevitable. And right now, it's fast, too. As soon as we adjust to one set of expectations about our employment options—what it takes to land a job and how long we can reasonably expect to stay with one employer—the landscape changes beneath us.

A hundred years ago, there was no fast food. Today a staggering four million people work in the fast-food industry, full-time or part-time.[1] There were hospitals, sure, but not with the range and number of jobs that contemporary medicine encompasses, from physical therapists to ER nurses to oncologists. Health care is the biggest growth industry in the nation. And, needless to say, the first modern computer hadn't even been invented—let alone spawned an industry of consumer goods, including our addictive smartphones. Today technology is embedded in virtually every industry, sometimes creating wealth while eliminating jobs. (Think of the self-checkout kiosks at the drugstore and the lost cashier jobs they represent.)

Our workforce has changed just as much as our employment options have. In our country's infancy, 80 percent of paid laborers were male, and our nation had unpaid male and female laborers who were enslaved.[2] But in addition to assuming the majority of child rearing and housework, free women of all races often worked in family businesses, or hired themselves out as servants or farm laborers. A hundred years ago, women held jobs such as garment work and manufacturing. African Americans and other nonwhite workers, as well as women, had little effective labor protection.

Times have changed profoundly. Today 35 percent of the labor force is Latino or nonwhite.[3] Women make up nearly half of the paid workforce.[4] Some states and cities offer legal protection from discrimination for lesbian and gay workers, but the majority don't have a policy that covers both private and public employers.[5] (There is no federal protection for private-sector jobs.) And while immigrants have always been a part of this nation's workforce, the mix of who comes to America has changed. Federal quotas used to restrict sharply the number of immigrants who were nonwhite or non-European. When my father came to America for college in the early 1960s, he later became part of a (small) early cohort of Africans who became naturalized US citizens. Now, albeit with fractious political debate on all sides, America's immigrants come from virtually every country in the world.

I give you this compressed and highly incomplete history for two reasons. One: there was plenty of "bad" in the good old days, and good even among the hardest times. For example, even during slavery, my maternal family consisted of proud, free farmers in Virginia—which became the seat of the Confederacy. Some members of our family still own those farms. Second, and more important for us here, history does not predict the future. Yet you can't even *try* to comprehend what lies ahead without understanding where we've come from. Right now, the crisis of American jobs is provoking widespread social stress, affecting families and communities, and stirring up already percolating debates about the role of women in the workforce, race, religion, and immigration.

I started reporting this book after a radio documentary series I hosted and produced in 2010 to coincide with the midterm congressional elections. The country was still reeling from the Great Recession. My public radio team and I drove hundreds of miles—across first Florida and later Arizona—reporting on how the economy was affecting politics. We found that, as in today's Europe, a lack or *perceived* lack of jobs can manifest as fear of the "other," whether that "other" is based on race, religion, or immigrant nationality. Politics continues to stir the pots of how we talk about jobs: the people who have them, and those who don't. Today the economic blame game has devolved into calling unemployed people lazy. In 2014 Speaker of the House John Boehner said, "I think this idea that's been born over the . . . last couple of years that, 'You know, I really don't have to work. I don't really want to do this. I think I'd just rather sit around.' This is a very sick idea for our country."[6] Jobs and whether Americans were working hard enough to find them also became a hot topic during the 2016 presidential campaign.

Yet the numbers don't say that Americans are lazy. In April 2014 the Economic Policy Institute, a nonprofit and nonpartisan think tank focused on low- and middle-income workers, analyzed federal data from JOLTS, the Job Openings and Labor Turnover Survey. As the analysis put it emphatically:

The total number of job openings in April was 4.5 million, up from 4.2 million in March. In April, there were 9.8 million job seekers (unemployment data are from the Current Population Survey), meaning that there were 2.2 times as many job seekers as job openings.[7]

Put another way: job seekers so outnumbered job openings that more than half of job seekers were not going to find a job in April no matter what they did. In a labor market with strong job opportunities, there would be roughly as many job openings as job seekers.

Even today, as this book goes to press, the average duration of unemployment is twenty-eight weeks. By comparison, in the years following the Great Depression, it reached a high of forty weeks in 2011, but before 2008 had spiked above twenty weeks only briefly. In other words, not only are jobs genuinely hard to find for many people, but also, since 2008, those out of work spend more time looking, although the situation has begun to improve.[8]

There's also the issue of "disruptive innovation," a term used to describe what happens when the wide adoption of a new technology creates jobs and wealth—but often destroys other jobs or industries in the process. Early in the 2016 campaign, candidates Hillary Clinton and Jeb Bush sparred over whether the ride-sharing service Uber—widely considered to be a disruptive company, and one then embroiled in legal battles over whether its drivers were employees or independent contractors—was a model that America should embrace or one that exploited workers.

Uber, founded in 2009, is now valued at $50 billion. By offering a smartphone-based platform for drivers to connect with customers—but not, in most cases, absorbing any costs such as insurance and not requiring drivers to have livery licenses—the company has changed not only ride sharing but also the taxi industry. In many big cities, taxi medallions were high priced and hard to get—sold in limited quantities by the city and resold by drivers. With the rise of Uber has come a drop in the value of taxi medallions, which some drivers viewed as a key asset the same way that other people viewed the value of their homes. A 2015 article in *USA Today* charted the falling value of a New York City taxi medallion from a staggering $1.2 million in the spring of 2014 to $870,000 a year later.[9] You don't have to disagree with the business model of Uber to see how taxi drivers who bought high could be bankrupted in this new era. Not all types of disruption are this dramatic, but our society is full of examples of how technology has changed the job market—including online delivery services offering both cooked food and groceries, and Airbnb offering an alternative to hotels. Part of working, earning, and saving today is keeping an eye on trends in the marketplace so that you can protect your own interests.

Not even the best analysts can predict every bend and curve on the economic road ahead. During the winter of 2014–15, there was a rise in hiring.[10] During the following summer of 2015, global stock markets stumbled, no doubt changing the hiring plans at some domestic and transnational corporations. My survey research from 2015 shows how profoundly anxiety about the economy is affecting Americans. For example:

- 20 percent of respondents agreed with the statement "I work multiple part-time jobs, but would prefer to work one full-time job."
- 27 percent disagreed or strongly disagreed with "I believe jobs in my current field will become more plentiful and easier to find in the next five years."
- 34 percent disagreed or strongly disagreed with "I believe that I will have better work opportunities in five years than I do today."
- And another 34 percent disagreed or strongly disagreed with the statement "I believe most Americans will have better job opportunities in five years than they do today."

We can get a sense of how people deal with uncertainty from what happened in America during the recent past, the Great Recession that began in December 2007 and ended officially in June 2009 (with a *very* long tail of long-term unemployment). It upended the fortunes of millions of Americans. I want to tell you about one of them: Hazel Shaw of Yuma, Arizona.

Hazel exudes a youthful exuberance after making a comeback from homelessness. You'd never know she's been through hell. She radiates joy, which I found humbling, since I can spend so much time on needless worry. When I met Hazel, she was fifty-eight, round faced and round figured, with nut brown skin and short, curly hair. She wore an intriguing little gold pin on her T-shirt: kind of a circle with an upturned curve under it. Turns out, it was originally an angel; now just the wings and a halo.

"Her body fell off," Hazel said with a gentle smile. "I wanted to keep her because she still had wings, so she could fly. I never threw her out, and I wear her every day."

The broken angel that can still fly is a perfect totem for Hazel. She spent what should have been her most secure career years living on her retirement savings and eventually moving into a homeless shelter. We met at the offices of the Yuma Private Industry Council (YPIC), a campus of low-slung buildings where the town's unemployed come to look for work. And there are a *lot* of unemployed in Yuma, Arizona, a hot desert city that used to be a gem of the Old West. It sits on the borders of both California and Mexico. When I visited her there in 2010, Yuma's unemployment rate was 26 percent.

Hazel has a master's degree in public administration and had worked doing human relations for the city government for over twenty years. She is more of a cautious career planner than a risk taker (a type we'll discuss extensively in the Work/Life Matrix section of the book), but life threw her a curveball: Hazel's father got sick in 2009, and she couldn't get a leave of absence, so she quit her job in human resources and moved to rural North Carolina to take care of him. She figured she'd eventually return to Yuma and pick up where she left off. But by the time her father died, the aftershocks of the Great Recession rendered her sparkling résumé just another useless piece of paper. People who value long-term job stability and favor caution in their choices can sometimes misjudge how important it is to remain aware of fluctuations in the job market. Thus, Hazel came back to Yuma and searched for jobs, but to no avail. Dollar by dollar, her personal and retirement savings dwindled until, finally, they were utterly depleted.

"The day that everything was gone, and I moved out of my condo, the only place taking anyone in was the family shelter at Crossroads Mission," Hazel said. Her son was in Phoenix, going to college and living with roommates, so he couldn't help her. "My landlord actually gave me forty dollars back from the rent so I could sleep in a hotel that night and at least take a shower and feel clean." The tone of her voice was soft, not at all self-pitying. "I went to a cheap motel and slept on a bed and cried all night. The next morning, at eleven o'clock, checkout time, I got in my car with all my belongings and went to the Crossroads Mission."

The shelter was generally well run but was filled with people who lived unstable lives, and some who took their frustrations out on others. There was petty theft, and tempers were short. Single mothers with children were also housed there, so Hazel often found herself barely able to sleep with the children crying around her. She spent up to seven hours a day at the YPIC center's computers, looking for work, but that didn't yield many job leads. (Computer-based job searches alone are not as effective as you might think, except in certain fields, such as computer coding.) But Hazel also started volunteering around the shelter, resolving conflicts and pitching in when Crossroads needed office assistance. Hazel also favors doing work that builds and strengthens community (or "high-social-impact work") as part of a team, and her unpaid service impressed the staff. The shelter gave her a temporary job as a clerk in human resources.

Hazel mused, "If anybody had told me five years ago that I would end up being homeless, I never would have believed it." But her focus on helping others paid off in unexpected ways. In April 2012 the fifty-year-old Crossroads Mission opened a new family shelter in Yuma. Today Hazel Shaw is its full-time human resources coordinator, no longer homeless, and earning a living wage. Her broken angel has flown once more.

Hazel's story is a triumph of human will, but it came at a great emotional and financial cost. Because she wanted to believe that relief was on the way and that the next good job was just down the road, she depleted her retirement savings completely. Now at an age when many people are planning their retirement, Hazel is making up for lost time. "Things happen, and you try to make the best of them," she said simply.

Today all jobs are "glocal"—affected by a mix of local, regional, and global factors. Yuma has to deal with the thorny issue of how the labor market functions on the border. Many local workers are seasonal migrants, documented and undocumented, from Mexico and Central America. Without them, the city would not be able to staff the lettuce fields growing improbably in this arid but heavily irrigated climate. The US military (army, air force, plus border patrol) is the largest local employer. As other sectors in the local job market have shrunk, the border patrol has grown rapidly in size due to a steep post-9/11 rise in federal funding. In the late eighteen hundreds, Yuma, located at a narrow point in the Colorado River, was a distribution and waypoint for goods shipped from other parts of the world and the nation. But modern roads and transit eroded that industry.

Hazel's story also illustrates the fundamental difficulties of combining adult caregiving, child rearing, or both with a steady job. Although we have a federal Family and Medical Leave Act, it allows a maximum of twelve weeks away from the job per year. Thinking that her work history would make her easily reemployable, Hazel didn't want to restrict her time with her dying father. Unable to forge an agreement about returning, she quit rather than take limited leave or force a formal firing. The latter option would have harmed her résumé, but at least she would have been eligible for unemployment benefits during her financial distress. Quitting a job, of course, disqualifies you.

One of the biggest debates right now about how we work and whether it makes us happy is whether we can live full lives while going gangbusters at work, including whether and how people can build families and succeed at the job. I ran a three-hundred-person, nationally weighted survey in August 2015—a follow-up to a larger one from the previous year—that asked questions about work/life synergy. Seventeen percent of people surveyed agreed or strongly agreed that work interfered with their role as a parent or caregiver, versus 24 percent who disagreed or strongly disagreed. Sixteen percent agreed or strongly agreed that it interfered with their role as a spouse, versus 28 percent who disagreed or strongly disagreed. One question asked them to respond to the assertion "I delayed or chose not to marry or become a parent because of my job or career." Six percent delayed marriage. Nine percent chose not to marry. Eight percent delayed having children, and an equal number chose not to have children—all of which they attributed to their work.

As one example of work/life issues laid bare, a *New York Times* article from August 2015 (the same month as my survey) painted a blistering portrait of white-collar employment at the online retailer and tech company Amazon. In addition to long hours and a performance review process that former employees says encourages anonymous "tips" downgrading fellow workers, the company's human resources policies around family and health came in for scrutiny. In one anecdote, a supervisor admitted telling a woman she would not succeed because she had children. (Both she and the supervisor later left the company.) The article also reads in part:

> A woman who had breast cancer was told that she was put on a "performance improvement plan"—Amazon code for "you're in danger of being fired"—because "difficulties" in her "personal life" had interfered with fulfilling her work goals . . .
>
> A former human resources executive said she was required to put a woman who had recently returned after undergoing serious surgery, and another who had just had a stillborn child, on performance improvement plans, accounts that were corroborated by a coworker still at Amazon. "What kind of company do we want to be?" the executive recalled asking her bosses.
>
> The mother of the stillborn child soon left Amazon.[11]

Amazon does not offer paid paternity leave, although some other tech-fueled companies have begun offering generous benefits, with Netflix changing its policies to offer up to a year of paid parental leave. The point here is not to argue that Amazon is the only company with these issues (CEO Jeff Bezos decried the "shockingly callous management practices" depicted in the story), but to show that even the most successful corporations are places where work/life problems can become profound.[12]

Government and corporate policies have changed much more slowly than the American workforce, which includes a far vaster number of working women and working parents than in the 1950s or 1970s. In her book *The War on Moms: On Life in a Family-Unfriendly Nation*, Sharon Lerner points out that China has nationally mandated paid maternity leave (ninety-eight days at full salary), but the United States has no such federal policy. She calls attention to nations such as Sweden, where parents are allowed to work reduced hours with benefits until their youngest child is eight. In Germany, which has a robust economy, expectant mothers get six weeks of fully paid prenatal leave and eight weeks of fully paid leave after a child is born. In fact, the mother's taking the eight weeks after a child is born is *compulsory*. Two parents filing for leave jointly can receive two months of paid leave at the same time once a child is born, and parents also have the security to take leave and return to their jobs until a child is three.[13] Simon Vaut, a German political strategist and liaison to the European Union, says that when his sister-in-law had a child, the couple followed that plan: both parents spending two full months with their newborn, and then both working part-time and having more time to nurture their growing baby. Vaut adds that policies like these actually encourage both family and economic growth. In some parts of southern Europe, where there are less-family-friendly policies, births have fallen below replacement level—meaning that populations will shrink (unless there is heavy immigration), and, likely, so will the economies.

This isn't just about working mothers. Clearly, these policies benefit working fathers too. Many psychologists who study death and dying say that the biggest regret men express on their deathbeds is that they didn't spend enough time with their children. Bronnie Ware, a palliative care nurse who wrote a book called *The Top Five Regrets of the Dying: A Life Transformed by the Dearly Departing*, says that almost all of her male patients told her they wish they hadn't worked so hard or so much. "They missed their children's youth and their partner's companionship," she said in an interview with the British newspaper *The Guardian*. "Women also spoke of this regret, but as most were from an older generation, many of the female patients had not been breadwinners. All of the men I nursed deeply regretted spending so much of their lives on the treadmill of a work existence."[14] Let's think of it another way: these men didn't make the choice to work too hard on their own. In many ways, this cohort of men (in families where women did not have to, chose not to, or were sometimes forbidden to work) saw their own overwork as inevitable.

Some men have had the power—both financially and in terms of desire and will—to put parenting first. Scott Carter is the executive producer of *Real Time with Bill Maher* on HBO. He's been Bill's producer for well over a decade, and although I'd been a guest on the show several times, I didn't know until I interviewed him for a podcast I do that he had quit working with Bill for a time. "We were working five days a week on *Politically Incorrect*," Carter says of the show, which was first on Comedy Central and then on ABC. "I never got to eat dinner with my kids. So I told Bill I had to quit. After the show got canceled by ABC in 2002, Bill called me up and told me he was moving to HBO, and he wanted me back. I told him I couldn't do five nights a week. He said it would only be one night a week, and I said yes." Carter also said that the executive producer of the popular sitcom *Everybody Loves Raymond*, which ran for ten seasons, made sure that his writing staff was out the door by six o'clock. "He wanted them to go home and enjoy their families so they had stories they could bring back—something to write about. I don't know why more shows don't do that," Carter said.

There are also key global economic questions around life/work balance, happiness, family, and particularly gender. In the words of Alec Ross, former senior advisor for innovation to US Secretary of State Hillary Clinton, "The best case for empowering women at all segments of the economy has less to do with fairness and more to do with arithmetic. There is no stimulus program, there is no austerity program, that can produce the kind of economic growth that empowering women at all segments of the economy can." In some parts of the world, the full participation of women in the economy would bring estimated double-digit gains in gross domestic product (GDP), or national value added via work and enterprise. In America, women's full participation would bring a rise estimated to be 5 percent—a huge bump up when you consider that our GDP was $17.8 trillion in the second quarter of 2015.[15]

Ross's wife, Felicity, won the Presidential Award for Excellence in Mathematics and Science Teaching. She later gave up the classroom to care for their three children during his travel-heavy years at the State Department. "A lot of people talk about relationships in terms of balance. The very sad, simple fact of the matter is that most relationships like ours don't exist in balance," he contends. "It requires extreme selfishness on one person's part, extreme sacrifice on another. We need to change a lot of our corporate policies around things like maternal leave. We need to make our workplaces more female friendly. And we also need to change some of our societal norms."

Not all women or couples want children, of course. That does not change the math that more family-friendly policies would be better for our economy, but it's important to acknowledge and celebrate the choice to be what some call "child free." Author Anna Holmes is now a columnist for the *New York Times Book Review* and was once editor of the women's online magazine Jezebel. At the age of forty, she told me that she was writing an essay about deciding not to start a family. "I am not disinterested in children," she says. "In fact, I like children a lot, and my friends who have kids, I'm obsessed with their kids. In fact, if you put me in a room with the kids, I'll pay more attention to them than to the adults. Maybe that's why my friends like me. I'm like a free babysitter," she says with a laugh. "I really enjoy the ways that children think, and I enjoy seeing the world through their eyes. But, well, I've rarely felt a maternal urge. I've never felt a deep-seated in-my-womb urge to have a kid." But she adds, "I don't think if I did have a kid that I'd want to have a child in New York City." While acknowledging that New York kids have some "pretty incredible" opportunities, the city life is also expensive and taxing on parents and children, who often lack regular access to the outdoors.

Yet the debate continues to rage over whether and how women can participate fully in the economy and still (in most cases) be a child's primary nurturer: on one hand, Facebook executive Sheryl Sandberg exhorted women to "lean in" (the title of her bestselling book) and have both family and career; while on the other, Anne-Marie Slaughter quit her high-powered government job as the first woman director of policy planning for the US State Department to care for her two teenage sons. She later wrote a controversial article for the magazine *The Atlantic*, titled "Why Women Still Can't Have It All." Likewise, a couple of personal examples from two women whom most people would consider privileged—MSNBC host and Wake Forest University professor Melissa Harris-Perry, and photographer, writer, and editor Deborah Copaken—offer very different perspectives.

After having a child in her first marriage, Professor Harris-Perry got divorced. She remarried in 2010, but by that time, she'd had had a hysterectomy caused by fibroid tumors. She still had her ovaries, but not a womb with which to carry a child. Yet in 2013 she announced that she and her husband were the proud parents of what she calls her "miracle baby," conceived with eggs harvested when she was forty. Harris-Perry says, "My daughter was born on Valentine's Day. And she was born via surrogacy. I had a lot of angst as a feminist about the idea of surrogacy as a journey. The question of what we think genes are, whether we think kids come to us via nurture or nature is tough. And I am certain after raising a twelve-year-old that there's a little bit of both."

Harris-Perry continues: "The woman who served as my surrogate, she and I had a series of books that we read as a sort of book club together. It was extremely useful for us to engage in reading other people's stories and to then talk about them with one another. It removed some of the emotional angst of saying, 'I feel this way.' Instead, you could say, 'I do not want to be like those awful, intended mothers who are in the book. Please tell me if I ever behave in that way.'" Today she commutes between her university and television jobs, while she and her husband raise their two daughters. But many women delay child bearing past the point where they have viable eggs—and then find out that they can't afford the expense of reproductive technologies. Many women have faced the choice between working and mothering, and made decisions they now regret or regard with mixed emotions.

Deborah Copaken wrote the bestselling memoir *Shutterbabe: Adventures of Love and War* about her years as a young war correspondent. She later went on to become a television news producer, a website editor, and a novelist. She also married and had three children, the oldest and youngest of whom are a decade apart in age. Now, following a divorce and becoming the sole breadwinner of her family, she is deep in debt and can't find jobs that pay remotely what they did when she was younger. While expressing clear and passionate love for her children, Copaken says, "I would say to anyone willing to go into media, are you willing to give up all monetary security? Having kids in a first world country should not bankrupt a knowledge worker. Think of how expensive child care is and how little companies help. My debt started on my maternity leave, and it just grew and grew and grew. Perhaps journalism will become a profession only for those who decide not to have children."

Let's turn from family issues to gender more specifically. Men were more likely to lose jobs in the Great Recession but also more likely to find new ones following it. According to the Economic Policy Institute, "Men lost . . . over 6.0 million jobs, or 8.5 percent of their total December 2007 employment, compared to women who lost 2.7 million jobs, or 3.5 percent. Since the economy started regaining jobs, however, the gender dynamic in job growth has reversed—between February 2010 and the June 2014, men gained 5.5 million while women gained 3.6 million jobs."[16] Some of the hardest-hit jobs during the recession were in fields such as construction. For example, if you recall the housing crisis that accompanied the recession, you may have seen the news images of half-built subdivisions sitting unfinished because builders had run out of money.

The wage playing field by gender has never been equal, nor is it today. In 2014, women earned 78 percent of what men do. That's up from 57 percent in 1973. What explains the gap today, since, theoretically, men and women have equal work rights under the law? It is due partly to the gender difference in life paths, particularly parenting, as discussed above; and part of it is "unexplained"—meaning, unlikely to be caused by anything except gender bias itself. The report *Behind the Pay Gap* by the American Association of University Women Educational Foundation found that among college graduates, 12 percent of the gender pay gap was unexplained by career paths and work experience. The report's authors add: "Among women who graduated from college in 1992–93, more than one-fifth (23 percent) of mothers were out of the work force in 2003, and another 17 percent were working part time. Less than 2 percent of fathers were out of the work force in 2003, and less than 2 percent were working part time. On average, mothers earn less than women without children earn, and both groups earn less than men earn."[17]

In 57 percent of married couples in the United States, both spouses work. Before Elizabeth Warren became a US senator, she and her daughter, Amelia Warren Tyagi, wrote *The Two-Income Trap: Why Middle-Class Parents Are Going Broke.* It explores what many people know from experience: that it takes two incomes today to provide the same lifestyle one income provided a generation or two ago. Embracing an episodic career means, among other things, not living beyond your means. In this context, a break in employment could be devastating if you don't realize that most careers are destined to have breaks in employment anyway, and plan accordingly.

In addition, many employers have shrunk vacation time and lunch breaks, and routinely expect workers—especially those who don't qualify for overtime—to work long hours. (Many studies, including one from a 1980 Business Roundtable, found that prolonged overtime decreases productivity in manual labor jobs.) Not just among dual-earner families but also among workers at large, the time crunch can weigh just as heavily as income. If we are crunched for both time *and* money, we have to do some soul-searching—as individuals, in workplaces, and as a culture.

It can be frustrating to consider the impact of government and company policies and globalization, when the issues seem far out of our reach. But the more we understand the big picture, the more we can pick wise options and find our allies. Many organizations across America are working on the national and local issues that affect vocational training, caregiver and parent benefits and leave, and tax policy, just to name a few things I've highlighted thus far. Each person has to make a reasonable assessment of how and how *much* he or she wants to engage with structural reforms in the workplace while earning a living. For example, a friend of mine got a senior management position in a large international company. An African American who had spent years in a small remote office, working with distinction, she moved to headquarters and hired a career coach to help her sort through how to deal with the demands of central management. One bracing bit of advice from her coach: *"You didn't come to liberate everyone else."*

What the expert meant by that provocative statement was that my friend had to take care of herself before she could help anyone else. So, if this newly promoted manager has a choice to (a) transform her company deeply from within, while shoring up her power base for big negotiations, or (b) choose smaller but worthy battles that put her out of favor with management, what should she do? The answer is both devastatingly simple and utterly complex. She has to pick strategies for navigating her workplace that are true to both her short- and long-range goals, so that she can have the highest transformational impact. Sometimes that means laying it all on the line and addressing issues head-on, but it can also mean documenting what's going on in the workplace and staging strategic interventions more meaningfully but less often.

During my own career, I have sometimes challenged management over issues of gender or race, among others. (One example was when a female-led group of employees felt that they were being shut out of a specific discussion with the CEO. I brokered a discussion, annoying the CEO, but the women-led group's idea was ultimately deemed the best thinking on the topic.) Unfortunately, the exchange wasn't good for my relationship with the executive, echoing an article I read later in the *New York Times*, coauthored by Sheryl Sandberg, "Speaking While Female," citing studies showing that women who offer useful suggestions or data often receive less favorable ratings from male managers.[18]

I don't regret speaking up *at all* on a level of principle, but I now realize there is often a choice between playing a long game and a short game when it comes to workplace fairness. Sometimes an immediate "win" in a battle creates an enemy who causes you to lose the larger war. How to champion ethics and equality in the workplace for all and at what cost is a topic we'll discuss much more in chapter 9, "Money and Morality."

Let me say this loudly and clearly: few people are getting off easily in this economy. Men (like Alec Ross, quoted earlier in this chapter) can champion gender fairness just as women do; white Americans can champion racial inclusion in the workplace, as my first boss, Mark Starr, of *Newsweek* did as he brought me in. I don't want to imply or pretend that the volatility doesn't affect men, white Americans, or—well—*anyone*. But you may also make different assumptions about your employability and have very different experiences in the job market depending on your race, gender, and sexual orientation; where you live in the country; or your educational and work histories. Much of this book is about tapping into your core strengths, while recognizing that your demographic factors (including race, age, region of the country, education) and psychographic factors (such as appetite for risk, desire to work alone or in teams) are going to affect your ability to find and keep the right work.

Your demographic and psychographic maps also affect how likely you are to advocate for yourself. For example, a manager at a media company told me that all of the white men he promoted asked for additional compensation, whereas none of the women or nonwhite employees did. It's not just about "leaning in." There's evidence that women who negotiate for raises—especially using the strategy of bringing in alternate offers as a base for negotiation—are viewed as pushy or disloyal compared with men who do the same thing.[18] So as you think through what you need from the workforce, I will give you honest feedback about the many factors—from personal desires to skills to societal stereotypes—that could influence your ability to navigate employment.

Carmen Rita Wong examines work from the perspective of a personal finance expert who not only crunches numbers but also listens to people grappling with how to structure their lives and careers, and to protect their families. A former television host on the financial network CNBC and the author of *The Real Cost of Living: Making the Best Choices for You, Your Life, and Your Money*, among other books, she is also the divorced mother of a young child. Carmen, who connects deeply and personally with many of the people who seek her counsel, takes an empathetic as well as analytical approach to what's happening to families during a time of profound financial and career shifts.

According to Wong, "The middle class is squeezed, and part of the reason why is the stagnation of wages and the cost of living. There's deflation"—a trend of lower costs—"on basic items like food and clothes and massive inflation on a couple of other categories. One is education, so you're seeing the costs of middle-class people with children go way up. Another is health care, which, even with Obamacare, is tremendous. This is especially true for the middle class, which is increasingly taking care of aging parents. Seniors suffered hugely in the crash in terms of their housing values and retirement funds, and they're falling back on their children, who are now middle-class adults. There's this really bad confluence of events where certain costs of the middle class, including education and health care, are going up drastically at the same time that they become more essential expenses. Most middle-class people would not consider education or caring for a parent or an adult child as part of their discretionary budget. Those have become essential parts of their budget."

The good news is that Wong believes people have reacted with increasing financial restraint following the Great Recession. "Discretionary spending has shrunk so much among the middle class that I don't know if it even exists. Among some of the big economic changes that we're seeing is a lot more people living within their means," she says. "Part of this is caused by the credit crunch and by a shift in mentality and habits. We've seen big drops in personal debt load, including credit cards and cars. People are also being more mindful in planning for things like retirement. What has really gone up drastically, almost to take its place, are student loans."

While a strong advocate of getting a college degree, Wong warns against the "higher education trap"—seeking an education at all costs, especially taking on too many loans or ones with exorbitant interest rates. "When I talk to large groups, usually middle-class women, I always hear them talk about how they make too much to qualify for financial aid but don't have enough to pay for their child to attend the college that they want to go to. They feel this crunch of the government and lenders saying they make too much money, but they also take care of their eighty-five-year-old mother and are the sole breadwinner because their husband has been out of work. There's just a whole run-up of things that are coming up against the middle class," says Wong. "I could tell them to sell their home and downsize, but that's easier said than done."

It's important to acknowledge the challenges of the current job market without viewing them as insurmountable. Episodic careers, and breaks in employment to transition and reposition, are increasingly becoming the norm. In the next chapter, we'll look at the indicators of where the American economy is headed, a critical knowledge base that will help you understand better how to chart your path.

3

The Economic Long View

MAKING SMART WORK choices today means embracing your inner futurist. No one has a crystal ball, but understanding the factors influencing the American job market is one very important way of examining your options. This can include looking at growth industries and regional job-creation patterns; global economics; and the changing cost of higher education. For a look at the big picture, I turned to economist Austan Goolsbee, formerly the chairman of the Council of Economic Advisers under President Barack Obama. Now a professor at the University of Chicago, and a partner in a firm called 32 Advisors, Goolsbee frames the choices ahead of us in terms of how much we have to take control over our careers and finances compared with the past. For example, there's a challenging give-and-take between employers and employees when it comes to training.

"In the future, where there's going to be a lot of mobility," says Goolsbee, "the willingness of people to want to invest in things [like skills training] that only work at one employer is going to go down. But at the same time, the willingness of employers to invest in job training when they're offering even general skills that you can pack up and take somewhere else is also going to go down."

Goolsbee continues, "So this thinking through lifetime learning is going to be important. Lifetime general skills will become increasingly valued *and* increasingly endangered"—in other words, unlikely "to be provided by your employer. In the old days, companies like Procter & Gamble had a leadership program where they hired people right out of business school. They taught them everything they needed to know about brand management because they're thinking, 'Hey, two-thirds of our guys are going to stay at Procter & Gamble for a whole career. But when the share that are going to stay for their whole career is down to five percent, their leadership brand management program is going to go way down." As Goolsbee sums it up, the impetus is now on employees to think through their own training and leadership paths. "How are you going to get brand management skills? You have to be thinking about that too."

So in addition to looking for a job, staying employed, and seeking better opportunities at that job, you have to think about the skills you are building and how you are going to pay—with time or money—to get those skills. You also have to see around corners, in the sense that you begin to anticipate how your field is changing. For example, I learned HTML (hypertext markup language)—the building block of website design—in 1995 in order to create a journalism site. I didn't create sites for other people, but at the time, it was a valuable skill I could have used on a freelance or staff basis to make money. Since 1995, advances in website development have created all sorts of intermediaries. so you don't need to know HTML to create a site. Instead, you can use tools like Tumblr or Medium that give you easy templates and create the HTML for you. So let's say that back in 1995, you were a hotshot at creating sites using HTML. If you didn't upgrade your skills, today you'd be making a fraction of your former income. In fact, I know several web designers who found themselves slowly painted into a financial corner because their skills became more common and/or outdated, and thus less lucrative.

So the conundrum becomes this: If companies don't want to pay you to upgrade your skills (fearing they will lose you to a competitor), but your career will be at risk if you don't keep up, how do you budget both time and money for training? Many Americans now find themselves working full-time and going to school for short courses; or part-time toward degrees; or even dual-tracking full-time work and full-time school. In some cases, this produces the desired additional income and opportunity. But in other scenarios, it simply means accruing debt and finding that the new skills you acquired are already outdated. This is a topic we'll discuss in depth in chapter 8, "Lifelong Learning, Lifelong Earning." But I bring it up here as one example of the challenges we face as individuals and as a society.

In many ways, we are moving toward psychological self-employment. What does that mean? Well, we each must think like the CEO of our own small company—let's call it Little Ol' Me, Incorporated—even if we have a full-time staff job. So while your staff job might not require you to go back to school or find other ways of seeking out new skills, as the CEO of LOM Inc. you constantly have to evaluate what's best for you in the long run. That involves not only issues such as retraining, but also budgeting for retirement and for periods of short or even prolonged joblessness.

We can't underestimate the importance of this mental shift. It's not about being less loyal to your employer, if you work for a company. It's about realizing that you can truly deliver the best value to a company and to yourself if you're well informed and well prepared. Anxiety is a productivity killer. In a study by the American Psychological Association, a third of workers describe themselves as significantly stressed out at work.[1] And a large-scale study of 22,347 employees in twelve countries by the business firm Towers Watson found that more than half of those who claimed to be highly stressed were disengaged, or what we commonly call "checked out," which means less attention to detail and increased absences from work. But only one in ten of employees who described their stress level as low were disengaged.[2]

Following the Great Recession, many companies cut jobs and expected employees to work more with less help. And this is where employers and employees often part ways. According to the Towers Watson study, half of stressed-out employees blamed their anxiety on understaffing, yet only 15 percent of managers saw this as a cause.

Some of America's business leaders are trying to find new ways to bring employers and employees' needs into alignment. Reid Hoffman (the cofounder of the massive online job engine LinkedIn), Ben Casnocha, and Chris Yeh coauthored a report called "Tours of Duty: The New Employer-Employee Compact." The Harvard Business School's executive summary of the work says in part:

> For most of the 20th century, the relationship between employers and employees in the developed world was all about stability and lifetime loyalty. That has recently changed, giving way to a transactional, laissez-faire approach that serves neither party well. A new arrangement is needed, the authors argue— one built on alliance (usually temporary) and reciprocity. The high-tech start-up community of Silicon Valley is pointing the way—and companies that wish to be similarly agile and entrepreneurial can learn valuable lessons from its example. Under the new compact, both employer and employee seek to add value to each other. Employees invest in the company's adaptability; the company invests in employees' employability. [The authors] outline three simple, straightforward ways in which companies can make the new compact tangible and workable. These are (1) hiring employees for explicit "tours of duty," (2) encouraging, even subsidizing, employees' efforts to build networks outside the organization, and (3) establishing active alumni networks

that will enable career-long relationships with employees after they've moved on.

In the war for talent, such a compact can be a secret weapon that helps you fill your ranks with the creative, adaptive superstars who fuel entrepreneurial success.[3]

Of course, what works for Silicon Valley might not work for Main Street, let alone distressed communities. But the idea of companies encouraging employees to build external networks of contacts is one that does run counter to much current thinking, where employees are often viewed as "fraternizing with the enemy" if they become too close to competitors or even merely companies in related fields. But today there's no question that the *new* new realities of work require broad social networks. More than the traditional job search (like job ads in the newspaper, Help Wanted signs, or even online), a networked job search—where you spread the word among your circle of contacts that you are looking for specific or general opportunities—is proving to be the winning strategy. However, a networked job search is only as good as your network, which we'll discuss in chapter 6, "The *New* New Realities of Job Search."

Economist Goolsbee sees the job situation improving, with caveats. "It was a really unusual, crushing recession, leading to far more long-term unemployment than we have ever seen before in the US," he says, but then adds that we're better off and steadier than we were in, say, 2010. The economic turbulence has also changed how people evaluate opportunity. "People have a taste for freelance that they did not have before," he observes. "The notion that people should be seeking to find one job that they stay in forever—that's just not the way the job market works anymore." In one study by the Bureau of Labor Statistics, younger members of the baby boom generation (those born in the years from 1946 through 1964) held an average of eleven different jobs just between the ages of eighteen and forty-six. Although the bureau hasn't run a directly parallel study of older and younger workers, the evidence is that younger people (millennials in particular) will switch jobs even more often, while older Americans switched less.[4]

Goolsbee adds, "Much of the tension that we've had in the country over labor market policy is rooted in the fact that the job market has transitioned away from the long-term career of one employer. Things like health benefits and pensions apply to full-time workers and are premised on there being career trajectories at one firm." But he says firmly, "We're increasingly not in that world. People are freelancers and contractors, and they're working part-time. I think that has proved challenging from a policy perspective. How do you ensure that people are going to have retirement savings? How do you ensure they're going to have health insurance? How do you ensure all of this kind of stuff when the system that it was premised on has broken apart or fallen apart?"

Goolsbee is hardly a pessimist, but his assertion that the old system has broken or fallen apart dovetails with the rise of the episodic career. Even the figures about young baby boomers changing jobs an average of ten times by the age of forty-six does not reflect the entire picture. A person who, for example, switched jobs eleven times but stayed in the same industry is very different from someone who moves from field to field. Increasingly, people are finding that out of desire, necessity, or a mix, they are leaving behind (or being pushed out of clear) not just jobs but also entire industries.

Let's throw a real curveball: the possibility that unemployment will continue to rise over time, but also that our society can find a way to deal with that and perhaps even improve by it. That's a theory being floated by some economists and technologists, although for their vision to manifest, there would need to be an alignment of economic and political factors—a very difficult task indeed. Before we look at the possible positive scenario, let's be clear about the current human cost of what some people are calling the "jobless future." A 2015 *Atlantic* magazine story called "A World Without Work" looked at the impact of technology on jobs, and the ways in which some people were finding new opportunities, flexibility, and creativity, while others fell into poverty and despair. It examined the work of economists Loukas Karabarbounis and Brent Neiman of the University of Chicago, who found that wages were no longer driving as much economic growth in America, with half of that decline linked to technology replacing humans. As the article's writer, Derek Thompson, points out, "In 1964, the nation's most valuable company, AT&T, was worth $267 billion in today's dollars and employed 758,611 people. Today's telecommunications giant, Google, is worth $370 billion but has only about 55,000 employees—less than a tenth the size of AT&T's workforce in its heyday."[5]

Americans are, in essence, needed less by American and multinational corporations as we transition into a tech-driven society. Albert Wenger is a partner at Union Square Ventures, which manages $1 billion in investment capital and has helped grow companies such as Tumblr and Etsy. He puts things this way:

"During the industrial revolution, we discovered how to use machines to replace human strength. That set up a positive cycle where we figured out how to make things relatively cheaply and how to employ people making things—that cycle of 'You have a job, you make a wage, you use that wage to buy interesting new things.' And we had a lot of innovation, like cars and televisions. It was very positive and produced the standard of living that many of us have experienced. So fundamentally, I am very pro-technology.

"Now we're entering this new phase where we can use technology to do things that have required the human brain rather than brawn. We can in many cases make things with very few humans, or in some cases with no humans. And that breaks the cycle, because if nobody's making a wage, what are they using to buy things?"

But Wenger does not believe the "jobless future" needs to destroy human lives. (Of course, the very term is an exaggeration. Even if it does lie ahead, there will be jobs, just not as many, and they will change in the skill sets they require more often.) First of all, he stresses, "Many jobs out there are not jobs we want humans to be doing. We don't want humans to be driving trucks for eighteen hours, be overly tired, then drive again. If a computer can drive that truck, it's a good thing, as long as we have an answer for what happens to that truck driver."

Wenger advocates a concept called universal basic income, or UBI, which would replace many existing social programs with a flat payment to all citizens that would cover basic living expenses. That would allow people to become entrepreneurs, retrain for jobs, and survive disruptive innovation while new jobs are being created. Proponents—many of them among the wealthiest Americans—contend that UBI could simplify government and provide for a new era of security, abundance, and creativity. "You decouple the most basic income—the one you need to take care of food and clothing and shelter—from everything else," he explains. "And once you do that, then we can embrace automation. It's no longer our enemy. Automation becomes our friend." In addition, many things that we once paid for can now be accessed for free, including online courses and educational resources that people can use to train or retrain for jobs.

Of course, the American political system is notorious for its gridlock, and although Wenger believes that UBI could ultimately unite the left and right by combining wealth redistribution with smaller government, a practical discussion—let alone implementation—seems a long way off. "If you try to construe how to get a universal basic income past the current Congress and the current dysfunction in Washington, it seems like a completely nonsensical uphill battle," he admits. "But if you think of it as investing long term in an idea that could grow over time and could appeal to a very broad part of the population, then it could have legs." In the meantime, however, many Americans are understandably anxious about how they will fare in our time of disruption and change.

Alec Ross, who assessed the role of women in economic development, also offers a sobering assessment of America in an era of globalization:

"It's never been more difficult to be working class or middle class in America, going back to the 1930s. I say that not as a polemic but just as a matter of statistical fact. The degree to which there is not just stagnation but the steady erosion of well-being, purchasing power, and quality of life for everyday working Americans is real.

Globalization cuts both ways. On the one hand, it creates opportunities for very quick upward economic mobility for people who have the skills to compete and succeed in an increasingly knowledge-based economy. But it really hurts those who lack those skills.

The ability to get a job based on the strength of your shoulders with which you can feed your family and for which you have health insurance—those good old union-wage jobs—are largely gone, and I really don't see them coming back, for the most part. In a global economy made up of 7.2 billion people from 196 countries, being American does not advantage you in the way it did in decades past."

Alec lives in my hometown of Baltimore. The people there, he says, "are not competing against people in Pittsburgh and Cleveland for jobs. People in Baltimore are competing against people in Bangalore, India. And so what this means is that education needs to become lifelong—it's not just something you do in high school or college. It also means people have to be comfortable with increasing mobility in their work lives. And the sum of it is that life is only going to get more difficult for working-class and middle-class Americans as our economy grows increasingly interconnected and increasingly global."

Ross favors revamping vocational education to help train current and future workers, and also points to the offshoring of revenues by companies from Apple to Burger King:

"Big companies right now are not incentivized to bring their capital to the United States and are not incentivized to hire domestically. So right now, more than a trillion dollars are abroad, with America's biggest companies basically in tax avoidance schemes. So if we can figure out a way to repatriate those dollars and tie the repatriation of those dollars to domestic hiring, I think that that will do more to structurally impact unemployment than just about anything else."

In fact, in September 2014, the US Treasury Department instituted new rules to make it harder for companies to slash their tax bills by moving overseas using a process called inversion.[6] It has yet to be seen whether the rules will work as designed, as some analysts are already saying that there are large loopholes.

So, are we living in a time of opportunity, challenge, or both? The American Dream is often summarized as a belief that your children (or the next generation, broadly) will do better than you or your generation has. A study by the Equality of Opportunity Project, led by researchers from Harvard and the University of California at Berkeley, found that mobility had not changed much over time—indicating, perhaps, that the American Dream was never as widely accessible as advertised. They did find that it varied strongly by region, with people in the Southeast having far less opportunity to rise in income than those in the Midwest. In general, the project concluded, "Areas with greater mobility tend to have five characteristics: less segregation, less income inequality, better schools, greater social capital, and more stable families."[7] In addition, the fifty-year-old global Organisation for Economic Co-operation and Development (OECD) found that income inequality "can stifle upward social mobility, making it harder for talented and hard-working people to get the rewards they deserve. Intergenerational earnings mobility is low in countries with high inequality such as Italy, the United Kingdom, and the United States, and much higher in the Nordic countries, where income is distributed more evenly."[8] A study of US Census Bureau data found that while better-off Americans have recovered from the Great Recession, others have not. "The top 5 percent of earners—households making more than about $191,000 a year—have recovered their losses and earned about as much in 2012 as they did before the recession," said a summary in the *New York Times*. "But those in the bottom 80 percent of the income distribution are generally making considerably less than they had been, hit by high rates of unemployment and nonexistent wage growth."[9]

American tax policy allows people who gain wealth from investments and inheritances to keep more of their money than people who earn it on the job. And the housing crash during the Great Recession meant that many working people and retirees who had counted on their homes to provide savings found themselves, at best, breaking even; being "under water" on mortgages that exceeded their homes' values; or, as a result of being under water, losing their homes to foreclosure. Thankfully, the number of foreclosures has dropped in most areas, though in some areas, including New York City and Florida, it remains relatively high. There are more arguments than this book is designed to address concerning wealth inequality; however, suffice it to say that while, according to studies from organizations such as the Pew Charitable Trusts, people still believe that the American Dream is possible, many are grappling with how to make it a reality.

There's a grim joke that says if your group of hikers is being chased by a bear, you don't have to outrun the bear—just the other hikers. So you could look at the challenging realities of employment in America as a chance to simply survive; to let others get eaten while you flee. Or, as I hope to communicate in laying out options (via data and stories in this book), we can begin to think collectively. Most of us care about our friends, family, and coworkers. We have two needs that might not always converge: what we need to take care of ourselves and our immediate family, if we have one; and what constitutes collective survival and "thrival." Many people are being urged, consciously, or unconsciously, to try to be the fastest runner in front of the bear of economic volatility. But many of the people in this book do work or service that, even when frustrating, helps others find opportunity.

Of course, the question remains: Where *is* higher ground for American workers? What industries, types of jobs, and types of careers are most promising? How do we navigate toward them, if they appeal to us; or if we feel drawn inexorably to a diminishing industry, how do we find our way within it?

Here's the lay of the land: first, technology is everywhere—in agriculture, education, construction, and the arts. Your specific career might not include technology at its core, but instead of thinking of tech as a sector, it's perhaps more helpful to think of it as a component of many different job types. Yes, being a computer coder or a bioengineer is what we may consider pure tech or science. But as a classroom k–12 teacher, or even teaching English or other languages, you'll be expected to make decisions about how, whether, and when to incorporate software and computers into your students' lessons.

Technological innovation and automation also affect which job sectors are growing and shrinking. In some cases, technology provides new jobs; in others, computers' inability to do everything that humans do (so far)—such as child care—preserves certain jobs. The Bureau of Labor Statistics generates ten-year jobs forecasts. Its 2012–22 projections indicate that the job market will grow more slowly than in the past.[10] In the bureau's words, "The overall labor force participation rate is projected to decline from 63.7 percent in 2012 to 61.6 percent in 2022, continuing the trend from the past decade . . . Slower labor force growth is expected to limit potential economic growth."

This indicates that America is a land that still holds opportunity, but probably not the level of economic growth we saw in the 1950s, when it was experiencing a postwar manufacturing, housing, and baby boom; or even parts of the 1990s, which included periods of intense growth as well as the lead-up to the dot-com tech bust in 2000. I wouldn't advise anyone to pick a high-growth career if it's something he or she hates, but choosing a high-growth field from a variety of appealing choices is certainly a great idea. The same Bureau of Labor Statistics report goes on to say:

- A third of the total number of jobs created in 2012–22 are projected to come in the "health care and social assistance sector." Think not only of doctors, nurses, and home health care aides, but also companies and consultants who help families figure out their best caregiving options. For example, entrepreneur Sheila Lirio Marcelo, a Harvard MBA who found herself part of the so-called sandwich generation—caring for young children and ailing parents at the same time—started Care.com, an online resource for families looking for caregivers. The aging American population, particularly baby boomers entering their senior years (although often still working or volunteering), makes health care a huge job sector.
- As context for health care growth, baby boomers are the largest single population to enter its senior years in American history. (There are seventy-seven million baby boomers, and the oldest among them began entering senior citizenship in 2011.)
- On the flip side, five employment areas are projected to shrink: manufacturing; federal government; agriculture/fishing/hunting; information; and utilities. "Information" is an awfully broad term, but in this case it refers to everything from publishing to television and film to some types of data collection.

There's another interesting note in the bureau's projections. First, the majority of jobs created overall are in sectors that don't typically require a college degree. But in a world where there are more job seekers than jobs, employers often hire college graduates preferentially for jobs that don't really require a degree. (A study by Georgetown University's Center on Education and the Workforce argues that 97 percent of "good jobs" created since the Great Recession went to people with bachelor's degrees.[11]) On top of that, the bureau adds, "occupations typically requiring postsecondary education for entry generally had higher median wages ($57,770) in 2012 and are projected to grow faster (14.0 percent) between 2012 and 2022 than occupations that typically require a high school diploma or less ($27,670 and 9.1 percent)." To make all that jargon clearer: more jobs that don't require a college degree will be created; employers are often hiring college graduates for those jobs; and the fastest-growing and highest-paying jobs do require a degree.

Despite the need to be mindful of higher-education debt, the report also says that jobs for college graduates will grow faster than those for high school graduates or dropouts. According to the National Science Foundation, an independent federal agency charged with promoting science and engineering, only 1 percent of college freshman intend to major in software engineering, a challenging but very secure growth profession. Of the computer science and computer engineering bachelor's degrees granted in the United States in 2010, 14 percent went to women, 12 percent to Asian Americans, 5 percent to Hispanics, and 3 percent to African Americans. These numbers should give us pause as America becomes more diverse.

Knowing what lies ahead will help you shape your own future. You can decide if you're in an industry where you'd be better off to go for full-time retraining or leave the field entirely; or if you need to sharpen your skills (for example, by taking online or short-term courses) to continue to succeed.

In part two, "Your Life's Work: Defining Your Path," we're going to shift gears, giving you a chance to ask yourself four key questions that could change your life. These questions form the basis of the Work/Life Matrix, a tool that will help you stay centered in your own dreams and desires, even as you take note of the massive changes in the job market. Author Aldous Huxley (*Brave New World*) wrote, "There's only one corner of the universe you can be certain of improving, and that's your own self." I personally believe that improving the self can also improve the world—whether that means your family, your community, your nation, or the globe. Americans work more hours, on average, than people in developed economies including Japan and most of Europe's nations.[12] Improving how we work, and our work/life synergy, will have a profound ripple effect not just on us but on our families, friends, and country.

PART TWO

The Work/Life Matrix

Your Life's Work: Defining Your Path

Part two begins an exploration of how we can take control of our work/life based on interviews with Americans of both modest and extravagant means who have found ways to succeed, often against great odds and *on their own terms. And in order to better align ourselves with success, we will use a new self-analysis tool, the Work/Life Matrix, to determine how psychographics—our attitudes and desires about how we work, not just what we do—affects our career choice.*

4

Mastering the Work/Life Matrix

Know Yourself, Set Your Goals, Play by Your Own Rules

THE EPISODIC CAREER combines economic assessments, original data, and deep dives into the human experience. I'm sharing with you what others have shared with me—a wisdom that emerges from story-telling. I like to say that being a reporter is a little bit like sitting in an invisible confession booth. People tell you the most unexpected and honest things, digging down to the parts of their hearts that have been broken and reassembling them before your eyes. Yes, there are the liars and the people who only want to show themselves as heroes. But after twenty-five years as a journalist, I've gotten pretty good at spotting those. What I am constantly touched by is how vulnerable and *honest* people are willing to be when you ask them the right questions.

After the devastating Great Recession that began in late 2007, I re-ported and coproduced, with WNYC and other public media and foundation partners, a series of political reports that all returned me to the question of work. I traveled to cities such as Yuma, Arizona, where, at the time, one in four people was unemployed—*officially*. The figure including what are called "discouraged workers" (people who have stopped looking for jobs) was even higher. Yuma is where I met Hazel Shaw, who became homeless but has since rebooted her life to become the head of human resources at the Crossroads Mission.

A team of reporters and I drove through Miami neighborhoods ravaged by the subprime mortgage crisis. A *Wall Street Journal* investigation found that in 2005–06, more than half of all home buyers who got saddled with costly subprime loans actually qualified for regular loans but, unbeknown to them, were steered by unscrupulous lenders into these moneymaking schemes.[1]

Work is about many things: being able to support yourself or your family; keep a home; make an impact on the world in ways private or public. And as we've discussed, work is a source of pride in American life. Even people who have been sidelined in the US economy embrace work as a source not only of income but also of identity. I'm talking about people in shrinking industries; people in areas with high regional unemployment; and parents who find that their salaries barely pay for child care. Yet we persist in working, not just because we must, but because we see employment—even with all its issues—as an essential part of modern life.

We're working longer hours than ever (when we can find work), and we're living in a digital, multiscreen universe, which some analysts say causes us to have "continuous partial attention." Right now, as I'm writing, I have a television on mute. It's not distracting me but providing me with some visual stimulation that allows me to pause as I think. For me, it's a visual version of the audio stimulation that many writers get from penning their works in coffee shops, and the human chatter has been shown to increase productivity in many writers. There's something very solitary about writing—but also something very human, even among us writers, about the need to be part of the crush of humanity.

As I interviewed people for the book, I began to notice patterns in their personalities and work preferences. Some people like not only to work alone but also to make *decisions* alone, regardless of how many people carry them out. Others gain from brainstorming ideas in teams. For some, work must align with a higher social purpose; and others use work as a means of gaining the money to make things happen, whether it's raising children, funding a local charity, or enjoying luxury goods. Other people like taking career risks, applying for jobs that often have a potentially high upside *and* downside. Many prefer creating projects to executing them.

For years, I participated in a circle of fiction writers called "the Finish Party," so named because we didn't just start writing books—we finished them. Having that group structure was extremely important, because the process of launching new projects excites me in ways that executing and completing them never does. Even in my team-oriented work, I love dreaming up new ideas much more than the steady slog of getting them done.

Some people are the exact opposite. They revel in every step that takes them closer to completion, whether it's on individual projects or as workers or managers at large firms. For example, I was at a women's fitness retreat and complained bitterly about having to complete my business taxes. A woman I'd barely met looked up at me as if she were six years old and I'd just offered to buy her a pony for Christmas. A bookkeeper by trade, she offered to help me with my taxes for free— that is, the *execution* of the paperwork—because she truly loved doing what she was good at, as much I love scribbling new ideas in my red Moleskine notebook.

As I met so many different types of people, I began to think of four different factors as something akin to the sorting hat in the Harry Potter series. One is whether you like to execute and complete projects, or whether you prefer to begin them. Another is if you like making decisions alone, mulling things over by yourself, or brainstorming with a team.

(This is regardless of whether you need a team to do the work.) There's the question of how much risk you're willing to take in choosing your jobs, and also whether you want to have "high social impact" or changing your community or the world directly through your work. Many people I interviewed over the years about their jobs grappled with their desires and choices in these areas. They're not about what types of skills you have or will build but about the natural center of gravity of what work means to you and how it suits you. Much of this book talks about tracking industries, acquiring skills, searching for and keeping jobs, and planning financially in our volatile times. But this critical section is devoted to grouping us into archetypes—sixteen, to be precise—based on the responses to four key questions. I hired survey researchers to develop questions and help me run a nationally weighted survey of two thousand respondents that asked fifty-eight questions, including the four that form the archetype system for the Work/Life Matrix. (For comparison, many presidential polls survey a thousand people to be considered valid.)

How many times have you heard the term "wage slave" or some other phrase equating work with bondage? Part of mastering the Work/Life Matrix is learning to "work freely." That's not to say that you should be free from work, but free from the chains of employment, free to have a personal mission, free to set aside time for your family as well as your own pursuits (art, sport, religion—whatever your passion). You can be free to develop a workstyle that gives you more pleasure and still maintains your financial security and can revolutionize your life, no matter what your income. Often we are taught to evaluate job possibilities by looking at our skill sets. Are we good with our hands? Do we like numbers? Yes, those things are important—fundamentally and *critically* important. But most of us have many different types of skills we can access and cultivate in order to build a life. In today's society, we haven't focused enough on *integrating* our work within the larger framework of our lives, including our ethics, values, desire to give back, and style of human interaction—all keystones of the Work/Life Matrix.

The Work/Life Matrix formulates your individual career goals, lifestyle, and personality into one of sixteen archetypes that will guide you as to your adaptability to certain careers. Your archetype will also gauge how flexible you are to the ebb and flow of the labor market. For example, are you someone who is willing and able to change jobs aggressively, and why or why not? (Some people intentionally switch jobs fairly often to make sure that their salary remains at the top of the market rate; others, because their industry is unstable; and yet others do so to seek new experiences.) The Work/Life Matrix can help you set your *trajectory* in an era of episodic careers, and also understand the power of *intention* you bring to your work. You might have a job in fund-raising for mission-driven reasons, while another person might be working in the same field seeking a certain wage and lifestyle (and there is *nothing* wrong with that). Having this kind of self-knowledge is invaluable in assessing how you will handle the inevitable ups and downs of any career path.

What's next? First, I'll ask you to complete the four basic questions. Then I'd like you to read the powerful stories of men and women who fit each of the sixteen archetypes. Although you might identify more with the ones whose characteristics and interests match yours, you will almost certainly find similarities with others. That's okay. Go with your gut. If you feel torn between answers, pick one but note what options you felt drawn to but didn't choose, so that you can read up on those profiles as well.

You'll get to read an in-depth work/life history of a person in each archetype; observations from others who rated themselves the same way; and, in the appendix, note some statistical variations between the archetypes. Most of us gravitate toward certain choices throughout life—whether it's the kind of music we like or much more practical matters, such as whether we consider ourselves savers or spenders. Likewise, how you approach the world of work is certainly shaped by personal effort and the luck of the draw, but also by how you view your place in the world of work. Note when you feel like you are in the "zone"—productive and focused; or filled with vague dissatisfaction; or just plain mad you have to get up and go to work! The tools in the Work/Life Matrix are designed to help you get past moments of uncertainty and definitely steer away from long-term dissatisfaction with work and plot new paths.

Please take out paper, a notebook, or the digital equivalent, like a note-taking app on your phone, and begin building your core Work/Life Matrix. Read each of the four questions below and choose the answer that best describes how you would *most likely* respond and the answer that feels the most accurate *most of the time*. You will be asked to select a letter that represents your response, and then print or type the letters in order from right to left, beginning with question 1.

THE WORK/LIFE MATRIX IN FOUR CORE QUESTIONS

All of us have elements of both of these within us. Choose the one that seems most natural to you, or that you would choose with all other factors in a job decision being equal.

QUESTION 1: Do you seek to (1) build your career with care and caution, step-by-step, or (2) take significant risks in order to get big payoffs (for example, working for a start-up or spending money to retrain for a new industry), which might mean having to absorb major losses of time and money if these risks don't pan out?

If you answered (1), mark *C* for cautious.

If you answered (2), mark *R* for risk taker.

QUESTION 2: Do you want to (1) have a high social impact and change the world for the better as part of your work life, or (2) get a sense of accomplishment from doing a good job as long as your work is not directly harmful to others?

If you answered (1), mark *H* for high social impact.

If you answered (2), mark *P* for passive impact.

QUESTION 3: Are you happiest as (1) an innovator or (2) an executor? The example of the ace bookkeeper who began wriggling with excitement at the idea of helping me with my taxes is a classic "executor." Other people I know love coming up with ideas constantly. They might be able to carry out those ideas but enjoy that part less; prefer to pass the ideas off; join forces with a team member more focused on execution; and may occasionally have a hard time executing their ideas. Those people are "innovators."

If you answered (1), mark *I* for innovator.

If you answered (2), mark *T* for team decision maker.

QUESTION 4: Are you mainly (1) a solo decision maker who seeks to do things your own way and perhaps by yourself; or, at the very least, do you prefer to make decisions on your own, regardless of who executes them? Or are you (2) a team-oriented decision maker who thrives on the collaborative decision-making process and the energy of those around you? For me, this is a tough question. In my broadcast work and some of my collaborative writing, I'm a teammate. But for the most part as an author, I'm a soloist. I would never give up writing, which has been a passion since I was a kid, but I'm happiest brainstorming with a team.

If you answered (1), mark *S* for solo decision maker.

If you answered (2), mark *T* for team decision maker.

Write down each letter in the order of the questions. My answers are:

R FOR RISK TAKER. I've worked most of my life as a journalist, which can be a risky occupation in and of itself (involving, in my case, visiting murderers in prison, interviewing white supremacists, and sparring with politicians). But it's more that I've invested my own money to start my own small journalism enterprises, and left what other people consider dream jobs (like being a television reporter for example) without another job lined up when I felt it was a poor fit.

H FOR HIGH SOCIAL IMPACT. I've always wanted my work to make a difference in social problems such as economic issues, politics, and race, in my case by doing journalism that helps people understand these issues and, for a time, directly by running a journalism-training nonprofit organization.

I FOR INNOVATOR. I love the thrill of coming up with ideas, and although I do finish (a half-dozen books and counting, among other things), I love that dreamy state of falling in love with a new idea.

T FOR TEAM DECISION MAKER. This was the hardest one for me to answer. Although my writing is a solo pursuit, even then I find myself turning to trusted allies—book agents, editors, research assistants, astute friends—to help me work out the kinks. When it comes to working on radio, podcast, television, and event-based projects, there's always a team, and much of the fun is brainstorming what we are going to do and how we are going to do it. I find that when I work alone, I miss both the creative energy and the solid grounding of other people who help me make decisions.

This makes me an RHIT: a risk-taking, high-social-impact-focused innovator who prefers making team decisions.

• • •

In completing this simple survey, you might feel that you fall on two sides of a question. If so, choose the answer that best describes you and your attitudes toward work, and then add your second strongest option in parentheses. For me, that would be T(S) for question 4. Then, as you look at the archetypes, you can see which ones fit you perfectly or at least moderately well. But don't hesitate to make a gut-level decision.

After answering all four questions, you will have identified yourself as being one of sixteen work/life archetypes in our matrix:

CHIS	CHIT	CPIS	CPIT
CHES	CHET	CPES	CPET
RHIS	RHIT	RPIS	RPIT
RNES	RNET	RPES	RPET

Mark down your archetype. In the section that follows, you can read about individuals who share the same Work/Life Matrix category. You'll also see some common jobs among people who, through survey and interview data, selected these archetypes; as well as possible points of accomplishment and potential trials and tribulations based on your type.

All of these men and women have learned to conquer the world of work on their own terms by staying true to their values, understanding their desires (whether it be in terms of compensation, entrepreneurial opportunities, or minimizing stress), and acting decisively when opportunities present themselves. The Work/Life Matrix is ultimately a self-analytic tool designed to help you find your happy place with work, given all the obstacles and market forces. It's that simple, and that complex, because none of us leads identical lives or has the same exact choices.

There are sixteen archetype profiles, all of them real stories from real people. I've chosen to present these stories in a form close to oral history, meaning that the people interviewed tell their own story with minimal interruption and use their own names. (In two cases, people decided to use a partial name or remain anonymous.) I intervene only when I need to provide context. Pure oral history is a form that journalist Studs Terkel mastered in his landmark 1974 book *Working: People Talk About What They Do All Day and How They Feel About What They Do.* I want you to really feel as if you're having a conversation with these people from many walks of life. You will "hear" some of the differences in education, region, and style as you "listen" to the interviews of people with different Work/Life Matrix archetypes.

WORK/LIFE MATRIX OVERVIEW

We can sort the sixteen archetypes (below) into four broad categories that will help you to use this tool more easily: CH types, RH types, CP types, and RP types.

CH types	CHET	CHES	CHIT	CHIS
RH types	RHET	RHES	RHIT	RHIS
CP types	CPET	CPES	CPIT	CPIS
RP types	RPET	RPES	RPIT	RPIS

CH types—cautious, high-social-impact—want to help transform society through their work, but they want to do it in relatively secure jobs. CH archetypes include many people in teaching and health fields.

RH types also want to help change the world with their work and are willing to accept higher risk in their careers. Under this category, among others, you find people who describe themselves as "social entrepreneurs": starting businesses that have an element of social change, as well as activists, organizers, and some types of artists.

CP types want more stable careers (*C* for "cautious"), and see their work as having passive social impact. Passive does *not* mean negative. It can be very powerful and liberating not to think that your work has to save the world. You can choose *P*—passive social impact at work—and make a high social impact through parenting, mentoring, volunteering, the arts, or other ways. Many people who are CP archetypes do prioritize family, faith, and other pursuits highly. In this category, you find workers and managers who are often passionate about doing strong work, often supporting others, but are not willing (in general) to enter high-risk careers.

RP types, too, view most of their work as passive social impact, but they are willing to take more risks. Many RP types exhibit an entrepreneurial streak.

There are many ways to parse the archetypes, but they're meant to be a useful tool that brings you closer to joy, happiness, and security in your work. If that simply isn't possible where you are, it can help you think through what to do next. Now let's explore stories from an astounding variety of real people who took the test and represent different archetypes.

THE CH TYPES: Cautious Careerists Who Do High-Social-Impact Work

CHET	"The Good Shepherd"
CHES	"The Right-Hand Man or Woman"
CHIT	"The Change Agent"
CHIS	"The Sharp-Eyed Analyst"

Archetype 1: CHET, the Good Shepherd

A CHET loves helping others (H, high social impact) in relatively stable environments (care and caution regarding risk, C) while executing (E) a larger plan as part of a team (T). I call them Good Shepherds because they see part of their role as helping others, no matter what field they are in, and don't mind if they are not the center of attention as long as they help guide their flock.

Jenny Ye, Data Journalist, New York City

Strong Ties to the Neighborhood Endure Through School and Work Years

"I was born in 1991 in New York and have lived in the same apartment in Chinatown my whole life. It's the same apartment that my mom and her siblings immigrated to in the 1970s. I went to elementary school in Chinatown and other New York public schools before going to Harvard University.

"My mom and dad are both immigrants from southern China, from the Guangdong Province. We speak Cantonese at home. My mom worked in garment factories in Chinatown when she immigrated. Once the garment factory industry left Chinatown, she found a job at a bank in the World Trade Center.

"My dad came to America in the eighties to go to school. He has a college degree in computer engineering and has worked as an engineer for the city since the early nineties. Even though I now closely identify with being a techie and studied computer science in college, I wasn't really encouraged by my parents to do that. I wasn't one of those people that learned how to code when they were five.

"Growing up in Chinatown is a big part of who I am. Going to a ninety-percent-Chinese American elementary school really made me very comfortable with being Chinese. I was really used to using both Cantonese and English, with English at school and Cantonese at stores with my parents. In high school, I started volunteering in Chinatown, helping with English classes and also getting involved with tenant organizing." In that capacity, Jenny used to explain to renters about their rights, especially when landlords tried to use illegal tactics to evict them. While still a high school student, she also "worked with different community organizations. This kept me really curious about politics at a larger level, which I then learned more about in college. I majored in computer science and minored in ethnic studies."

Mixing Paid and Volunteer Work

"Now that I'm back in Chinatown, I'm still volunteering as an interpreter and really invested in giving back to this community. I am aware of how quickly things are changing. Most of my best friends from elementary school, middle school, and about five of my closest friends from high school are all back in New York, and most of us live in Chinatown. I'm very lucky to be back in the place that I grew up in with my closest friends, who are also invested in this community. We'll eat and hang out at many of the places we went to growing up. Through working at WNYC, I am also learning so much about other parts of New York." WNYC-AM and WNYC-FM are New York's flagship public radio stations, broadcasting programs from NPR (National

Public Radio), the British Broadcasting Corporation (BBC), and other radio services. In addition, WNYC produces original local programming. Jenny, a producer on the station's data news team, works closely with WNYC reporters, helping them incorporate data analysis in their on-air pieces.

"I have a lot of work," she continues, "both paid and volunteer right now, but I do prioritize getting enough rest every night and making sure that I have time for myself. I'm super lucky that John Keefe, my supervisor at WNYC, is someone who says, 'All right, it's sixish; we should all go home.' I work ten to six, and I teach an early class for high school students twice a week in the mornings. Ten to six gives me a lot of time at night. I wake up early to read and work on things outside of work.

"My weekends are 'real' weekends, which is lovely and amazing. Sadly, a lot of people I know from school are working at their jobs on their weekends. I feel really lucky with my schedule right now. It's flexible enough that I can do things outside of work that I care about. They're things that inform how I think of data journalism and think of stories. When I'm working with the high school students, I try to bring out what they're interested in.

"I teach through a program called TEALS—Technology Education and Literacy in Schools," she says. Founded and administered by Microsoft, the program recruits working professionals to volunteer teaching computer science in high schools. The classes are held early in the morning, so volunteers can get to work. In the 2014–15 year, TEALS operated in 131 schools spread across 18 states and the District of Columbia. "Students go every day of the week. It's a real class," Yee says. "For the teaching team, we rotate. No one volunteer is there every day. There is a teacher with us every day, helping with the classroom management. He meets with us every week to plan lessons, and he is also learning the curriculum. That way, in the future, he can be a teaching assistant or teach the class."

A Grounding and Security in Technology

"In high school, I had a required intro computing course that we took sophomore year. I was initially dreading having to take this course, but it started to click. After taking that intro course, I took the AP. After that, I didn't take any computer science for two years. I started the computer science major at Harvard during my sophomore year. By that time, I was very involved with IOP, the Institute of Politics, but I remembered how much I loved computer science in high school. I decided to try and start again. I was still a math- and history-ish person, and I really wanted to integrate the politics I was learning about at the IOP and my CS courses.

"I looked for opportunities where I could use code in some way relevant to cities. When I learned about WNYC, I realized this was that opportunity. The summer before, interning at WNYC, I was on Google Public Sector's engineering team in DC, which does election results. We were working with cities and governments that were releasing data to make that data easily discoverable in Google search, Bing search, and other things like that.

"Knowing that technology is a growth industry gives me a personal sense of security. I'm twenty-two and driven by impact and curiosity. In New York, I think about my impact on Chinatown, on other immigrant com-munities, and on the city in general. I am curious about things or about neighborhoods that I don't have as much interaction with. I will never stop being curious in New York City. I love it here. Right now, the people around me really drive me too. I not only have close friends from elementary school and fun people at work who are really smart, but I'm still meeting like-minded people. They remind me that the city is huge. And that's what moti-vates me."

CAREER PATH AND CHALLENGES

CHET individuals often prioritize others' needs ahead of their own. That might be good in some cases, but not when it blocks a CHET worker's ability to protect his or her own career and earnings potential. CHETs also have to remain vigilant about continuing lifelong learning, so that they are best positioned to stay in their career of choice as it evolves. Jenny Ye is well aware that she is in a high-growth industry, computer science, but CHET archetypes (Good Shepherds) in fields with less growth potential can find themselves losing financial or career ground as they focus on work with high social impact.

JOBS AND CAREERS OFTEN HELD BY CHET SURVEY RESPONDENTS: educator (k–12, college, and vocational levels; librarian; educational specialist), health occupations (nurse, doctor, physical therapist, family health advocate, psychiatrist/psychologist), social worker.

THOUGHTS FROM OTHER CHET RESPONDENTS

- *"Leaving my previous employer after fifteen years and a pretty important position, I went from an executive staff position to caring for underprivileged kids at a residential school. Best decision I ever made for my career. I have learned that servicing others less fortunate and being mentors to students is much more satisfying and rewarding. It's not about how much one makes in life."*

- *"I returned to graduate school twenty years after undergrad and fifteen years after first master's degree to get a degree in library and information science. It allowed me to pursue what I really wanted to do. I'm completely satisfied with my decision in terms of what I do, but it has affected my flexibility with retirement age. I will have to work longer to be able to afford to retire."*

- *"One thing I learned early was to follow the chain of command. I was given a task to coordinate a big recruitment event for the college where I worked. I went to a staff member in another office to talk about aspects of the program, and my boss was angry that I didn't run it by him first. I was doing what I was supposed to do, but he thought he needed to be informed."*

- *"If you are not happy or fulfilled with what you do, it will affect your work performance."*

Archetype 2: CHES, the Right-Hand Man or Woman

A careful careerist (C) concerned with high social impact (H), the Right-Hand Man or Woman is primarily an executor (E) of a company's or supervisor's agenda, yet is empowered within the job to make many day-to-day decisions on his or her own (S).

Terri Wilder, AIDS Activist, New York City

Learning a Work Ethic in Childhood

"I was born in Athens, Georgia, in 1967. My parents were attending the University of Georgia. My first job that I ever had in my whole life was baby-sitting, like a lot of young girls probably do, but then I started this hair barrette business. People would weave ribbon through them, and then the ribbon would flow down in people's hair, and sometimes they'd put beads in them or tie them in a bow. That was a trend in the eighties, and my grandmother would go buy the ribbon and the barrettes. I would make them and sell them to little shops. I'd make my money, and I'd pay my grandmother back.

"But the first job where I got a real paycheck and paid taxes was when I was in high school. Before Blockbuster was the place to go get videos, there were still some mom-and-pop stores where you could rent Beta or VHS videotapes. I worked at Channel 1 Video. That job put gas in my car, and I'd buy my Gloria Vanderbilt jeans or Calvin Klein jeans or whatever that my parents wouldn't buy, or go do stuff with my friends on the weekend."

Entering Social Work

"When I graduated with my bachelor's in social work in 1989, I got a job at this horrible, horrible, *horrible* nursing home in south Atlanta. It was really depressing. It was not in the best part of town. And I got paid seven dollars an hour. I only stayed a couple of months. I thought, 'I cannot get paid this much. This is ridiculous. God, I just killed myself to get a bachelor's—I guess I need to go back to school.' So I did. I went back in '91 and got my master's in social work.

"In the late eighties, I started doing volunteer work at AID Atlanta, which is still the oldest and largest AIDS service organization in the Southeast."

Deepening Work on HIV Prevention and Services

"I was very interested in HIV and all the sociopolitical issues that surrounded it. Gay men and sex and drugs and stigma and homophobia and racism and sexism. I'm kind of a little bit of a bulldog when it comes to my personality. I've kind of got an activist spirit, and so I always will fight for people, and it just seemed to be a natural fit.

"Eventually I made it to Minneapolis, Minnesota, and I worked at Hennepin County Medical Center in their HIV clinic. I was very, very happy there. I thought I was making tons of money as a social worker. I was making thirty thousand dollars a year. And I just thought, 'God, I'm rolling in the dough.' Eventually I got this full-time position at the HIV clinic, and I finally felt like: 'I'm a professional social worker, and I have a job and health insurance, and I can pay my bills.'

"The job made me feel very fulfilled, but eventually the winters really got to me. My boyfriend and I broke up. I hit a depressive period and moved back to Georgia. I actually was very sick when I first moved back. I had fibromyalgia and really couldn't work. Then once I started getting my health back, I started volunteering again in HIV at AIDS Survival Project," an Atlanta-based advocacy and support group.

"I ran their two-day education empowerment workshop for people with HIV, and I just loved it. People with HIV would come for a workshop, and they were scared to death because a lot of it was 'Oh my God, who's going to see me? Who am I going to see? If we see each other, then we're both going to know we have HIV.' And by the end of the workshop, you could just see the anxiety had melted. They knew they were going to live. We had just given them all this great information. They now felt a sense of community.

"Today I coordinate clinical education so that medical providers are trained in the highest standards for treating people with HIV. So although I don't have direct contact with people with HIV like I did in my previous positions, I know that, through these trainings, it trickles down to affect the person with HIV's life. I still feel good about what I do. I still feel it's important."

Balancing Budgets in an Expensive City

"Do I get paid enough? When I lived in Atlanta, Georgia, I worked at a hospice for a while and got paid forty-three thousand dollars, and I was thrilled with that. I thought that was awesome. But then I moved to New York City in 2009. In your application, you list all of your salary history, and I remember that when I was interviewing, the interviewer said that this job started at sixty-three thousand. But he said, 'I wonder if compensation is going to come back and tell us we can't give you the minimum because your salary in Georgia was forty-three thousand.' One of the things I said to him was, 'That job that I had in Georgia, if I was doing it in New York City, I might be getting paid seventy thousand.' They did end up giving me the sixty-three thousand, but he was like 'I think you're going to have a hard time living here on that.' And you know, when I first moved to New York City, I used my credit card a lot. And then later I was working at the New York City Department of Health, and within two years, you get an automatic raise.

"After switching jobs, I got another raise that bumped me up to almost eighty-three thousand. The MD that I work with literally makes three times more than I do, but he gets to leave at five thirty. I'm often staying at work until eight, nine, or ten o'clock. I realize he went to medical school.

"There used to be a time where MDs weren't these gods in white jackets. And so I often wonder if social workers could be as organized and really send the message out that we're valuable and that we're essential to community. Maybe just by pure marketing and smart messaging, maybe eventually social workers could get paid as much as doctors. I just got appointed to the Governor's Task Force to End AIDS."

Life Choices, Family Choices

"I'm turning forty-seven Wednesday. No, I do not think I am on a good path toward retirement—at least not right now. I happen to be a part of a family that has a lot of money. My dad has a lot of money because he inherited it. If my dad didn't help me, I would feel stressed about retiring. I live in one of the most expensive cities in the world."

Terri pays $2,700 for her apartment, which, believe it or not, is actually below the average price of a one-bedroom apartment in Manhattan. "I'm by myself," she says, "and I don't want to get into 'Well, if I had a boyfriend or a husband . . .' because then I start having an internal feminist fight with myself. But the reality is that if I was partnered, or if I did have a husband, my expenses would be very different.

"I would like to have a kid. Because of my age, my doctor and I tried to get some of my eggs and freeze them and then inseminate. But because of my age, we got *one*. And it did not take. So I'm probably going to have to purchase eggs.

"I went to my parents about a year and a half ago and said, 'I want to have a kid, and I absolutely cannot afford to do this without your support.' My dad said he would help me. I mean, I should get to have a family even if I'm single, but I can't even afford to do that.

"That psychologically messes with you a little bit. Like, you're forty-six years old, you're not sixteen, like 'Dad, can you give me some money so I can go to the movies with my friend?' It's 'Dad, can you help me pay vet bills and fertility bills?' And if you look at my salary on paper, I actually make more than my father. My dad's a musician in the Atlanta Symphony Orchestra. So on paper I actually make more than him, but because he had an inheritance, he's able to help me.

"I've never worked as hard in my life as I have since I moved to New York City. There's a hustle here, and I feel the stress of that hustle. If you're not working hard, somebody else is going to pass you, and they may get that job, or that promotion, or that raise, or that acknowledgment that you should have gotten. So you'd better stay late—but they're not going to pay you more."

CAREER PATH AND CHALLENGES

CHES individuals are deeply passionate about the mission-driven aspects of their work, but as executors, they are often not in complete control of the policies of the organization they work for or with. This can cause frustrations when the CHES worker's goals differ from the organization's. The role of the Right-Hand Man or Woman is essential to charismatic leaders who are visionary but not detail oriented. The Right-Hand Man or Woman has to be clear about prioritizing his or her goals as well as that of the organization or leader; and also prioritize self-care and personal goals.

JOBS AND CAREERS OFTEN HELD BY CHES SURVEY RESPONDENTS: researcher/science research analyst, education (professor, teacher, special education specialist, academic advisor), day care and child care, nonprofit management, criminal justice (police officer, judge).

THOUGHTS FROM OTHER CHES RESPONDENTS

- *"Trusting people with anything is a mistake. Do it yourself and keep to yourself, especially in a supervisory position. Keep your own counsel, or if you must, speak with someone outside of your company."*

- *"Choose a field that you enjoy, and if you find that it is not what you thought, don't be afraid to pursue something else. Being happy in your job is worth more than the money."*

- *"Be prepared for constant change."*

- *"Be adventurous, look for meaning. You're never going to starve."*

Archetype 3: CHIT, the Change Agent

The Change Agent (CHIT) wants to find new ways to solve social problems. He or she seeks to innovate (I) new ways to help others (H, high social impact) by working with a team (T) and has a relatively cautious desire for job security (C).

Alfred Marshall, Construction Worker and Labor Advocate, New Orleans

Growing Up in New Orleans Public Housing, and Seeing Things Change

"I've lived in New Orleans for fifty-two years. We are southern people, and we got a big family. In the B. W. Cooper Housing Development, everybody was kin to everybody. When you walked out the door, going anywhere, from the Iberville development to the next one, you were connected in some way to everyone—it's either a cousin or an in-law. That's how deep rooted the South is.

"Growing up in the Calliope/B. W. Cooper/Marrero Commons project— its name keeps changing—it was a beautiful community. We had a village, including fifteen hundred units with two bedrooms, adding up to five thousand people in one area. It was nothing but love. We had gardening, and you could leave your doors open. It was a respectful thing. It was a village. I miss those times. We didn't have much, but we had support from others. But I saw that change in the late seventies.

"We lost our way when drugs came in. That's when all the disrespect started happening, the killing started happening. Today I am determined to try to begin to fix that by organizing and having young men stand up for themselves and demand better for themselves."

From Prison to Organizing

"I went off to prison for three years. Inside the prison system, we were only provided a TV, and all the young men would fight over it. There was no read-

ing material available. With the help of two other guys, we passed out peti-
tions and won a library. It was through that that I knew, if anything was ever
broke, I wanted to try to fix it.

"When I got out, I still wanted to organize, but I didn't want to go back
to jail. I needed a new method. I became a construction worker and organizer." Soon he learned about STAND with Dignity, a project of the New Orleans Workers' Center for Racial Justice (NOWCRJ). STAND is an advocacy
group that does government outreach and labor organizing, and writes reports on issues facing unemployed residents and low-income workers, primarily African Americans like Mr. Marshall. "When STAND came in," he
reflects, "it showed me that there was a better way to organize." He's been
working with the group for three years.

"During Katrina, we had to evacuate. I went to Houston. After coming
back a year later, we came back to the place where we used to live. It was
fenced off, and there were a lot of Latinos living in our old homes. There
was no electricity, but there was plumbing. The authorities wouldn't let us
live in our apartments even though we seen other people residing there,
using our clothes and stuff. We were even threatened by the local police
and the National Guard that we could lose our vouchers for emergency
housing even if we tried to clean up our old homes or something. That was a
blow, coming back.

"We ended up living in an apartment in one of these communities for
three months, but they only got twenty-five percent of that community up
and running again with electricity. And they made commitments about the
building process, but I was one of the twenty-five percent who watched
them come in and tear it down. Just part of it was damaged, but nothing
was wrong with other parts that they were destroying. Maybe the first floor
got a little water, but it wasn't like you couldn't restore it.

"And I couldn't find work at the time. They said there was no work, but
we see Latinos and everybody else was working." Today another part of the
New Orleans Workers' Center for Racial Justice focuses on Latino workers,
through its Congress of Day Laborers. NOWCRJ tries to forge alliances be-

tween poor black and Latino laborers via its two groups, easing some of the tensions Alfred saw.

As Alfred recalls, "Certain guys started acting out, robbing people that had jobs because they want to work. Or they felt, 'Why should I work if I'm going to only be paid $7.25 an hour? If I'm going to build something, pay me for doing it!' We built this country before, and black people understand all the work they put in building, and they want to get paid for the work. The Latinos—or the 'new slaves,' I should say—do work for low wages. Blacks were being excluded from the workforce, not because we didn't want to work, but we didn't want to work for wages that was poverty wages.

"In 2011 the NOWCRJ staff came into the housing authority and the project where I used to reside. Big corporations came in and made promises that they was going to allow the community to rebuild and live in the new community. There was light for the neighborhood."

Asking for a Share of the Business of Rebuilding New Orleans

Section 3 of the 1968 Housing and Urban Development Act mandates that in projects using HUD funds in certain neighborhoods, "preference must be given to low- and very low-income persons or business concerns residing in the community where the project is located."[2] According to the law, Alfred explains, "thirty percent of all new hires must be low- and very low-income people, so that made me get involved. We went to the New Orleans Housing Authority for two years, banging them on the head about needing a better policy that would have on-the-job training, so some young men can get training rather than just a job. We won it, but it's just something that's on the books, because New Orleans is a right-to-work state. It's blocked at the state level, so it's not being implemented.

"We also had to go tell people that we need second chances in New Orleans. We had men who had been convicted speak at the city council. We went to the contractors and developers, demanding that they remove the convicted-felon question from the application, so that these guys get an opportunity to work. We actually won. Once we accomplished that, we became even more proactive. We started to demand training.

"Contractors, trying to keep costs low, started claiming they did not need more people, but instead they needed skilled people. We had one guy who was fired. And so three days after getting laid off, during work hours, he was hanging out in a park. Some guys shot him and a two-year-old girl playing nearby.

"A lot of guys were laid off and started going back to doing bad things. I tried to get them to focus their energy on getting the training piece of policy passed. I told them we needed to keep fighting, but I lost some funding. I was trying to educate fathers while my son focused on the youth his own age."

A Personal Tragedy Sparks New Growth

"Then I lost my son who was helping me right behind me. He was murdered. We were trying to keep the hope. But we lost that little girl, the young man, and my son, and this took away from our movement.

"It's really been hard to get young men to see the big picture. My son, Sadiki Navarre, was a twenty-four-year-old man. Coming up, he was the honor roll student, and he was a people person. He wanted to go to the University of Miami after high school, but I couldn't support him because of my addiction at the time. Later I got clean and I got back into his life.

"I showed him the way to go through a three-year apprenticeship program, and he became a plumber. That was paying him good money, and, for the most part, he was a happy-going person.

"He'd go down on Magazine Street, where white people are at. In that neighborhood, he established some white friends. After he was killed, they honored him. They named a drink in honor of Sadiki, and if you ever go over there and order that drink, it's free.

"He would see people as human beings. He didn't discriminate because you was gay or because you was white. He didn't care what you were. He engaged with you. He was a loving person. And he's so dearly missed.

"Every year, he would give these big parties and invite people from around the city to come, free. So, we gave him his last party this year on New Year's, and the party had four hundred fifty people. We got a lot of memorabilia going around in honor of him. My son saw the negative things I was doing when I was an addict and wanted better for me, his mother, our community.

"He took a leadership role and always envisioned a world where people had a good time. In our community, he had young guys that he came up with that were warring. Gang violence. He was right there with them trying to make peace all the time. I found out after his death that there have been several occasions where he stopped guys he knew from killing other guys. He said, 'Man, don't do it. It isn't worth it.' His slogan was 'Living is better than people killing, people dying.' I'm very proud of what he stood for and what he accomplished.

"He convinced young men to put down their guns and stop warring for about a year and a half. Unfortunately, one of the young men decided that they wanted to war again. My son was brutally killed coming home from work by one of the gang members from the other side, so the war kicked back off. What was the mind-set of the young man that really did that?

"The man who shot my son said, 'I killed him because I wanted to make a lot of people mad.' It was that quote made me angry. Should I retaliate? Or should I find out what is the real mind-set? What triggers a young black man? Now I am trying to organize them to see that the only way we are going to get opportunities for young men in their early twenties is for them to come together. They are feeding on all the negativity.

"To fix this, I first talk to parents and youths about how to restore justice and conflict resolution. I get them in a room to understand conflict. I can't ask them to stop doing stuff without putting something in place that's going to bring money or bring some kind of consolation to the conflict that's happening with them.

"Today is worse than the aftermath of hurricane Katrina. The walls of despair are getting higher and higher, and young men are drowning. If you peek under a bridge, you can see the homeless rate has gone crazy. People are drowning in sorrow because of the lack of opportunity, lack of housing, lack of jobs. We see more temp service jobs than anything. You have to sign an agreement with the temp service saying you won't leave them for the next two years. We are seeing that the plantation is still in effect. You are tied into one slave master until he make all this money off you. Then he'll cut you and let you go.

"Today at STAND with Dignity, we are building a movement. I want to go to the mayor and all these dignitaries who are in control and have the young black men tell their stories.

"Our victories so far include getting the felony box removed from job applications and getting a three-dollar-per-hour wage increase from developers. A victory is having young men speak in front of Baton Rouge about the minimum wage being too low. I felt victory when we had the opportunity to go to DC and have young men speak to the National Partnership for Action to End Health Disparities, part of the federal Department of Health and Human Services. We had young men tell their stories to people around the world. It's a victory having young men be proud to tell their story. It changes how you see yourself."

CAREER PATH AND CHALLENGES

Change Agents often seek to provide opportunities for others (high social impact) within the context of a larger company or nonprofit in a cautious career path, sometimes one based on a lack of opportunity or a current or previous hardship. They delight in building and working within teams, adding their own ideas and innovation. In the best of circumstances, that makes them expert navigators of interpersonal relationships—in Mr. Marshall's case, among current and former gang members as well as construction workers and labor organizers. In hard times, a social strategist might be frustrated by his or her teams' dysfunctions.

JOBS AND CAREERS OFTEN HELD BY CHIT SURVEY RESPONDENTS: military, law enforcement, higher education.

THOUGHTS FROM OTHER CHIT RESPONDENTS

- *"When I came around in corporate America, I was the only black person around, and there was no coaching or mentoring or advice giving. I mean, you were on your own. If I look back today, I absolutely have no idea how I made it. I didn't know how not to go to work. Because that's what my father did."*

- *"I spent a year in Vietnam, and I think that's another thing that helped me learn how to persevere."*

- *"You have to know what your personal brand is."*

- *"I think the key to collaboration is humility and leaving your high horse at the door."*

Archetype 4: CHIS, the Sharp-Eyed Analyst

The Sharp-Eyed Analyst is a cautious careerist (C) who nonetheless seeks high social impact (H), likes to innovate (I), and works best making decisions on his or her own (S), often gravitating toward ways to promote new ideas while retaining fiscal stability. The Analyst can, for better or worse, make people feel both enlightened and uncomfortable when he or she points out a system's, or even a society's, flaws and hypocrisies.

Anna Holmes, Author and Founder of the Website Jezebel, New York City

Writing as an Early Passion

"I went back to my hometown in northern California about two months ago to help my mom pack up her house, so I had to go through old stuff.

And I found a book—I use the word *book* loosely here. I'd written and illustrated it when I was probably eight or nine years old. It was about a girl who befriended a dolphin. I mean, what more clichéd story is there, but I did it.

"Consistent writing for pleasure, which is to say not for school, happened in my late teens and then amped up a bit when I was in college—just my sitting on my futon in some dingy East Village apartment with my ten-pound Apple laptop, writing essays about whatever was concerning me at the moment, which I would sum up as guys, life, work.

Usually when I write, I write for money. Sometimes those two things connect, in that I'm writing for myself and also I get paid. But I'm not as prolific as I would like to be, and, in fact, I feel that the older I've gotten, the less prolific I've become. I've suffered more from writer's block than I did when I was younger. You'd think that writing would become easier as you practice it, and as you live life and have more things to say, but I feel like with me it's kind of the opposite.

"The first book I ever did, which came out in 2002, was an anthology of letters written by women to men at the end of relationships. It's called *Hell Hath No Fury: Women's Letters from the End of the Affair.* I called it like an anthology of breakup letters, but not all of them were calling off a relationship. Some of them were written for the express purpose of the letter writer to find some sort of catharsis or to find a narrative in the story of her relationship that she could then grasp onto and help her understand why things had gone the way they did.

"Researching that book was great because I was not only going through those kinds of previously published anthologies of people's letters, but I was looking through archives. I was wearing those white gloves, actually touching people's letters and transcribing them. I started working on the book in 2000, and it came out in 2002, so certainly people were using email by then. There was something sad and also exciting about looking at these letters, because you could already tell that they were on the way out."

A Site of Her Own—Founding Jezebel

In 2007 Anna founded the website Jezebel, which featured women's commentary and essays. It found an enthusiastic audience of women in their twenties and thirties. The workload was intense, says Anna. "When I was running it, we were putting up fifty different posts a day. I left in 2010. Then in 2014 I published *The Book of Jezebel: An Illustrated Encyclopedia of Lady Things*. It's an encyclopedia of the world according to the sensibility of the site. I'm not saying that it's comprehensive. It's very pointed and opinionated."

Reflecting on Jezebel's core readership, she observes, "Younger women are in many ways more media literate. They have the vocabulary and tools to talk about the ways they're represented by media. I mean, I certainly don't remember those sorts of discussions going on when I was a young woman. A lot of the reason they have the tools is because of the internet and because of websites that have jump-started those conversations. Jezebel was one of them—not the only one.

"In the United States, there's a certain awareness of being watched when you're a female that hits you around the age of eleven or twelve. Part of that has to do with the kind of very complicated social relationships that you start to encounter in junior high school. Part of it has to do with going through puberty and not feeling totally like yourself or not understanding what's happening to you. There's much more going on now because of things like the internet, Instagram, Twitter, and Facebook.

"As much as I like technology and new media, I think that they have a negative side as well. And I'm really glad that I avoided growing up in an era in which Facebook existed. You know, the only thing that really existed was the telephone, where I would bitch to my friends about whatever was going on in my life."

Race, Class, and Identity as They Relate to Education and Career

"I grew up in Davis, California, which is a college town near Sacramento. It was a safe place to grow up, and they had good education. But by the time I was about nine or ten, I started hating it because it was so homogenous. I was biracial, and there weren't a lot of biracial kids back then. I liked having one white parent and one African American parent in just the same way that there was something I liked about being taller than most people.

"When I got to New York University in 1991, I traveled alone because it was too expensive for my parents to come with me. I was pretending to be tougher than I was. I did not admit that I was afraid to travel across the country. I didn't admit that I was afraid to go to college in general. When I moved to New York, there were still areas of the East Village that were considered dangerous.

"But you know, the city was nothing like it is now. I mean, there were certainly plenty of wealthy people here then, but I feel like it is much more a city for the wealthy now than it ever was, and it's very depressing to me. It's depressing to me that the one-bedroom apartment that I rented in 1992 on First Avenue and Tenth Street—which I shared with a roommate, and I think we each paid four hundred dollars a month—probably goes for thirty-five hundred dollars now. I don't know if a working-class student could do that now."

Life, Work, Love, and Family—Finding Balance

"Right now I'm writing a five-thousand-word piece for an anthology about people who are childless. I'm forty. I love kids. Something I would love to try someday is to write a children's book, just because they were so formative for me in terms of my curiosity about the world and the stories they had to tell. But I'd never—well, I've rarely felt a maternal urge.

"I was married, now divorced. And my life has changed a lot. I'm enjoying living alone. I see my friends more. During my marriage, I'd been running Jezebel, which was healthy for me in some ways but not so healthy for me physically. And it probably wasn't mentally that healthy for me to be sitting inside a second-bedroom home office for eighteen hours a day working.

"My relationship was not doing well, so I decided to quit running the site. But I decided that it was important for me to not only get out and see friends again but to do something good for myself physically. And at first that just required my walking around more than I ever had. Then it involved me walking for exercise, and then it involved me taking yoga classes. I became a happier person. I was reminded of the importance of physical activity in terms of feeling like I knew myself. I started eating better, and I didn't drink as much wine as I had been, and I was exercising a lot, and it really did help me get through a very difficult time. As my marriage ended and after I left my job, I had to take care of myself in a way that I hadn't taken care of myself in a very, very long time."

CAREER PATH AND CHALLENGES

The Sharp-Eyed Analyst derives a lot of satisfaction from work done in relative solitude that could have a lasting, positive impact on society. At the same time, the solitude of the work—at the very least, the decision-making and innovation part, but often the entire process—can exacerbate health and wellness issues connected to work.

People who get too deep into their work can ignore their own needs, particularly at times when they focus on the social impact of their work. Anna Holmes, for example, is very much mission driven in exploring women's lives through writing and literature. While the Sharp-Eyed Analyst is a cautious careerist, some CHIS individuals risk seeing their jobs become defunded or obsolete if they forget to keep tabs on the health of their industry. Generally, however, they are committed to using ideas as a means of achieving social impact while also seeking to adapt to new business realities and find new opportunities.

JOBS AND CAREERS OFTEN HELD BY CHIS SURVEY RESPONDENTS: researcher, counselor/therapist, educator (k–12 or college), business or nonprofit consultant or board member.

THOUGHTS FROM OTHER CHIS RESPONDENTS

- *"I returned to school after several years to attend medical school. When switching careers, plan ahead! Ask people in that field as many questions as you can. Fear not! Ask for help!"*

- *"All the accolades are nice—that's just gravy—but that's not as significant as this journey that you're going to take throughout your career and life, trying to get better at what you want to do."*

- *"Do you have equal access to education? Do we have equal opportunities to build wealth? Do we have equal opportunities to earn fair income? Those are resource-distribution questions, and they are critically important. Legislation has been part of moving us toward a more egalitarian system, and other kinds of legislation can move us away from it."*

THE RH TYPES: People Who Combine Risk Taking and High Social Impact, Often as Entrepreneurs or "Intrepreneurs"— That Is, Creating Change, with High Autonomy, Within Existing Systems

RHET	"The Bridge"
RHES	"The Maverick"
RHIT	"The Promoter"
RHIS	"The Empire Builder"

Archetype 5: RHET, the Bridge

An RHET thrives on delivering high social impact (H) by executing (E) plans to help others as part of a team (T), with an eye on taking calculated risks (R) to achieve larger social goals. The "Bridge" refers to the ability many RHETs have to bring together people in an organization who may have different goals and communication styles.

Michon Lartigue, Fund-Raising Consultant and Writer, Washington, DC

The Sometimes Heartbreaking Balance of Family and Work

"I work for myself right now—just hosted a big event last night, a fund-raiser for one of my clients. Just to give you a sense of how I got here, my first in-house development director position was in Colorado Springs, Colorado, where I grew up. I moved back from 2009 to 2011, when my father was diagnosed with cancer. Not long after, my mother was diagnosed with cancer too. Having a job was ideal, particularly because I was dealing with significant crises in my personal life. First my father had a heart attack. Then he was diagnosed with cancer. At one point, he lost more than fifty pounds in about eight weeks. The doctor asked, 'How are you feeling?' And he said, 'Fine.'

"I had to really straighten things out right there. He was *not* fine. He was dying. During that time, my mother was diagnosed with breast cancer. But I moved back to DC on Christmas 2011. I had gone into therapy and learned that I needed to take care of myself. I didn't love my family any less, but I had to go on with my life.

"In that first year I moved back to DC, my father died from yet another heart attack, and also my grandmother—both within the first two months of the new year. Later that year, I broke my foot. But my mother's cancer treatment went well. And I decided I had to see the light and just keep pushing.

"But as far as my job in Colorado Springs as a development director for a nonprofit, I learned a lot of things that I keep with me:

"Strong and effective leadership determines the tone and health of an organization. I experienced an ideal case of this as well as a very challenging situation, when they went through a process of changing their mission.

"You can create work/life balance, especially when supported by leadership.

"Board member support—or lack thereof—truly impacts the health of an organization.

"Timing and candid assessment really matter when working to execute large-scale visions.

"It is important to value people who operate in every aspect of an organization."

Self-Knowledge Is a Key to Career Direction

"I also learned a lot about myself. I had a lot of responsibility on the job and a lot of personal stress. But it helped me make sense of my priorities. Things I learned:

"I do not want to be an executive director or CEO of an organization.

"I have the skills and talent to serve in executive management leadership positions.

"Crisis and grief can deeply impact your professional life, even when you are composed and a great worker.

"I no longer want to work in environments where crisis dwells. I don't mind navigating challenges or conflicts that are addressed, but I will no longer work in environments where leadership allows crisis to remain unaddressed.

"I began doing my own consulting in the fall of 2013, after first having another great job, this time in DC," she says. "But I was inspired to pursue my own dreams. And I feel more settled now."

Higher Education

"College was more of a social experience for me than academic. I had been so focused in high school, as well as very protected socially, that I was ready to just *be*. I attended the University of Oklahoma in Norman, Oklahoma.

"I was a broadcast journalism major initially. I enjoyed aspects of it, particularly as it related to production in radio and TV. I was exposed to mentors who both encouraged and *discouraged* me from going into the business. After a visit in the production room during a newscast, I questioned my ability to be in the business; I was afraid I wasn't tough enough. In 1995, after both the Oklahoma City bombing and the O. J. Simpson trial, I struggled with the business significantly and took a required course on magazine and creative writing. The professor told me I had talent in this arena and suggested I switch from broadcast journalism to professional writing. OU was one of the few universities at that time to have a bachelor's program in professional writing, which was described as nonfiction for magazine publication, and fiction writing. I loved it.

"My freshman and sophomore years, I was a fairly focused student, but also involved in Black Student Government, the National Association of Black Journalists, and the Know Thyself Society," a black student leadership organization. "I was involved in local and regional student government and found leadership roles that I enjoyed. But I also, by end of sophomore year, was into partying, and by the end of my junior year, I think I was a 'professional partying political activist.' I tried to recoup my senior year, knowing that I needed to graduate at the end of it. But I had been through so many 'life' circumstances that I lost the vision of how academics could impact my 'real' life. My father also started to experience some significant challenges financially and, I know now in hindsight, with depression, so I started to become more serious and focused on my future—even though I had absolutely no clue, vision, or idea of what that meant. The only thing I thought was that I would be a writer at some point. I left OU in the fall of '96 and moved home to Colorado Springs for eight months, and then in July 1997 moved to Washington, DC.

"Since I moved to DC, my professional positions have been: executive assistant at a nonprofit; consultant, writer, editor, event management; executive assistant at a small production company for author and political pundit Dr. Julianne Malveaux; senior development and fund-raising associate at two different organizations; founder of a nonprofit organization, Voices Under Forty; and director of development at two different organizations.

"Now I work independently as a nonprofit consultant, doing fund-raising and program management, and as a writer-producer.

"I learned different things from all of my jobs. For example, as a senior development and fund-raising associate, I worked at two different organizations. But both times, there were internal crises that made it difficult for me to do my job. Well-meaning (or not well-meaning) leadership can really be damaging to the structure of an organization and to people working in the organization. But I learned how to still build relationships even as the organizations were in crisis. I also learned quite a bit about fund-raising, creating organic and authentic connections, and how the process of raising resources really works.

"I learned how critical it can be, in a professional environment, to know who you are and your strengths and challenges. I think it is important for people to identify and rely on their own self-definition of their professional worth. This doesn't mean you don't take advice, criticism, or information from others. But I learned to create a bottom-line self-assessment so that I would not be at the whims of other people's opinions.

"I learned to identify those moments when I feel professional fear and to navigate them with clarity. For example, when I first started raising money, I was so scared about the responsibility. This translated into me not being flexible enough with myself and others sometimes, especially during times of conflict. When I realized that, I changed that and can now identify when I am operating from fear. I'm a strong person, and I have a truly diverse set of skills. I enjoy and am good at fund-raising. But sometimes it's easy for me to become professionally lazy, in the sense of not cultivating new skills."

Life Lessons for Workers and Entrepreneurs

"If I was talking to a teen about careers—someone the age I was when graduating high school—I would tell them to truly determine what it is they love to do and shape a path that incorporates that. They also need to cultivate courage. They will face professional moments where they will have to be very brave. I don't think that's discussed enough.

"And this is important: they need to understand money, not only as it relates to salary but also how it flows in and out of their company. Also, technology has changed the game and they have to keep up their tech skills. But I would add that being amazing at all things technologically does not trump or negate the importance of developing people skills and relationship-building skills. Finally, they should honor whatever job they are doing, menial or high powered. Treat people well at every level.

"Oh: I'd also mention that executive assistants are the keys to the universe when trying to connect with busy high-profile folks. Make sure to treat assistants very well!

"When it comes to money, I'm certainly pulling my own weight. But as far as planning for the future, like retirement, I don't feel secure in the traditional sense. It's more about a faith in the future. I understand and value the traditional purpose of early retirement, and saving now for later—all of things that you hear from financial experts. At the moment, my life does not operate in the traditional sense professionally or when it comes to money. I'm okay with that, and trust that my path toward retirement will be stabilized and abundant. But I wouldn't say I feel secure.

"Life experience has shifted my 'future' perspective quite a bit, and so while I think that retirement is really important, I also know firsthand that you really don't know what you will be dealing with during that time. It's nice to be prepared, and it helps if you don't have to worry about money, but you just never know the shape that our world and financial markets will be in when retirement approaches."

CAREER PATH AND CHALLENGES

RHET individuals are naturally torn among their team player and executor sides—both of which are about creating an environment where a group gets work done—as well as their risk-taking side, which can sometimes bring them into conflict with peers and superiors. RHETs should develop the capacity to take honest feedback from those around them about their performance, so they can continue to align their work behavior with their high-social-impact goals.

JOBS AND CAREERS OFTEN HELD BY RHET SURVEY RESPONDENTS: skilled trades (construction, pipe fitting, contractor), education professions management, arts (performer or administrator), religious community leader.

THOUGHTS FROM OTHER RHET RESPONDENTS
- *"You see people becoming more sensitive and more open to the ideas of equality in lots of different ways, and you see people who are really committing their lives toward working toward that change and putting their lives on the line."*

- *"I've learned many years ago to divorce my own personal feelings from whatever the finished product is, because sometimes people appreciate things I do that I don't appreciate."*

- *"I love the communal aspect of work."*

Archetype 6: RHES, the Maverick

RHES individuals can work in very traditional companies, with autonomy, as they prefer making decisions solo (S). Natural risk takers (R), they are not concerned if people think their work is too "out there," but/ and they also care about giving back to society (H) and delivering on the promise of what their duties entail (E).

Sex Therapist and Phone Sex Worker[*]

Working with an Invisible Disability

"I'm from abroad, and I actually spent a lot of my twenties on disability support pension for a chronic pain and fatigue condition, so I did jobs around that. I worked for the railroad as a station assistant, I worked as a nanny, worked as a housekeeper, and I have a degree in sexology, and I had my own sexual health business. Coming to the US, I worked in warehouse packing for a while, I worked for a few years as a clinic assistant for Planned Parenthood. I have my own business now, doing sex therapy and calls on a telephone sex line.

"Health and symptomwise, the main disabling thing I deal with is pain and the fatigue that goes with all the effort put into coping with it. During my twenties and into my early thirties, I would go through cycles of not working and find that when I had unlimited rest, I would cope just fine. Then I would feel like a lazy loser for not being in the workplace or at university, and I would go back to full-time work or study and find that within a month or two, I could not cope at all. Then I would struggle through for six months or so, especially if I was at university. I would finish a semester, then I would collapse and spend a couple of months in bed for up to eighteen hours a day.

"By my late twenties, I learned to take things part-time so that it would take a lot longer to get overwhelmed, if I did at all. However, days when I would have flare-ups would be horrible.

"These days, my pain is ten percent of what it used to be. I still have bad nights, but now, because I work for myself, I can nap and get my energy back. I wish there was more flexibility in the workplace around people's needs. I went through university with an excellent disability support department. I was registered as a student with a *proven* disability, even though no one could see it. No one ever questioned whether or not I was actually disabled when I asked for what I needed. If more workplaces could be like that, they would have an awesome worker in me.

"At home, my degree started off being in rehabilitation counseling,

---

[*] Name and locations omitted at subject's request

working with people with disabilities. Partway through, I got frustrated with how little attention was being paid to social and sexual concerns of people with disability. I changed majors and got a sexology degree. Then I started a company about sex and disabilities. I did a lot of public speaking and advocacy, but the biggest thing was that sex work is legal where I grew up. I actually trained sex workers who were interested in working with people with disabilities. It was great."

A Profession with Flexibility—but Not Her Desired Field

"I came to the US to get some help with my health. I was going back to get my master's degree so I could be a sex therapist here, because my sex therapy qualifications from abroad don't transfer over to the US. While I was doing that, I was looking around for work. Now I run my own service. It's kind of awkward to admit, but now I'm a sex therapist on a phone sex line. I can name whatever price I want, but the company that arranges the calls takes about a third of whatever I make.

"A third of the time, I do actual sexual therapy, which is fantastic because I'm reaching clients who normally wouldn't go to a sex therapist. About two-thirds of my work is just straight phone sex. But when my partner's son came to stay with us last week, he doesn't know what I do, so I take time off. Now this week work is slow because most of my regular clients have gone off and found someone else. They'll be back, but it might take them a week or three to get bored with someone else. I have great difficulty taking vacations, partly because of the work that I do.

"It's very, very difficult to have a career with a disability. It's very hard to find work that fits around my needs, but working for myself has been the best solution for me. I really try not to take time off because my business really slows down if I do. I was ill from May through September of this year and had to take time off. I had the same problem in 2010 when I was working for Planned Parenthood, and that was really difficult because I had to be on my feet all day. I really enjoyed the work, but I would come home, sit down, and cry because I was in so much pain and was so exhausted. Now if I need to log off to do something, I can.

"For people with disabilities, working for yourself when you can is definitely the way to go, especially if you have a condition with flare-ups. You can work your ass off when you're feeling well, and when you're feeling ill, you can take better care of yourself. The big difference here in the US is that you don't have a lot of the support for people with disabilities. Back home, out of each dollar I earned, they would take fifty cents for my disability support pension. Here I could have very well have no safety net if I can't work."

An Immigrant's Perspective on American Careers

"Compared with where I came from, people in the US are more career oriented. It's necessary, because in the US, there's a lot more incentive to stay in one job and to move up because of the benefits attached to a job. Where I grew up, benefits are not attached to your job—the government provides them—so you can choose anything you want as a career and change it as often as you want. It's not going to impact your ability to access health care. Here, there've been times when I wanted to do a job and have not chosen it because I couldn't make my own choices about health care." (Although the Affordable Care Act has changed that dynamic, some people find they have much better benefit options within a company than getting it through the US government exchanges. She was interviewed after the ACA took effect.)

"I have a teenage stepdaughter from a previous marriage that I've been talking to a lot about careers," she says. "She's looking at going into the health care field, and I've been advising her to find real people to talk to about their jobs and how they suit their personalities. The mesh of your personality with your job affects how much you enjoy it. Also, I'm telling her to look at how much a job pays before she goes and puts a degree into it. Why put a degree into a job that will pay you forty thousand dollars a year when you could put a full degree into something that will earn you a hundred thousand dollars? That is, if you would enjoy both jobs. I do want to enjoy my career. It's so much of your life. My job back home didn't pay nearly as well as my job now, but I got a lot of travel in, and I really enjoyed the opportunity.

"The last place that I worked, we went from five employees to three and a part-timer in the space of the year and a half that I was there. We were already overworked before, but it became insane. You'd always do an hour of unpaid overtime at the end of work. We all just ate on the job. When we complained about it, they said, 'You can find another job if you want to.' No one left because it was 2008, and who's going to try to find a job in the middle of an economic crisis? When people are desperate, employers will take advantage of that. I despise most workplaces and most of the people that I've worked for. You also get no vacation, or if you get two weeks of vacation, they'll stipulate that you can only take five days at a time. By comparison, six weeks of vacation is mandatory where I grew up.

"Having that time off is good for your health and mental health. There's something that changes in your mind after about four weeks of vacation; four weeks of doing whatever you want to do with your life. You truly say, 'Okay, I've had enough vacation now, and I'm ready to go back to work.' That completely changes your attitude about going back to work."

CAREER PATH AND CHALLENGES

The RHES, or Maverick, has very clear ideas about how he or she wants the world to work or change. The caring Maverick is a natural leader in the executor mode, a soloist who needs a lot of autonomy. The biggest risks for the Maverick are feeling disillusioned by the system he or she is a part of, or feeling limited by the ability do work in his or her chosen field due to market conditions.

JOBS AND CAREERS OFTEN HELD BY RHES SURVEY RESPONDENTS: web developer, remote or freelance office support, health care professions.

THOUGHTS FROM OTHER RHES RESPONDENTS

- *"Went to grad school at forty-seven. It turned out great, as it led to my current career as a mental health therapist."*

- *"Show up on time and expect to work hard. Then, if you have an easier day than usual, it will be a welcome surprise."*

- *"Follow your heart."*

- *"Don't choose a career based on money. If you are passionate enough, the money will come."*

Archetype 7: RHIT, the Promoter

A Promoter, or RHIT, wants to "promote" not for the sake of self but rather for bigger ideas, often of justice. He or she seeks to take calculated risks (R) and innovate (I) new ways of working in a high-social-impact (H) field such as education or politics, working closely with a team (T), and often leveraging media or face-to-face or social networking to rally people to the cause about which he or she cares.

Betty Reid Soskin, National Parks Ranger and Civil Rights Activist, Richmond, California

Living History

"I'm a National Parks Service ranger at the Rosie the Riveter World War II Home Front National Historical Park in Richmond, California. At ninety-two years old, I am this country's oldest full-time national park ranger. I lead tours, speak to groups, and answer questions about living and working in the area during World War II.

"I am firmly rooted in my family and therefore in life. My family comes from New Orleans." But in 1927 the worst flood in the history of the United States left some two hundred thousand African Americans living along the swollen Mississippi River homeless, including Betty's. "My family lost everything," she says in a matter-of-fact tone. "That August," she continues, "my mother arrived in Oakland with three little girls and everything we owned in double cardboard suitcases to join her father, who was here since the First World War. He was a waiter at the Oakland Athletic Club.

"If you went back to when I was eighteen, I'd have been graduating from high school in Oakland. I'd have been the child of a service workers generation," by which she means what many black families called being "in service" to white families and individuals, some of the few jobs available at the time. "Our fathers and our uncles were the Pullman porters and the waiters and the redcaps and the janitors. Our mothers were the domestic servants. I would have followed that course. My older sister, who was four years older than I, worked for her first five years as a domestic. Her husband was a chauffeur, and she was the housekeeper. They worked on the premises as a couple and saved up for a down payment on their first home. This was the route into the middle class for black people.

"That's what my life would have been. At twenty, even working at a union hall—which I did—was a step up. It was probably the equivalent of today's young woman of color being the first in her family to enter college. I filed change-of-address cards for black workers who came into that union hall. I was a member of Boilermakers Auxiliary 36. The unions weren't yet integrated racially—and were not for a couple of decades beyond that."

Work Rooted in Community

"If you can scroll ahead with me to about thirteen years ago, after many, many years and many lives, I was back in Richmond, and this time as a field representative of a member of the California State Assembly. I helped to determine what kind of legislation might be needed for the five cities of West County, over which our office sat. And it was in that role that I became connected with the National Parks Service as a consultant.

"The genesis in creating the Rosie the Riveter park was as a homage to the women who had worked on the home front during that war time. It was women who did much of the flesh-and-blood work of manufacturing, shipbuilding, and all sorts of things during World War II, and Rosie the Riveter represented that. It was a part of the campaign to attract women into the workforce, but there are many, many women who are not included in that image. Ordinary women had been working for a long time in traditional jobs that were assigned to women: librarians, secretaries, teachers. Black women, for instance, had been working outside their homes in slavery. So there was nothing that attracted black women into the workforce based on that Rosie the Riveter image, and I certainly didn't relate to it.

"I had raised four children to adulthood by the time I joined the National Parks Service, and outlived two husbands. I came here as a consultant to the planning group from the Department of the Interior. I was the only person of color within a group of planners from the National Parks Service and the Department of the Interior. It's a park that is formed of scattered sites that fall throughout the city and were almost universally sites of segregation. What gets remembered is determined by who's in the room doing the remembering—and I'm the only person in that room who had any reason to even know it. From the outset, I was able to provide some aspects of the story that had not been recognized.

"Having come here at the age of six means that I entered a school in Oakland, California. I had never been to a formally segregated school. My education all the way through high school was open. I pretty much grew up as a second-generation American. My neighbors and friends were Italian, Portuguese, and Creole families from New Orleans. We were kept pretty much together as a social group. Even though segregation obviously existed, and it's been part of our lives forever, it was not formal here. It was by gentleman's agreement. It was subtle, so I wasn't confronted with full-blown racial segregation before the age of eighteen or twenty.

"I married a man whose family had come out here during the Civil War. His great-grandfather had been a boot maker on Market Street in San Francisco. Mel was in his third year at the University of San Francisco, majoring in history and playing left halfback for the school football team, the San

Francisco Dons. We were pretty much privileged, middle-class African Americans until World War II started."

Race, History, and Employment

"This is when I personally met formal discrimination for the first time. My husband volunteered to fight for his country. But he found himself in the mess hall because all a black navy man could do at the time was cook for his country. He refused. He lasted only three days. He appeared before a panel of psychiatrists and counselors. They gave him an honorable discharge, forty-five dollars, put him on a Greyhound bus, and sent him back home.

"He had volunteered to fight. He did not volunteer to cook, and he simply did not know until he got back that this was a black man's role. While he was gone, I had been working for the FBI in the San Francisco Federal Building. Then when he was volunteering to go back into the service, I transferred to the air force without realizing that the air force only hired African American women in the canteen or to clean restrooms. I didn't know that. I discovered while Mel was gone for those three days that they had made a mistake, and I had been hired in a clerical position. But I was not fit for this position.

"The lieutenant in charge of our section called up to his desk the young white clerk whose desk abutted mine. She came back and told me that he had found out I was colored. I walked up the full length of the basement offices and confronted him. I said of course I was colored, but why didn't he know that?

"He said, 'Don't worry; it's all right, Betty. I've checked with your coworkers, and they're all willing to work with you.' For me, this was an insult. I figured they might be willing to work with me, but would they work under me if I was eligible for a promotion? At which point, I walked out on the air force. So Mel and I were both confronted with what was out-and-out racism within about a week.

"Next, we went into business for ourselves, swearing that we would never work for another group of white folks. We owned a little duplex in Berkeley. We had bought the building when we married in May of 1942. In June of 1945, we knocked the walls out of our garage. We put orange crates to hold the records and a cigar box to hold the cash register. We went into business selling what was then called 'race records,' because there was suddenly a market for black culture.

"Ninety-eight thousand people moved into the Bay Area during the war years, fifty thousand of whom were African Americans. They brought with them black culture but were not able to get any of the music that they could get back home. Suddenly we were in a very successful business.

"The store was named Reid's Records, and it's still open today. The very first hit was Wynonie Harris's 'Around the Clock.' They were lined up around the block to get it. We'll celebrate our seventieth anniversary this year. My youngest son is the proprietor.

"Through the Parks Service, I work on history that is so recent that it doesn't have a curriculum. It's only now beginning to come out, in master's theses or doctoral papers. This means that it's important that that history be told accurately and truthfully in order to revisit those years of 1941 to 1945. We need to get a baseline, to measure all the social change that this country's been through over the last seventy years.

"I'm also sometimes a public face of the park. I do outside speaking engagements. I do two bus tours a month, which means that I have a twenty-five-passenger bus with a swivel front seat that's quite special. We travel around the scattered sites in a two-and-half-hour bus tour.

"The only exercise I get is jumping in and out of my car, but in my family, we live a long life. It's genetic. My great grandmother was born into slavery in 1846 and died at 102 in 1948. My mother was born in 1894 and died at 101 in 1995. I was born in 1921 and am still here. I think that those genetics are undeniable. My children and my grandchildren are my biggest fans. They love that I am still working."

CAREER PATH AND CHALLENGES

The Promoter (RHIT) is devoted to getting ideas and innovations out in the universe. Successful Promoters cultivate a strong life outside of the world of work: faith, family, creativity. Some also take on less intense assignments, though generally they are go-go-go! Promoters who lose sight of their high-social-impact side can risk coming off as self-promoting rather than as being attached to their larger cause.

JOBS AND CAREERS OFTEN HELD BY RHIT SURVEY RESPONDENTS: writer, artist, educator.

THOUGHTS FROM OTHER RHIT RESPONDENTS

- *"I've learned I can guide and inspire the people I work with."*

- *"Young people need strong soft skills, like interpersonal skills, because those are useful in multiple careers."*

- *"I took a chance to go for an interim job that became permanent."*

Archetype 8: RHIS, the Empire Builder

RHIS individuals are willing to take massive risks (R) and innovate (I) by launching new companies or ventures based on their own ideas (soloist, S). Their focus on high-social-impact (H) work often makes them world changers.

Justin Dangel, CEO of Goji, an Online Insurance Agency, Boston

"Yeah, I do think differently than other people," says Justin Dangel. "I know the way I think about math and numbers is different from the way most people can do it." Justin, born and raised in Boston, attended the exclusive private school Buckingham Browne & Nichols, where he played football. Then he went off to Duke University.

How an Internship Became a Passion

"While I was still in college, I went to work one summer in the Ukraine with a man, George Yurchyshyn, who ran an investment company. He wanted to help reform finance in the Ukraine. And one day, in 1994, I got a call that his car had crashed in Kiev, and he was dead. He might have been run off the road for his anticorruption work. Here I am in my twenties, and I have to decide what to do. So I stay and keep his firm going until someone else can come in. A lot of people would have left. So, yeah, I'm proud of myself for that.

"Yurchyshyn believed in the power of businesses to help build the sort of society he wanted to see there: the start-up of new companies not only in the way of job creation, but also in their missions, as vehicles to transform society. When he was killed, along with other people in the company, who were in the car, it was a pretty scary situation. But those of us who remained decided to stick it out, and with the help of some affiliates in the United States, we were able to help keep the fund and the company going. That changed the direction of my life, because I would have gone straight into public policy if it weren't for that, but I ended up being an entrepreneur."

Resilience and Launching Businesses

"Resilience—sure. I think every successful businessperson has it. You fail. My first business, Voter.com, didn't turn out the way I wanted. We had big ideas, and we hired Carl Bernstein," the famous *Washington Post* writer known for his work in exposing the Watergate scandal in the early 1970s. "But there were things I could have done differently, things I regret. Our goal was to use the tools of the internet to help campaigns and others get their message out and help inform voters.

"It was the late nineties. There was a lot of hope about the power of the internet, and we raised a ton of capital. And from a service perspective, we accomplished a lot of what we wanted to do. It wasn't as successful as a business, but it was an important early step toward building the digital political universe that exists today, and I'm proud of what that company did. I don't think there's a contradiction between running a mission-oriented business and a successful business. Most founders start companies with a broader mission than making money, and I don't think it's a contradiction to want the two.

"Then I cofounded Canback Dangel Analytics," a management consulting company now known as Canback & Company. "I sold my share of the company to my partner. It's still around. And it was a great way for me to get some seed money for what I wanted to do next."

Creating a Business, Creating Domestic Jobs

"I wanted to create jobs with my next company. So in 2007 I started the company I run now, Goji, which was called Consumer United at first. At that time, it was clear that people were getting squeezed by financial services. The cost of buying other things was going down, but financial services were going up. So we jumped into auto and home insurance and took two to three years to perfect it. And by the middle of our fifth year, we were the largest auto and home insurance agent in the country, and we still are. We have a price comparison service and a large call center, to give advice to people on what their best insurance options are and how to reduce their costs.

"We get customers that find us online, but we also hire a lot of people to make calls to homes. We now employ hundreds of people in our call centers in Boston and Las Vegas. In Boston, we started with part of a floor; now we rent the whole floor. Creating domestic jobs was something I was proud of. Most of the people who work in our call centers are recent college grads."

Learning from Failure

"Usually when you start a business, it doesn't seem that risky because you believe it's going to work. If you're any good at entrepreneurship, you have a hopefulness at the outset, but you also have some notion that if you stay in the business for any length of time, you'll keep taking risks out as you build. It's a question of your optimism when you start a business—that you can change the world and make it better in some way. Almost every company starts with 'Doesn't it suck that . . . ?' or 'Wouldn't it be great if . . . ?'

"The desire to be an entrepreneur is more like a *need*—where people can't stand the idea of not doing anything important. For me, the idea of getting stuck in a regular career track, where you have a boss, always felt a lot riskier than starting my own company.

"Any entrepreneur who tells you that things going wrong isn't stressful is crazy. But it's less risk taker versus playing it safe than it is optimist versus pessimist. Entrepreneurs tend to start with that natural resilience. Being resilient—some of it is just about imagination. When things aren't going your way, you have the imagination to say, 'Here's how things are now, and here's how things could be in the future. And I like that future and I'm going to start steering in that direction.' That's why your entrepreneur can be more resilient than the typical person."

Is America in Decline?

"I think things are on a great track in America," Justin enthuses. "The country continues to build new technologies and ideas at an incredible pace that both make life better in the United States and the rest of the world. We'll continue to be the most important country in the world economy for at least the next century to come."

He advises, "People should think less 'Can I carve out a financial reality for myself?' and more 'How do I want to spend my time, and what kind of person do I want to be?' The advice I give to college students is, be conscious of the decisions you're making and when you're making choices that aren't making you happy. The financial reality is impacted by student loans and debt that will materially impact their lives. But the most important thing is for them to figure out what they want to do. And the way you do that is by trying different things. I thought I wanted to be a politician and run for office; and then I thought I wanted to be a venture capitalist; and it turned out that I really liked being an entrepreneur.

"The people who try to pursue actualization through work and are invigorated, those are the ones who win, and it's not about money they make—although I do think they make more money. Ask yourself, are you doing something you like? The bigger question is: Whither the American Dream? There's an evolving concept of what the American Dream means. In the 1950s, it meant buying a house and a car and a washing machine. Now the American Dream is more like Jay Z's story: you start off with very little and become a superstar.

"But it's very real that there's another phenomenon going on in our society: people who don't have as many options; often people who aren't college grads. For people who have fewer options and want security, it's a hard place to live. We have to be careful our country still can produce the kind of middle-class and lower-middle-class life that existed in the fifties and sixties, but it's more challenging now. We are an economy where private-equity ownership is two to three times the phenomenon that private-sector unions are. The leverage labor has to negotiate for better treatment has gone down.

"We in this country work too hard and value work too much. When you're the boss and you love your job, working sixty-five hours a week is one thing. But there's also more pressure now on people who don't share the upside of the business."

CAREER PATH AND CHALLENGES

The Empire Builder is a rare archetype. Few people can stay true to their vision and keep their own counsel as much as the Empire Builder does, particularly in the face of huge challenges arising from high-risk long-term strategies. The key for any Empire Builder is to retain enough of a trusted circle (family, mentors, advisors) who can respectfully push back against the Empire Builder's more extreme plans. Empire Builders can also run themselves into the ground physically or mentally meeting the challenges of the job.

JOBS AND CAREERS OFTEN HELD BY RHIS SURVEY RESPONDENTS: entrepreneur, nonprofit director, scientist, professor.

THOUGHTS FROM OTHER RHIS RESPONDENTS

- *"Learn to communicate. Anything can be taught and learned, but the ability to communicate is a rare skill, especially with younger generations who are used to simply texting and using social media. Learn the difference between formal and informal communication methods."*

- *"Your position and title do not equate with power in an organization."*

THE CP TYPES: Cautious Careerists Who Don't See Their Work as Having Inherently High Social Impact, but Who Often Make a Social Impact by Volunteering, Donating, or Other Methods

CPET	"The Team Player"
CPES	"The Taskmaster"
CPIT	"The Steady Hand"
CPIS	"The Masterful Realist"

Archetype 9: CPET, the Team Player

CPET individuals are the ultimate team players (T), looking for ways to work more cleanly (executor, E) within a seemingly secure field or company (cautious careerist, C), for personal gain and satisfaction (passive social impact, P).

Ben Deneweth, Marketing Analytics Manager, Greater Chicago Area, Illinois

Small Company, Big Flexibility

"I work for a small marketing analytics firm," says Ben, an MBA, or master of business administration. "I didn't have any experience in the field when they hired me, but I had the education and mind-set they were looking for, and was a fast learner. I didn't really know what I was getting into, but I learned to love it. We create new knowledge and do real science—but in a way that makes real money.

"I also like working for a small company with fewer office politics and meetings for meetings' sake than the big company I worked for before. I work from home and personally think that's great too.

"After working here for two years, I got promoted to being a manager, which I've been for a little over a year. I perform and lead marketing analytics projects for CPG clients"—that's consumer packaged goods, anything from cookies to small electronics that are sold prepackaged in grocery, department, and other stores.

"In this job, I've learned the importance of doing things right, even if you don't think it matters. Early in my career, I made a change to some media that I was measuring to see if it made a difference, and that change, even though it was incorrect, was left in our final analysis. It was, in the grand scale of things, inconsequential, but one thing in our analysis did not make sense because of it. The client noticed, and we had to restate our entire results and admit we made a mistake. It taught me to not make those mistakes in the first place by being more organized and thorough, but also to be more questioning of your own work and to double-check anything that maybe doesn't make sense.

"My first job after business school was as the web analytics specialist for a major airline. I always wanted to work for an airline, and I was hired by the marketing department and assigned to this role because I had some web analytics experience from my internship at Northwest Airlines."

Lack of Clarity in a Job Is Frustrating

"The position was fraught with a lack of resources, an ill-defined role, and unrealistic expectations, given the resources. My role was to run reports using the web analytics platform and to communicate web analytics requirements to IT and to manage our relationship with the web analytics software vendor. It wasn't working out, and I was let go after a little over two years.

"In my position at the airline, I learned that the job is a lot more important than the employer. I liked my employer, I liked a lot of the people I worked with. But the position was just poisoned. It taught me to realize that and that if I ever find myself in a similar situation, to try to get out as soon as possible.

"If I was talking to a teenager, I'd tell them that first of all they need to learn as much as they can and to always keep learning. You cannot predict what skill sets you will need in your career when you are starting, so learning as much as you can about as many things as you can is the best way to be valuable to a company. Secondly, I would advise them not to become too friendly with their coworkers. It's the tendency of younger workers to become close friends with their coworkers as they would their classmates. I feel that this clouds their judgment with regards to their career, especially when it comes to leaving a job."

Loyalty and Work

"I agree that companies show little loyalty to employees. This is a market necessity. Older workers get angry about this, longing for the good old days when they could work the same job with the same mediocre effectiveness for thirty-plus years. Nowadays, jobs simply don't last thirty years, and this scares them. Younger workers do not know another way, and they know their employer will not be loyal to them. And if they are wise, they show their employers no undue loyalty in return."

CAREER PATH AND CHALLENGES

The Team Player is an asset to whatever company he or she works for. Many end up in middle management, able to deal with the demands of "managing up" to supervisors and "managing down" to direct reports. However, companies sometimes undervalue Team Players, who are not motivated by the spotlight, in favor of more flashy or self-promoting workers.

JOBS AND CAREERS OFTEN HELD BY CPET SURVEY RESPONDENTS: sales, food service and restaurant occupations, office administration, management.

THOUGHTS FROM OTHER CPET RESPONDENTS

- *"Pay close attention to detail."*

- *"Upon retiring from teaching, I became an insurance and investment agent for almost fourteen years before completely retiring."*

- *"Be open to suggestions and also ask questions. Be open and also be flexible."*

Archetype 10: CPES, the Taskmaster

The Taskmaster is a soloist (S) within his or her area, someone able to make things happen (E, an executor), ideally nestled within a stable company (cautious careerist C), or able to roll with the punches. Ultimately, he or she is focused on maximizing his or her job stability, growth, and compensation (passive social impact, P).

Laura Gibbons, Call Center Payment Specialist, Missouri

Be Flexible

"My first job was actually an interior design consultation business I started, and contracted out of, for approximately three years. My tasks included managing the business as well as creating estimates and managing projects for clients. After closing that business due to financial reasons, I moved on to a low-level customer service position at a local call center. I am currently a payment specialist at that same call center, and in the three and a half years since starting my employment there, I have also had two additional part-time administrative/office positions.

"The biggest thing I have learned is that flexibility and adaptability are key to continuing to progress in a career. If I had not learned to adapt to sudden changes early in my life, my career changes and frequent additions to job responsibilities, as well as changes in my personal life, would have been more difficult to weather.

"My advice to any teenager is twofold: always do your best, regardless of the task, and always have a backup. You never know when something is going to happen that changes everything, and, as I learned in college, if you don't have a backup plan, it is very difficult to rebound from sudden changes. In a career today, you really can't afford to take a significant amount of time recovering, unfortunately. You should always do your best, because doing less than your best is to fail yourself and everyone who has put time, effort, and faith in you."

Benefits Are Hard to Find in Local Employment

"Only a handful of employers in my area offer full-time employment or benefits; for the most part, employees are limited to part-time hours, with few, if any, benefits. Due to the lower cost of living in our area, wages tend to be lower overall, even in positions that require specialized training or degrees. Many families have two or three jobs per household or rely heavily on public assistance programs to fill in the gaps.

"From my personal experience, my current employer at the call center limits employees to a part-time temporary basis in such a manner that excludes employees from any sort of benefit. Employees do not receive actual sick time but instead get the equivalent of three attendance penalty–free days per year, and annual wage increases do not keep pace with the levels of training and experience that many employees develop. After three and a half years, my hourly wage is still equal to that of an employee who has only a week of experience.

"The key problem at our local call center is a lack of adequate communication between employees and management, and then between local management and corporate. It makes the employees feel as though the company does not take their needs or abilities seriously, and puts management in a tough situation between what the employees want to know and what corporate will allow them to say. I have heard similar statements from people employed at other local employers: that there is a lack of communication, or they feel that their managers or employers don't care about the position they put employees in. That's especially true when they reduce hours or benefits yet expect the same production quality and levels from employees who are now financially stressed and often working two jobs trying to maintain their finances and cover the benefits they lost. And those managers or employers are trying to keep their employees as much as they can while meeting requirements for costs, profits, and production. Many of my friends and fellow employees see employers as out for their profits, and nothing else, having a total disregard for the people who have worked hard for them—sometimes for decades."

CAREER PATH AND CHALLENGES

The Taskmaster thrives by bringing top-notch value to a company or team, particularly a growing one. He or she is a Soloist rather than someone who seeks the consensus of a team. While his or her concern is mainly about quality of life (passive social impact), that concept of quality of life includes a focus on excellence. The potential downfall of the CPES is that he or she will find other people at the company unable to match his or her standards, which can produce frustration or even burnout, especially if the company does not reward employees well.

JOBS AND CAREERS OFTEN HELD BY CPES SURVEY RESPONDENTS: sales, retail, law enforcement, health care, accounting/auditing/analytics.

THOUGHTS FROM OTHER CPES RESPONDENTS

- *"Document, document, document. Always have clear documentation to justify the actions you have taken."*

- *"Consider moving. I moved to a new city to pursue more and better job options, and I'm glad I did."*

- *"I am an administrator at a university. Deciding on a 'career' as a teen is next to impossible. Take some time to work before going to college."*

Archetype 11: CPIT, the Steady Hand

Innovating (I) with a team (T) gives the Steady Hand satisfaction that transcends the limitations of working for a more risk-averse entity (C), while focusing on personal goals (passive social impact, P).

Resa Goldstein, Actuary, Saint Louis

Dealing with Stress and No Benefits

Resa Goldstein, twenty-five, works as an actuary, using statistics to calculate risk—for example, with life insurance tables. Right after college, she explains, "I had a contract position in a pension department basically doing what I'm doing right now. I worked there for two and a half years, but because I was a third-party contractor, I had no benefits. For about six months, I was a financial analyst for health care evaluation so I could get benefits, and now I'm back on my career track as a full-time actuary at a new company.

"The biggest thing that I've learned is that most companies don't have loyalties toward their employees anymore. When I was a third-party contractor, I was basically doing the same exact job as everyone in my office, but I was getting paid less than half of what they were being paid. I had zero benefits, zero time off. Nothing.

"Then the second job I had, which was my first salaried position with benefits, I was literally screamed at every single day and told I was worthless. The company I'm with now does want to invest in their employees, but I've worked in the past with companies that don't. That was surprising for me, because my father was someone who worked for the same company for over thirty years.

"I dealt with the stress on my old jobs until I found something better. I didn't really have a choice, to be honest. I was literally was in a corner. I needed benefits because my health insurance was going to quadruple with Obamacare [the Affordable Care Act], so I needed a job to pay for it. [Note: many employers subsidize medical insurance costs, so a subsidized employer option might cost less than an Affordable Care Act option.]

"For over three years, I would go on interviews every month or so, but nothing ever panned out. I found this job because it was a company that I had interviewed for five months before, and then they finally brought me in for a second interview because they were hiring again. I got lucky, I guess.

"The place I work now supports progress in my career. And they definitely say that they prefer to hire people for life instead of just cycling through employees. There's a bit of a gap with my group obviously because we're younger, but a lot of the people that I work with have been there for over fifteen years, so for me that shows a lot. It shows that the people they hire want to stay. Whereas the miserable job I was at before, ninety percent of the workforce had been there for less than a year."

Seeking More Certifications to Advance

"I'm happy where I am right now, and I don't see myself leaving this company, because even if I wanted to, I don't think I'd be able to. I'm definitely going to work on getting my certifications and advancing my positions." (Actuaries can take a series of increasingly advanced and specialized exams to gain certification for higher-skilled and higher-paying jobs.) "I feel like I definitely have the flexibility and the work/life balance that I want," Resa continues, "so at least right now I don't see any reason why I would change. That's what I wanted, so I'm happy.

"Anyone just starting their career, I would tell to go into STEM." That's a popular acronym for the fields of science, technology, engineering, and mathematics. "I would also tell them to make themselves versatile. I have seen a lot of my friends that just get a degree in something, and then they don't use it at all. Or I see a lot of people struggling to get a job because they didn't get a useful degree—something that was more like a hobby instead. We definitely need more people in STEM careers. I was talking to my dad, and he said that when he graduated college in the 1970s with an engineering degree, he got a job immediately." Even though STEM careers are valued highly, says Resa, "it's just not like that anymore. There's a lot of people with degrees, especially bachelor's degrees, but they're losing their worth as something that shows you have ability. On the other hand, just having a master's doesn't mean you're more qualified. I don't think that a higher degree means higher qualifications, necessarily. I think it's more just a piece of paper and a social standing.

"I feel like a lot of people my age are struggling to find a career and really pin down what they *want* to do, what they are *able* to do, and what they can do that will keep them in a job long term."

CAREER PATH AND CHALLENGES

The Steady Hand wants to be part of a stable system, and finds it difficult as a cautious careerist to deal with uncertainty in the job market. He or she enjoys teamwork, with an ability to gain higher positions or innovate, and can be frustrated by a lack of career opportunity, particularly as someone who works primarily for self-support and self-sufficiency (passive social impact).

JOBS AND CAREERS OFTEN HELD BY CPIT SURVEY RESPONDENTS: scientist, engineer, teacher.

THOUGHTS FROM OTHER CPIT RESPONDENTS

- *"You are always being watched. Even if you are sure you aren't, act like you are—you never know."*

- *"Keep options open; try several careers, and travel!"*

- *"Find a passion and figure out how to get paid for it. Always do your best work no matter what the job is."*

Archetype 12: CPIS, the Masterful Realist

The Masterful Realist prioritizes personal goals (passive social impact—P—rather than mission-driven work), seeks an environment to express his or her innovation (I) and make top-level decisions (S), while still retaining a career trajectory that is cautious (C) and steady. "Masterful," in this case, relates to both mastery of the job and a deft sense of corporate culture.

Elaine Chen, Corporate Marketing Communications Manager, New York City

Frequent and Fearless Job Changing

"I was raised in Delaware. I'm forty-six. Since college, I've had fourteen full-time permanent positions—not including the part-time jobs. That is a lot by American standards," she acknowledges.

"After college, I was a paralegal; then went to law school; was a lawyer, briefly; a tech journalist; a digital agency strategist; a copywriter in a direct marketing agency; an in-house marketer—there were a couple of transitions in that process. I remain in marketing today. Once I got into the agency world, all of my jobs have been fairly related.

"Going from law to journalism to marketing were significant changes. I never really wanted to be a lawyer. My parents told me they would take me out of Harvard University if I did not basically have a major with a career path they approved of—which is a lot of pressure to put on a seventeen- or eighteen-year-old who's been killing herself to get into this kind of school. I picked law, with the full understanding that I was being told, 'If you have interests and you enjoy music or art, you can do that in your spare time, but work is for making money, and law is a stable and profitable career.'

"But after a year at my first job, I got laid off. We graduated from the Fordham University Law School class of 1994 into a horrific economy. When I got laid off, certain friends said to me—and it was true—'I know you're upset now, but you're going to look back and say this was the best day of your life. You *hated* being a lawyer.' No one's going to quit a job in a bad economy. Most people stumble along because it's a huge amount of risk to change jobs.

"So, at a relatively young age, with low overhead, I lost a job. I started seeing an occupational counselor who dealt with career transitions.

"I enjoy being a writer. That's why I picked law over medicine when my parents asked me to pick a career. I found an entry-level job as a journalist at twenty-five thousand dollars per year. It was the only job I was offered, so I was going to take it!

"For close to a year, I also did a lot of odd jobs. I taught a Kaplan law school admission test prep course. I was a 'mystery shopper'—paid to shop and evaluate the experience that different companies offered. I was a paralegal working on tobacco smoke litigation testing.

"Today I work in corporate marketing communications. Marketing is a huge, varied discipline. There are lots of types. I work on technology-based communications known as product marketing. We want to make sure that people have heard of our product. There's an acronym we have: AIDA. It stands for what motivates people: awareness, interest, desire, and action. I go to trade shows and industry associations. I work on 'sales enablement': supervising what kinds of product sheets we produce and so on. I also volunteer my time supervising web design and marketing for an education nonprofit."

Don't Overthink Things

"So many people want a job that's a 'good fit.' But I would say to people, partly in jest, 'As long as you get along with your boss, and you don't have to work horrible hours, jobs are all the same.' People often dramatically overthink this whole idea of what's the right career and 'What's right for me?'

"Everyone has certain core skills. If you take someone who is fantastic with numbers and hates writing, and make them write all day, they will be miserable. So you need to find something that addresses your core skills.

"I think of myself as a good writer. I like to think of myself as empathetic. As a marketer, I use this all the time. You need to see yourself from the perspective of the people you are marketing to. I tend to be creative; I like not having to do the same thing every day. I like things that are new: technology, media research. I tend to want to sleep in a bit. If I had to work on Wall Street and be there at seven thirty every day, I would be fired! People don't think about these practical things enough." This is part of what we call workstyle: the mix of work and lifestyle concerns.

"Some things that may bother you about your job may be small things," Elaine continues. "But not getting along with your boss is a key thing that makes people unhappy. It's been a very long time, with a few exceptions, that I've said 'I hate my career.' Instead, I think, 'I need to change my job.'

"It also takes a lot of self-awareness to say, 'Hey, what's the problem here? Is it that I'm in an industry that's a bad fit? Is it that I'm in a job that's a dead end? Is it that I don't get along with my boss?'

"There have been times—for example, when I was in advertising— where I felt like, 'This isn't going to work.' We had bosses we had to make happy with this crazy creative work, and making the clients happy was less important. I felt like I was disappointing people every day. Advertising is unstable in general; there are layoffs all the time. So I decided I wanted to go 'in house'"—meaning, working for the marketing division of a company rather than for an advertising agency. "It took me a couple of years to make the tradition, but I did it."

The Interpersonal Side of Work Is Important Too

"You have a lot of perspective if you've worked fourteen jobs. Going from one job to another to another, you do realize you can keep those friends after you switch jobs. At this one dot-com where I worked, we had all these horrible layoffs. It was clear this company would not survive. I was having a conversation with my group, whom I had handpicked. We had worked together for many months. I told them, 'Let's have a conversation about where you guys are in your careers and where you want to be. To the extent I can make the transition we are all going to go through easier, I will.' One woman said, 'I would want us to all be together, even if we went to another company.'

"That was a very emotionally moving moment for me. You try to think you would be a good boss and make the world you work in a better place. It was inspiring.

"What I took away from that was a company is just a company. If I get run over by a car in the street tomorrow, the company will not come to my funeral, but I expect all of my coworkers would want to be there because of the relationships we built. Those relationships help you succeed.

"Screwing over a person for a company is *not* a good idea. It's not just about being fair or being good—which, of course, you should be. But corporate life is so unstable now. I've seen people get rewarded for playing the company game. But that doesn't mean that the company or the boss is still going to be there, even in six months.

"I had a boss I really respected in advertising. He'd had IBM and AT&T as clients, and lost them both. He said, 'You know what, Elaine? If you told me that IBM would no longer be selling computers and AT&T would no longer be selling landline phone service, I would have said you were crazy. But industry shifts like that might be why we lose our jobs.'

"Now, you can look at my career and ask why I've moved around so much. There are so many people who just say, 'I'm going to ride the wave.' But sometime it's better to leave the downward spiral of a company with huge problems before it hits bottom."

Sometimes a Job Is Just a Job

"It's also important to understand that at the end of the day, this is just a job.

"A job is not who I *am*. A job is not my whole life. I may enjoy my job, and there may be things that are wonderful about it. But if the company is having significant financial trouble, or they want to get rid of you, the company you enjoyed is already gone. The best you can do is re-create what you liked about it somewhere else.

"I might be considered to be throwing in the towel too soon, but at the end of the day, I don't think that is true. Staying too long is bad. So is taking things too personally—thinking 'They screwed me!' even when sometimes it's partially true. I can get angry, but I try not to internalize things that way. At a company doing badly, you as one individual just have a tiny bit of control, unless you're the CEO. Sometimes they *have* to lay people off. You are just a small part of things, and the decisions from the top can be capricious.

"For example, there are a lot of reasons you might get fired. Your salary might be higher than someone else's in the same job, even if you have more experience. Maybe the other person has some unique knowledge, so they can't be fired. Some employers consider things that shouldn't be considered." (Later in the book we talk about employment discrimination and ethics in the workplace.)

According to Elaine, "I do believe you should pay it forward. A lot of people have helped me, and I've helped a lot of people. Networking is something people talk about all the time, but I don't think I'm that good a networker. Maintain a network from companies where people appreciated your work. Used LinkedIn. Be that person that people get along with. To be hostile doesn't help. Lie through your teeth if you have to, but make everyone think you like them!

"I'm kind of an informal career counselor. People come to me because I have been through so many successful transitions. I ask them:

" 'What do you like? What do you need? What do you stone-cold absolutely *have to have*?'

"When it comes to salary, for example, those are three totally different amounts of money. But a lot of people don't go through that thinking until it's too late. You really need to do that math the day you get laid off—or *before* you get laid off.

"I do think the economy is getting better. But there's so much uncertainty. God only knows what's going to happen."

CAREER PATH AND CHALLENGES

The Masterful Realist loves to innovate and build part of a larger established entity, which offers relative security for someone fond of the cautious career path. He or she is willing to make unilateral decisions, even with the goals of the team in mind. His or her goals are geared primarily toward living a good life all around, rather than working for a mission-driven company, but many Masterful Realists give generously of their time and money for what they believe in.

JOBS AND CAREERS OFTEN HELD BY CPIS SURVEY RESPONDENTS: sales and retail, food service, administrative support, human resources, k–12 education.

THOUGHTS FROM OTHER CPIS RESPONDENTS

- *"My biggest decision was to leave sales management and return to sales. As a manager, I had no quality of life. I was responsible for people, places, and things I had no control over."*

- *"Don't make your job your life. To the company, it's about the profit. Period. You are a minion who is only there to fill a role, perform a function, and contribute to the bottom line, and management really doesn't care about you, or how you do it. Just do it, or get out. So, at the end of the day, you have to make your work a means to something more in life. It has to be for family or to support your charitable giving."*

- *"Don't limit yourself. I never thought I'd be doing what I'm doing, and didn't even know my job existed. I kept an open mind and was willing to take risks to get where I am."*

- *I learned many new skills as a temp worker and was offered a permanent job on almost every assignment. Good way to scope out the company, boss, and coworkers before ever making a commitment. Also, keep one's nose in one's own backyard when it comes to jobs, what others are doing, and so on. I saw my boss on one job go down the line and fire one after another. When she came to me, she simply said, 'You, you stay. You come in here, you do your work, mind your own business, and then leave.' Another great lesson, for sure!!"*

THE RP TYPES: Higher-Risk-Taking Individuals Who Choose Passive-Social-Impact Work

RPET	"The Chief of Staff"
RPES	"Mr./Ms. Get It Done"
RPIT	"The Cocreator in Chief"
RPIS	"The Groundbreaker"

Archetype 13: RPET, the Chief of Staff

RPETs don't mind if their jobs have passive social impact (P), as long as they can achieve tangible goals (their executor side, E) as part of a team (T). The RPET is willing to take risks (R) to be compensated well for his or her expertise.

Greg Jones, Utility Consultant, Conroe, Texas

Many Jobs, Many Cities

"The jobs that I've had as an adult? That covers a lot of water. I started in education. I actually taught business and computer science courses at the university level at Georgetown University and Indiana University. From there I went into banking and was in charge of what was then called data processing; then became senior VP of operations there. Then I got out of banking and went to work for American Express and ran their data centers in south Florida. Then I went back into banking in the Miami area. Then I got out of there and went to work for utilities in Illinois, and I was in charge of their information technology department.

"I then moved down to the South Texas Project, which is a large nuclear site. Got called back to the corporate headquarters and worked for them." Greg's list is far from over: next, he went into what's called shared services consulting, where companies rely on consultants to set them up with vendors who do aspects of their businesses, like human relations. "From there," he continues, "I went into Millikin University in Illinois as a senior VP, and then went back into utility consulting, and that's what I've been doing since. It's hard because I travel quite a bit. My family is someplace other than I am."

Career Lessons

"The key thing is to always go for opportunities that hold your interest. I certainly put enough time into work on any given week that it'd better be something that's meaningful. The second thing is, if the work has meaning, don't be afraid to even take a step backward. I've done that a couple times in my career. I've actually gone down in terms of position because the work was that interesting, and I knew it had to have an impact on the organization. Because of that, it all turned out to be better in the end.

"The third big thing is to keep your ears open, listen a lot. As you can tell from my background, I've been in a lot of different industries. Each one of those has been a learning experience. You have to listen quite a bit. Listening is pretty darn important, especially to the people in the industry and the people that have been in that organization for quite a while. One of the best pieces of advice I got from somebody early on in my career was: 'Keep your mouth shut for about the first three months that you work someplace. Because you'll learn a lot more, and you won't sound stupid when you open your mouth.'

"I would say one of the key things I've always tried to do is to get a mentor early; someone who is in a fairly senior position. Obviously, the higher up you go in an organization, it's a little harder to find those people because there are fewer of them. But I always tried to find a mentor who could help coach me, if you will, about what the culture was like, how to get along. The culture is a lot more things than just how the people feel.

"Another piece of advice that I got early on in my career was that I stayed close to the money. If you understand the finances of whatever organization you're working for, if you understand how they make and spend money, then you probably understand a whole lot more than most people working there as to what's going to happen with the company.

"I've always looked at the work and whether it was of interest to me. Go for the learning piece of it, don't go for the paycheck. A lot of people hop around in careers just to get a bigger paycheck, and, quite frankly, they don't learn much. They might as well have just stayed where they were for their whole life. If that's what you're doing, then you're really not growing. You're just staying stagnant, and all you're really doing is trying to increase your investment portfolio."

Changes in the Workplace: Episodic Careers

"Over the past six to eight years, more people are very, very anxious about taking a job at a new organization. They'd rather stay where they are. They see a huge upside risk if they go someplace else and it doesn't work out. When I started working—I tell this to young folks all the time—there was an agreement, if you will, between the employer and the employee that you'd come in every day. And if you did your job—guess what?—everything would be okay. And the only person who could break that would be the employee, who could say, 'I'm going to work somewhere else. I'm giving my two weeks' notice.'

"Now, over the last twenty to twenty-five years, that agreement is being broken on both sides. The organization will say, 'I'm sorry. We're downsizing, and you're not around anymore.' So the old agreement that people had when they went to work is gone. People are very skittish now, especially because of the economic conditions, of either picking up and leaving or taking another job."

Work by Generation: Millennials and Boomers

"I think about younger employees. I'm sure my dad's generation was skeptical of us, but for the Millennial generation, work is a means to an end. It's family, it's travel, it's friends. It's not the value of proposition of 'Gee, I want to work hard for the organization,' whatever that might be. One of the things that I think is very difficult is that because they take that attitude, I think you're starting to see a lot more specialization than generalization at a time when organizations are looking for a lot more people that can cover a wider spectrum.

"Take a look at how many people who are sixty-two to sixty-four years old and up are still working. Part of that's because they can't afford to retire on their investment portfolio, but another big part of that is that the organization is probably asking them to stay on because they haven't trained people at the lower levels to get that generalist experience. I think that's going to be a very difficult void to fill here in the next twelve to fifteen years.

"I think that goes back to the unspoken agreement between employer and employee that has been changing in recent years. Organizations now have no problem telling people who have been there—sometimes a long time, sometimes a short time—'I'm sorry, your job is gone.' We've become kind of callous about that.

"As a result, people have grown dissatisfied because the other piece of that—and I work a lot with utilities—if you go back in a time machine, say, to the late 1980s, utilities were part of the community. They were the people that sponsored the baseball team, they were a part of the chamber of commerce, they ran the Rotary Club, they sponsored a lot of things. Well, guess what? The people paying the rates for utilities don't want to do that anymore. They just want their electricity." Greg sees many companies that were once integrated into the life of communities no longer putting their time, money, and energy into those connections. Perhaps as a result, or at the very least in parallel, he sees employees becoming less invested in a larger sense of mission. "More and more organizations are looking like just a place to work as opposed to a piece of your world," he says. "There's no higher calling, if you will.

"I think the other thing that is very different now is the technology that we present to employees. It used to be that if I needed to do stuff, I either needed to physically get on the phone or go down and see someone. Now, especially with younger people, they don't even think of picking up the phone anymore. They send an email or text. We've taken the personalization out of it, so no wonder people are less satisfied. You don't have any feeling of belonging."

Work/Life Synergy

"I talk to a lot of young people about that, because a lot of them are wondering what's happening in our industry. The first thing that I tell them is that you really need to decide where your career fits in your life. Are you going to be a career-driven person? In other words, is work going to be a major component? Or are you going to say, 'My family comes first, and I recognize that may hold me back at times, but I'm okay with that because, quite frankly, I don't care if I'm the next VP or next director or next head manager or general manager'?

"I really encourage younger people to answer that question for themselves. Otherwise it's going to get terribly frustrating, and I do think it adds to the dissatisfaction. People who don't understand that might say, 'Well, my role is to come in here and do a job, and I'm going do as good a job as I can, but at five o'clock, I'm going out.' Then they get upset that they don't get the same promotions as the guy who is putting in twelve- or fifteen-hour days, leading projects, and things like that. They say, 'Well, gee, I've been around here longer.' Sorry, that doesn't cut it anymore.

"I've made choices between my career and personal life at times. And they haven't always been the best choices, either, looking back. If you're going to strive for the higher levels of an organization—and I still believe this is equally true today as it was twenty years ago—you'd better have a good sit-down with your family, and they need to understand the implications of that. You do too."

CAREER PATH AND CHALLENGES

The Chief of Staff is very practical about what work is and isn't. RPET individuals work best in teams and tend to focus their career risk taking on personal advancement and compensation rather than on high-social-impact work. The latter approach can bear fruit when an emotional distance from the job allows them to see clearly. One potential pitfall for RPET men and women is that they might become jaded if they're constantly surveying the job landscape and don't find the opportunities they seek.

JOBS AND CAREERS OFTEN HELD BY RPET SURVEY RESPONDENTS: entrepreneur, health care professional, artist.

THOUGHTS FROM OTHER RPET RESPONDENTS

- *"I left a company I was at for seven years because there was no room for advancement. Terrible choice—should have let them lay me off and not have to rush into another job. Instead, I have been struggling for the last twenty years."*

- *"Find something you love and try to make money at it. When you are young, shoot for more, because the debt and family obligations aren't there."*

- *"I had a work-related accident. Nobody cares if you are following the rules; the accident is a permanent black mark."*

Archetype 14: RPES, Mr./Ms. Get It Done

The RPES individual takes the lead (soloist, S) on implementing (executor, E) higher-risk strategies (R) for his or her own gain or for a larger company, focusing on individual and companywide benchmarks of success (passive social impact, P).

Aaron Keough, Senior Account Manager, Energy Company, Sacramento, California

An Episodic Career in Multiple Fields

"I began my adult working career as an armored guard transporting large sums of money on an assigned route. From there I moved into an online marketing/account management position. That position was with a start-up that didn't work out, so I moved into working as a security guard for a couple of different companies before landing a job as an account manager for another start-up company offering a calling center service for insurance agents. I additionally worked at a movie rental retail location at the same time to help earn income for my family. I briefly moved into a sales rep role for that start-up company, forcing me to leave the second retail job before moving on to a water company as a delivery route salesperson.

"The water company was purchased by a larger water company that led me to selling water only instead of delivering, and I grew tired of that quickly. I earned a position as a sales manager for an energy company and from there moved to another start-up in the energy sector that quickly failed. My most recent job has also been my longest, at a major US utility company providing both electricity and natural gas.

"The least satisfying of the jobs were the security jobs because I was working graveyard hours for next to nothing in pay trying to support my wife and two children. The most satisfying is my current position because I'm able to help people, have stable pay, and am able to take care of my family and now four children."

Education and Networking Lead to New Opportunities

"When I first moved to California, I had planned to finish my undergraduate degree (I was about half complete), but I was considered an out-of-state student and just started working instead. I planned to just work without a degree the rest of my life until I was at the water company with two children, and came the erudite thought: I wasn't going to ever be able to increase my income and support my current family and a potentially larger family without completing my undergraduate degree.

"I made the decision right then to go back, so I enrolled at University of Phoenix and went pretty much nonstop for two years to complete the degree, including the majority of that time working in a job that required a four-hour round-trip commute. I remember many nights eating dinner at a makeshift desk posting about different aspects of psychology, finishing at a late hour, and going to bed. The other major decision came after the energy start-up I came to failed so quickly and my family was left without any income, depleted savings, and no real prospects for another job. I must have filled out two hundred job applications, networked with everyone I could, and contemplated moving my pregnant wife and three kids back to Ohio, where I'm from, to try and earn a position with old connections. Finally, after a lot of exertion, a lot of prayer, and a lot of faith, I earned a position with the utility company, and thus far things have worked out very well."

Lessons from the Job

"The biggest lesson I've learned is through job experiences. What I mean is, each individual worker has a path they travel down, and what works for one individual won't work for another. Some people work great in a team setting, while others work great independently. I do well in established organizations that have set guidelines and allow for creative thought but not lackluster implementation of creative thought. Working at three different start-ups provided a lot of flexibility, time with my family, and the empowerment to get the job done the way I knew it could be done. It also provided a great deal of stress, and that stress came in a variety of ways: not knowing if I would get paid, not knowing if the pay date would change, would I have benefits, how much longer would I have a job, and so on. Some individuals thrive in that workplace, but I certainly didn't, and I am much more productive in the position I'm in now."

Advice for Young Professionals

"Life isn't going to be nice to you, give you a participation ribbon, tell you everything will be okay, and forgive your accidental errors. Life is brutal, only rewards top performers, makes you struggle through job loss, and will fire you for mistakes. Make the decision now to be better than your peers. Work to be the best at whatever your passion is in life. If you want to work on a waste management pickup route, then plan today to be the best worker that route and company has ever seen. If you want to build the next Golden Gate Bridge, then study to be the best engineer you can possibly be and then work to show your peers what you've learned and why you should be charged with building that next Golden Gate Bridge.

"Do not let your ethnicity, race, handicap, or other difference be a difference. Strive to be great, and people will recognize your greatness. Life would have you easily believe that if you're different you can't make it, but I would tell you that differences are the reason our country is great and why great companies succeed. The creativity of thought and subsequent products, services, and policies stem from those that dared to be different."

CAREER PATH AND CHALLENGES

Mr./Ms. Get-It-Dones wield their power in the service of a larger entity or a client, even if the company is their own. They are great at executing the company's or client's vision while retaining autonomy over strategy, and are often happiest when exploring new issues or sorting through new problems. The Get-It-Dones have the tenacity to stick with plans through the implementation, and are willing to shut down projects that are no longer useful.

JOBS AND CAREERS OFTEN HELD BY RPES SURVEY RESPONDENTS: engineering, publishing/writing/editing, management.

THOUGHTS FROM OTHER RPES RESPONDENTS

• *"Don't sit back and wait to be promoted. Your career is in your hands. The more you know, the better and more poised you are for the next change."*

- *"The scarier it seems, the more you should do it."*

Archetype 15: RPIT, the Cocreator in Chief

The Cocreator in Chief is willing to take risks (R) in pursuit of personal goals (passive social impact—P—rather than mission-driven work), leading the charge for innovation (I) with a team (T).

Baratunde Thurston, Comedian, Entrepreneur, and Author, New York City

"For me and for many people, how I saw opportunity and my path starts with my mother. She would always say 'Build your own.' This was a mantra for creating a life. She was always an employee of someone, but she was very creative, always sang, and loved manipulating tech stuff.

"It's about having more control over your own fate.

"She was also always encouraging me to just try stuff. Many parents want you to be an accountant or to be a doctor or to have some other stable profession, like an engineer. Many parents are very conservative because of their work experience: 'You need to get yourself a job with a good company and some benefits.' That was not my mother's perspective. I always felt supported doing all this stuff onstage, music, writing, tech. She was even pushing me, saying, 'Why don't you audition for this?' That was very influential."

Multiple Jobs and "Side Hustles"

"In terms of how I see the world, I have always had this little weird side-hustle thing. I think there's a race component to that; there's a black, urban East Coast thing pushing me to have creative economic opportunities. Everybody's got many jobs. My chief influences—positive and negative—always had multiple things going on. Some stuff under the table, some stuff next to the table, and the men who were in my life, none of whom was really my father, but friends of my mom and pseudo uncle characters, they were couriers and bassists and photographers; they were bike repairmen and cellists. There was always this combination of how people made their living and their lives. I didn't know too many people who just did one thing.

"Growing up in an environment where the hustle was normal, where some kind of side gig was just the default, I absorbed this as how you do things. When choosing a major, extracurriculars, to jobs and sales experiences, there was always this quilt mind-set, as opposed to this sort of solid comforter. I wrote about this in my book *How to Be Black*." The book, which made the *New York Times* Best Sellers list in 2012, reveals a rather unique life: raised in a drug-scarred neighborhood in Washington, DC, he attended the exclusive Sidwell Friends School—the alma mater of several kids who called the White House home—and then graduated from Harvard University. For Baratunde, now thirty-eight, the educational experience at Sidwell "was building on top of the neighborhood experience and the home experience. It just turbo-boosted it with confidence," he says.

"Instead of the hustle coming from a place of pure necessity or even desperation, it came from a place of opportunity, liberation, and entitlement. Which is: Yes, we can. Yes, we must. Actually, there's no other way. Most of this started at Sidwell first and then at Harvard, mainly because you're more impressionable when you're younger. And the entitlement came from seeing everyone else vacation here and drive this car and challenge this teacher. Seeing this made me expect it. It was normal.

"Challenging authority, such as your teacher, was not a nineties thing; that's a newer thing. But for the set of people that I went to school with starting in seventh grade, there was a healthy skepticism of authority and assumptions, facilitated and encouraged by authority. The assumption is that you're smart. That was also really helpful. So the piece that was missing for me is how to take all that passion, all that freedom, all that assumption that you can achieve your ambitions, and really effectively monetizing it. I've done okay at that. But I'm not great at it. And I've realized that for all the hours I've spent, for all the mental energy I've devoted, for all the inspiration that I've had and received, I'm not a millionaire, I'm not a billionaire, but I'm doing all right. I've got some debt, I don't own any property, I don't have a big retirement—I don't even *have* retirement. But I'll be fine.

"The third-level lesson is how do you leverage all that to actually create. In other words, not just to create ideas but also to create wealth.

"I felt I had achieved a level of escape velocity. I graduated from college in 1999. I'd had entrepreneurial inclinations for quite a long time, dating back to high school, with a lot of sales activities. I was selling everything from candies to verb conjugation tables; I was always hustling on the side."

Entrepreneurship, Failure, Debt—and New Ambitions

"After graduation from college, I went into a very traditional environment, this strategy consulting company. It was small, so it wasn't as formal as a bank, but it was cut from a similar mold. After a year, I left to try to start something. And it was an abject failure. I went into a financial hole, spending my modest personal savings, getting into credit card debt, and even had to borrow from my then girlfriend to cover my rent. Not only was I in a financial hole, but it was in 2000, when the economic bubble had just burst. Timing was horrendous. Heading back into the working world, I told myself, 'When I do this again, I'm going to do it better. I am going to have better partners and a model that makes more sense.'

"That was 2000, and I didn't do it again for twelve years. Now, I'm a weird case because even as I've had employment through institutions, I've also had my own brand franchise on the side. Being an author is very entrepreneurial, doing speaking and stand-up comedy is its own thing, so I had my own LLC throughout all that." A limited liability corporation (LLC) is a form of corporate structure often used by solo entrepreneurs.

"By my next major exit in 2012," he continues, "I'd basically assembled a much longer list of skills, a much deeper network, a much better understanding of who I would work with, and more of an actual business model in mind, as opposed to just a business idea."

By this time, Baratunde was working for the wildly popular satirical newspaper and multimedia brand *The Onion*, which, he says, "was in line with my passions. I also had options to work for big new organizations, agencies, and tech companies, but I knew I couldn't take those jobs. I needed to work for myself, combining my passions. There was no other home for this vision, and so I had to create a home for it.

"To describe that 'home,' I run a company, Cultivated Wit, that combines comedy, digital technology, and design, applied in a number of ways. We're funnier than your average marketing agency and smarter when it comes to the internet. We produce media, we write, we make shows, we produce live events, and we create software products that are tools for creative people. Our motto is 'We make fun, and we're the future.' No one else was focused on comedic marketing.

"Even today, in terms of my own life, I always have my *job* job and a little something else. I still have a bit of solo layer on top of everything else. My book writing is me, my stand-up is me, and even some of my hosting remains a sort of solo arrangement.

"For most people I know, it's hard to separate work from love and life. And there are many different ways of seeing how your work fits into your life. For many of my friends and network, work is a passion project. They are living through their work in a positive sense, it's all-consuming, and they are proud of it. It's like the World Cup, and they are waving their flag, saying, 'I am what I do, and I do what I am.'

"There's another set that sees work as something that allows them to be who they are. It's money, not work, that allows them to be who they are. And within that, there are big spenders, who are creating a big-ass pile of discretionary money to go live. They fly around, take vacations, hike, cook, and they're sort of buying life with their work.

"Then there's the other end of the spectrum: people who do not make much money. For them, work is to provide food, shelter, the occasional break, and entertainment or clothing. There's no hint of passion. It is a job. It is required."

Work, Inequality, and Gentrification—Being Priced Out of Opportunity

"As far as the future of work, I am afraid for New York City, and for most cities. I live in New York, but my work takes me across a lot of cities, especially DC, Boston, Detroit, San Francisco, and LA. *Inequality* is a word being used a lot more, but I also see an extreme split in people who are owning and making and loving what they do, regardless of compensation level, and healthily above the survival rate, and those who are scraping and just getting through life."

Baratunde lives in Fort Greene, Brooklyn. a neighborhood once home to rapper and former crack dealer Notorious B.I.G., whose song "10 Crack Commandments" includes the line "Don't you know Bad Boys move in si- lence and violence?" Today, amid boutiques, restaurants, and parents push- ing double strollers, a mural of the slain rapper is one of the few signs of the neighborhood's grittier and arguably more creative past—one which in- cluded the local founding of Spike Lee's production company. "In a year and a half," says Thurston, "the storefronts have shifted: an auto body shop is now a Hungry Ghost Coffee Bar and Café. The bike shop, which itself was a gentrifying force, is becoming a café and bakery. So what needs are being met within a certain geographic area? Fixing your car? Nope: serving your caffeine needs. It indicates a huge shift as to what's happening in the city. I am going to end up in the world Gary Shteyngart wrote about in the novel *Super Sad True Love Story,* where the world becomes this amusement park designed with an elite mind-set.

"It becomes really boring when you don't have artists and actual work- ing-class people in your city. I don't think a lot of people feel this, because it's hard to say, 'We need poor people in the city.' You don't wave that flag like 'Bring us your poor.'

"But you need that grit, that hustle, that dynamism. If everybody's super comfortable, and everybody's drinking five-dollar coffees, there's no drive anymore. Creative inspiration comes out of conflict, comes out of the desperation, out of mobility, not stagnation. A city that's all broke is not good either. No one can climb those hierarchies to create interesting stuff. But a city that's all 'top end' is just too lazy, too comfortable to be creative.

"That's the worst-case scenario for New York: rents keep going up, college kids don't do their internships here anymore, and broke people from around the world don't come here to pursue their dreams. Some other city will catch the spark, and in fifty years, we're talking about the renaissance that was New Orleans, or was Detroit.

"Being a creative is a hard life to pursue. But at least I have control in my life. We need a world where people can adapt to change on their own, but there's a cushion as well. Because a freelance-only lifestyle is crazy risky. I'm able to weather it more than the average freelance-lifestyle person, but even still, I didn't have health care for a year and a half. And I have health care now only because of Obamacare."

CAREER PATH AND CHALLENGES

The Cocreator in Chief is very mission driven in the sense of producing an excellent product rather than a specific social outcome. Nonetheless, almost by definition, these entrepreneurial types reshape society constantly, whether through ideas or software or architecture. The challenge for RPIT individuals is twofold: one, picking the right set of partners and institutions; and two, deciding how much to work independently within the structure of being team driven. Changing teams can be the most difficult part of a Cocreator in Chief's workstyle.

JOBS AND CAREERS OFTEN HELD BY RPIT SURVEY RESPONDENTS: entrepreneurship, sales, health care professions

THOUGHTS FROM OTHER RPIT RESPONDENTS

- *"Every good decision I've ever made, the universe has just kind of told me."*

- *"Even if you have a job, you're going to have a hard time making ends meet. That's a reality for a lot of people."*

- *"When I graduated college, I really didn't feel prepared for anything."*

Archetype 16: RPIS, the Groundbreaker

RPIS men and women don't mind if their job has passive social impact (P), as long as they can innovate (I) with a large degree of autonomy (soloist, S). The RPIS takes risks (R) in order to receive outsized awards.

Ellen Hongo, Senior Director of Collaborative Business Solutions, Reno area, Nevada

A Military Career Opens New Doors

"Going all the way back, I spent some time in the navy doing aviation electronics. Then I got into management consulting, and spent the bulk of my career doing that for a variety of industries around the world. I've also worked quite a bit in high-tech.

"The area that I specialize in is called knowledge management. It's really about business process optimization but through better access to intellectual capital, better collaboration within the organization. I've consulted on it and have been senior director of collaboration at Automatic Data Processing, or ADP.

"The biggest thing I've learned on the job was that I wanted to stay open. I had quite a few friends who always knew what they wanted to be, like 'By this age, I'll be this or I'll be that.' To me, it just seems like they missed out on so many things in life. I would say, as far as career advice, keep your eyes open. I've done a lot more interesting things than people who planned things out because I had more of an open mind about what's available.

"Also, as a woman, I've never felt any discrimination that I couldn't get ahead or been treated differently from men. Actually, being in the navy helped. When I would meet people and tell them I had been in the navy, I got acceptance. Even in the navy, I never felt like I was treated any differently as a woman. If you worked hard, you were treated with respect. The opportunities were there.

"Networking is really important to building relationships. A lot of people network with the intention of getting something out of it. But if you really network with the intention of helping others and not for personal gain, it's reciprocated. Your networks tend to come back to you with all sorts of great opportunities. They don't forget you. A lot of my most interesting opportunities came from people that I had worked with in the past or had helped in the past, even past clients of mine.

"I'm fifty-three," says Ellen, who refers to herself as a "tweener": someone born toward the tail end of the baby boom but too early to be considered a member of Generation X. "I don't really associate myself with the boomers or Generation X. I think that the landscape is very different if you look at Millennials and the fact that we're moving toward more of a contract workforce. There's not this idea that you join a company and stay for twenty years. Networking becomes even more important because it's not about permanence that you're looking at in a career, you're looking at opportunity, growth."

Look Sideways to Move Up

"It's important to look sideways as well as up," Ellen advises. "Moving up isn't always the best thing for you. Sometimes broadening your career or jumping sideways will allow you to go up faster if that's what you want to do. I've had a lot of experiences where I've jumped sideways, and it's far more interesting than just staying on the same career path and doing the same thing.

"Again, I would really stress the importance of networks and reputation," she says. Maintaining a personal brand is important because "you're going to be jumping around much more frequently" according to projections about the future of the labor force.

"I think a big difference between generations is the fact that you don't have the permanence. When I was getting out of college and going around, if you didn't have five years on a résumé, people would think you were a job-hopper, and they wouldn't take you seriously, or there must be some issue because you don't stay at a job very long. I don't think that exists today.

"Many times, the average person stays at a job for two years. There's a lot of talk about the 'contract nation' of workers and the fact that we're now going to become a generation of contractors versus the long-term view. You have a lot more opportunity in the short term, but at the same time, it gives you a little bit more uncertainty because you're not looking at staying ten years at a place.

"I think that companies will lay people off at the drop of a hat. I think it's the first thing that goes whenever there are financial issues. Companies don't put the same investment into people that they did years ago."

Consulting Offers Flexibility and Growth

"The beauty of consulting is that you're going to be working in different industries, encountering different problems. I started my own consulting firm, which opened up even more opportunities because I could choose the clients that I wanted to work for. High-tech, consumer goods, oil and gas—I've worked in all of them. For someone who gets bored really easily, it was always a new challenge. Even though I knew the subject matter that I was consulting on, I had to learn the new industry. I really enjoyed the fact that I worked across all sorts of different industries. I found that if you really know what your confidences are and what you're delivering, it can really transcend different industries. It wasn't that difficult.

"At the time, the big trend was business reengineering, which was really about optimizing processes—really looking at the balance sheet. But they forgot about people, and they forgot about knowledge. That's when there were a lot of layoffs. I just realized that there's a way of really optimizing business profitability without having to cut people and to always focus on the engineering approach of the process. I liked the more human approach. At the time, it was really a new thing in the marketplace, so a group of us started the consulting firm to really focus on that. It wasn't yet a major service area; there weren't any other consulting firms.

"I still have my own consulting firm. I'm working for ADP as an employee, but my business partners continue to run the firm. The biggest challenge in running a firm is business development, and getting the right people into the organization is a little harder. Also, I think people change jobs so quickly that trying to implement a program, you usually end up losing the people that you're working with halfway through, so it's harder to create that continuity."

CAREER PATH AND CHALLENGES

Many RPIS workers prize the feeling of being well rewarded for innovating and doing big things first in their field. RPIS men and women focus on excellence rather than on social value, which makes for a highly productive individual who can often create companies and contribute by mentoring or partnering with others.

JOBS AND CAREERS OFTEN HELD BY RPIS SURVEY RESPONDENTS: sales, management, consulting, creative professions (arts, writing, and performance).

THOUGHTS FROM OTHER RPIS RESPONDENTS

- *"Left a stable IT corporate job for insurance and financial sales. Returned seven years later. The experience gained was valuable to an IT career, but it will take me years to recoup personal financial health."*

- *"You have to have patience. You will work with people who are not qualified to water plants. You still have to work with them. You conduct yourself always to the highest standard. Never let them pull you down. Ever."*

WORK/LIFE MASTERY

Each of the people whose life journeys you've explored in this Work/ Life Matrix have mastered the art of "working freely." They are self-aware and know what their belief systems are and what they want from life. And even if they haven't achieved all of their goals (and who has?), they are aware of their optimum matrix zone. They're dealing with challenges that many of us face: the economy, interpersonal relations in the office, business negotiation, and/or family and personal demands. Despite that, you can see there are many ways to find your "home at work"—that is, the place where your skills are appreciated, your needs are met, and your personal goals (financial and otherwise) are achievable.

I hope you read through many of these stories, rather than going to your archetype alone. Everyone who shared his or her hard-won experience has lessons that apply broadly to the evolving era of careers. As you examine the lessons that come from the archetypes, also think about the people in your life who have found satisfaction at work. Study them and seek out their advice. By the way, don't be put off if they can't help you directly, at least at the moment. Those who have a lot to give often have so many people to mentor that they can't take on any new responsibilities without failing at their own jobs or shortchanging their own families. But seek actively to put yourself in the company of people you admire—not just ones who are considered well known but also those who are rooted in everyday wisdom.

In the following chapters of the book, we'll turn back to some of the big-picture issues facing contemporary jobs and careers. Use the frameworks of the Work/Life Matrix and episodic careers to think through how you approach the increasingly complex questions about work we have to answer. We can work together to share the solutions we've found, to inspire one another, to forge a future. In order for each of us to do our part, we also require self-knowledge—to pursue our own dreams as well as help our friends, family, coworkers, and country achieve theirs.

Learning how to navigate episodic careers in a time of disruption is critical, not just in our individual lives but as our communities and our country change. Just as you can seek people who have developed work/ life mastery as role models, you can also become one for others. In part three, "Making Decisions with Heart and Smarts," we'll talk about critical inflection points in episodic careers and how we can navigate them. In part four we'll look at "The Right Work for America" and the questions about money and morality, success, and retirement that we're grappling with individually and collectively.

PART THREE

Making Decisions
with Heart and Smarts

When faced with the big tactical decisions about careers, you can tap into your heart, look at your dreams and desires, and see where you fall on the map of the Work/Life Matrix and other self-evaluation tools. Or you can get into your head, plug into all the data from studies and government news releases, employment trends, and dive deep into the Help Wanted ads (and online job search engines). I believe the best path is to combine both looking at who you are and seeing what's percolating in the larger world. Though I'm bit of a data nerd (both running my own surveys and distilling research from others), I believe that what makes us thrive—on the job and off—comes from within. How do you combine knowledge of the world with your own emotional intelligence? In this section, we'll address three common thorny issues that require "heart and smarts": how to cultivate emotional resilience in the context of work; how to find a job when searching for work; and when, whether, and how to leave a job or career.

5

Resilience Is Everything

Recovering from Layoffs, Screwups, and Other Career Disasters

I'm pretty sure none of this would have happened if I hadn't been fired from Apple. It was awful-tasting medicine, but I guess the patient needed it. Sometimes life hits you in the head with a brick. Don't lose faith.

—*Apple founder Steve Jobs, from his 2005 commencement speech at Stanford University*

NO ONE GETS a free ride in life or work. Not even people born with silver spoons in their mouths or the self-made wealthy will pass through this world without some scars. Of course, there are paper cuts, and then there are cleaving moments when life leaves you gutted.

In the *new* new realities of work, the survivors and thrivers will be people who can recover from setbacks big and small; who can learn from their mistakes; and who do *not* become bitter when they lose a round in the job wars through no fault of their own. (See CPIS archetype Elaine Chen.) We have only so much control in this world. This chapter seeks to identify what you can work on predicting and controlling, and what you sometimes simply have to forge through and learn from.

Many people I spoke to for this book demonstrate resilience: what some people call the ability to bounce back and others might term "grit," which isn't limited by income or any one demographic factor.

- Carmen Rita Wong grew up in a family that went from comfortable to struggling after her stepfather lost his job. The lessons she learned helped make her into a personal finance expert.
- Philip Wingfield was highly educated but became one of the long-term unemployed. Yet he turned his lessons about unemployment into a whole new career.
- Adam Freed wanted to be—and became—a TV reporter. A dispute with management left him jobless, but it also led him to a lucrative new career in tech.
- And Kristine Danielle went from being a heroin-addicted street prostitute to a skilled welder, because she knew that the way she was living would kill her, and she had the strength to believe in herself and change.

As we look at these people, we'll analyze what resilience is, how we can cultivate it, and how it can change our careers and personal lives for the better.

• • •

"Confronted with Life's Hardships, Some People Snap, and Others Snap Back," reads the subheadline of an article by Diane Coutu in the *Harvard Business Review*. She quotes the CEO of Adaptiv Learning Systems, Dean Becker, whose company trains workers to be more resilient. "More than education, more than experience, more than training, a person's level of resilience will determine who succeeds and who fails," Becker states. "That's true in the cancer ward, it's true in the Olympics, and it's true in the boardroom." Resilience can involve everything from accepting that life can be harsh to having a sense of humor, being able to attract allies, and improvising when the going gets rough.[1]

Having led an episodic career that includes different types of jobs and workstyles, with a mix of freedom and anxiety, I would also add that a critical aspect of attracting allies is *being able to tell the truth*. If you are in need, don't pretend you aren't. After I left a technology job that wasn't working for me, and toward the end of a fabulous four-month fellowship at Harvard's Institute of Politics, I set a goal of reaching out to three people a day—whether I had talked to them in years or not— and telling them I was looking for a job, open to switching fields, and generally in need of help in finding the next branch to land on. I chose to extend my stay in Massachusetts to be near a dear friend while she was having cancer surgery, so I had plenty of time for outreach.

When I emailed and called, I didn't pretend I knew what I was doing with my life. I didn't pretend everything was fine. I was confused about what I should do next, even though I had many valuable skills. The workstyle of journalism as I'd done it to date was no longer working for me. I didn't want to be told anymore to get on a plane in the middle of the night to cover a story. I didn't want to regularly miss holidays with my family in order to meet deadlines. Nor did I want to work purely for money. I'd tried that, and when my heart isn't in a job, neither is my head. For all its logistical hassles, journalism brought me deep passion and connection to ideas and ideals. I wanted a new path to that connection.

A couple of weeks into my outreach, a friend told me I had two weeks to apply for a professorship at New York University's Journalism Department. I would get benefits for teaching one class a semester and could continue to freelance in radio, television, and writing. I applied, somewhat nervously, and got the position. Teaching is exciting and humbling. I've had great semesters, where I feel I innovate in the classroom, and ones where I feel I haven't pushed my students enough. But one student told me upon graduation that he viewed me as his "teacher, mentor, and friend," and it reminded me about the human connection that accompanies learning.

The workstyle of this job requires discipline, as it is predicated on combining academic work with ongoing efforts in journalism. In my case, I write books and columns, and sometimes I podcast and do television. I have to manage my finances so that I can hire researchers, transcriptionists, and occasional accounting/office help, while evaluating whether the work I have coming in justifies the expenses. It's a juggle. In return, I get the warm fuzzies from mentoring students and the freedom to continue to explore ideas that challenge me and my audiences. My life isn't perfect, but it's *true*. I'm true to my quest to learn and disseminate information, and I wouldn't have been able to do it if I hadn't shown my soft underbelly—the fact that I needed help figuring out things. If I decide to do something else with my working life, I hope I'll be able to acknowledge what I need and ask for help in seeking it.

Networking gets a bit of a bad rap because it's often done poorly, mechanically, with little real human connection. But in my life and career, networking is a way of maintaining relationships with people who interest you. You help some of them more than they help you, or vice versa, but there's a genuine connection. Sometimes it's a peer relationship; other times a mentor or mentee relationship. Storytelling—listening, reading, watching—can also show us ways of applying other people's hard-won lessons to our own lives. Now, many of us will get burned at one point or another. If we are truly open, we might end up trusting someone we shouldn't. But in general, in a networked job world like ours, judicious connection often fosters intimacy, which then fosters a willingness to aid. In other words, you gotta give to get. That applies to your contacts, but also to your stories and your wisdom.

Carmen Rita Wong, a personal finance author who offered some perspective on the economy earlier, has lived a life that illustrates the power of resilience. Dominican American, she grew up in a family with one brother and four younger sisters. "One of the most seminal moments in shaping how I think about work comes from watching my dad. I saw him as the epitome of the American Dream," she says. "He was educated at the University of Detroit, took us out of the city to a house with a picket fence, and went to work in a suit. He worked in tech, not as a high-ranking guy, but he made enough to have a good life. Then he lost his job in the crash of '87.

"I picked up the phone on that October day when the market crashed, and he said, 'Tell your mom I'm coming home early'"—that is, to announce the catastrophic layoff. "My mother left four girls at home and went to work waiting tables to help put me through school."

Carmen's father didn't want to take a job that he saw as below him. "He would come home and say that he couldn't take a job because it paid too little or some other reason. Even as a young kid, I was like 'Take the damn job, man! Do you see this economy? Do you see what's going on?' That, in turn, made me feel like there's nothing below me," she says, a precursor to the way she assiduously sought out work as an adult, whether high profile or not, sometimes better paying than others. In college, says Carmen, "I was a work-study kid and worked every break, long weekend, and vacation. Every moment I wasn't studying I was working.

"When things get dire in terms of work, the pride has to go, and you have to realize it's temporary," she says. "The demotion and the pay cut are all temporary."

The tragedy of the situation is that Carmen's hardworking mother died young. Her mother lost her health insurance after Carmen's parents divorced. "She ignored a lot of symptoms and hid others very well," Carmen says of her mother's health, "but she eventually ended up in the emergency room with stage four cancer and full organ shutdown. She said she didn't go to the doctor because it cost too much money, but we would have helped her. There's this major independence in my family, which is kind of a sickness in and of itself because it's really the fear of asking for help."

Today Carmen Rita Wong, divorced with a young child, is thriving creatively and financially. She seeks to give back to others both through her writing, including the book *The Real Cost of Living: Making the Best Choices for You, Your Life, and Your Money,* and by working with non-profits such as Dress for Success. Recently she's been writing novels and working with the film industry. "Resiliency has been key to everything in my life," Carmen says. "It's actually a big part of why I went to grad school for psychology." She credits her grandmother with giving her unconditional love and adoration, helping build her capacity to recognize her own self-worth and bounce back from adversity. "Do you believe that you can change things, or do you believe you are a victim of what happens to you? It's something that I'm trying to hand down to my daughter, who, like kids tend to do, says, 'It's not my fault! I didn't do it!'

"Resiliency is huge," Wong says. "I wish I could inject it like an inoculation into kids."

What is resiliency? When applied to physical materials, the term involves the capacity to withstand stress and bend or stretch—but not break—returning to the original form. It's elasticity and strength. But in the world of jobs and our psyches, resiliency often means evolving into a *new* form. We don't just return to who or what we were. We often find strength in new jobs and careers, tapping into what we have done, finding new focus, and sometimes returning to aspects of ourselves long dormant.

Someone who exemplifies resiliency to me is Philip Wingfield. We first met when he stepped up to the microphone to tell his story at one of my town hall forums on the future of employment at New York Public Radio. After years in the education industry—as a freelancer, not a staffer—he was suddenly unemployed and without benefits. He had worked regularly on a contractual basis primarily with community colleges, which allowed him the freedom to teach domestically and abroad and to travel extensively. His career risk-taking side means that Philip often prioritized flexibility and freedom over stability. However, the lack of security threw him into a position where he had no safety net when his contracts ended, and there was nothing to replace them because the colleges had cut back. Like Hazel Shaw, whom you read about in chapter 2, Philip had lost his job and gone through all of his savings. He didn't become homeless, but he borrowed rent money from friends and waited every week for sustenance at a local food pantry. But something astounding happened as he stood in line: he started giving out job advice to everyone around him. So when we heard about an opening for a job placement expert at the Gay Men's Health Crisis (GMHC), a social service agency that grew out of the AIDS epidemic but now serves a wide variety of men, women, and children, he sprang into action.

Being a career counselor might seem an unlikely fit for a man who has traveled to forty-eight countries and speaks four languages. Philip is a free spirit—hardworking and adventurous. Raised in Puerto Rico and New York, he grew up bilingual and taught English as a second language.

"Being unemployed is a mind game," he reflects. "The first thing you have to eliminate is the shame. I started going online to get some advice and discovered I am one of eight million people unemployed in the US. There is no shame in that for me, though there may be for the country."

Philip isn't unemployed anymore, but his journey has transformed his life and ultimately brought him to a new perspective on an old passion of his: activism and organizing.

"I began a traditional job search," he explains, "but it was frustrating because there's so much garbage online that it's hard to find the gold nuggets. I have a lot of respect for GMHC, having worked with HIV causes back in the eighties." Activism combines Philip's high-social-impact and risk-taking sides. "So," he continues, "I realized that this was really an ideal job for me. I put my heart and soul into the cover

letter and expressed my interest in working for this specific organization, highlighting my work with nonprofits and HIV advocacy."

Highlighting his own story of activism made him stand out as a candidate. After speaking to human resources on the phone and three
face-to-face interviews, Philip got the job.

"I didn't have any contacts there, but I was really focused," he says.
"In any job search, especially if you're entering a new field, you have to
make yourself relevant." Today he is still learning to merge his maverick, activist side with the workflow of a large nonprofit.

Philip is handsome in a bookish way, with glasses and lush, dark hair.
He'd turned fifty-four when I met him but looks a decade younger. He
approaches his new career helping others with a palpable intensity.
Many of his clients are women, and he recognizes that they've lost self-
esteem during the endless rounds of facing officials who are more interested in getting them off the welfare rolls quickly than in guiding them
onto a long-term, sustainable path to success.

"The whole social service system is designed to create compliance,"
Philip says, referring to the way that government agencies require aid
recipients to remain in compliance with often very complex, sometimes
nonsensical rules. "Once clients are in compliance, they are really not
thinking clearly about how to strategize, they are simply waiting for the
next command to fulfill. I try to break that cycle of compliance and re-
actionary behavior," he says, focusing on getting his clients to think
about their best options, not the best that the government thinks they
can do.

For example, one of his clients, Tawana, is a beautician. Her social
service caseworker wanted her to take a low-paying job quickly, but
Philip urged her to delay it so that she could try out for a more promising position as a salon stylist. She succeeded in waiting to hear back
about her tryout, and was hired as a stylist, her true vocation and one
with much higher earnings.

Philip's attitude about his clients is a continuation of the spirit he once brought to activism: never take no for an answer if you believe your community can do better. Though employed, he still considers unemployed Americans to be part of his community, and he offers plenty of wisdom on the subject.

"You can never anticipate when you're going to lose your job," he observes. "And if you do, people expect to land their next gig in a month or two—that's the old pattern. But that's not the case today, and it's causing severe social problems for the long-term unemployed." Today the average unemployed person takes more than six months to find a job, which can be devastating emotionally and financially.

"When you're out of work," Philip continues, "you begin losing structure. That's the first thing to go. You think: What should I do with my time? How do I prove that I'm looking for a job? Then, as time progresses, you start facing reality. You focus on your financial obligations. You become very, very lean in terms of keeping financial expenditures to a minimum. You get a roommate. After that, you become socially isolated because your friends are going out to dinner, and you're not. So now you have to address the mental problem of how to make yourself visible when no one can see you, because when you've become unemployed, you tend to recede into the shadows. That's when I had an honest conversation with my friends; I said, 'This is what I'm going through. This is what I need from you: buy me a drink, take me to dinner. I need to feel people around me. I can't feel ostracized.'"

Philip's friends responded with generosity and gave him all the support he needed to keep looking for work. Of course, not everyone has close friends with the means, time, and willingness to help. Unemployed people without support systems are the most vulnerable of all. In fact, many of Philip's clients fit this description. Sometimes he tries to step in and become part of their network, but he also shows them how to expand it themselves.

"One of the cornerstones of really tackling the employment crisis is not just job creation," he says with characteristic passion, "it's also thinking about how to seize opportunities. The old pattern of bouncing back into a new job after a couple of months is broken."

• • •

From a different vantage point in today's disruptive labor market, Adam Freed has been able to participate in both a shrinking industry (journalism) and a growing industry (technology), cultivating new skills all the while. After years in management, he is responsible for hiring employees and often, at new or rapidly growing companies, creating new positions and hiring for them. That requires the visionary quality of knowing what types of people a company will need in the near future, as well as how much their skills will cost, and being able to create and implement "org charts," or diagrams of who reports to whom.

Freed is now the CEO of a company called Teachers Pay Teachers, which offers lesson plans and classroom materials created by teachers, allowing them to earn revenue off of their products and offer high-quality instructional materials to others. This wasn't the kind of job Freed seemed headed for a few years out of college. Right out of school, he worked for a Spanish freight broker. "The most fun part to me was the opportunity to learn a new language," he recalls. "I arrived all perky and ready to speak my mediocre Spanish, when they told me that they don't speak Spanish because it was a Catalan company." The Catalan people live mainly in northern Spain and have their own language and culture, one that was brutally repressed until the 1970s and has since undergone a proud resurgence. "I would study Catalan all day or all night after I got off work. It also was the first time that I really understood something about different cultural attitudes toward work. It opened my eyes."

Freed then took an entry-level job in media—mainly transcribing tapes, and not very stimulating intellectually. "The first real lightbulb went off four years postgraduation, when I got my first TV job working for Japan Broadcasting, or NHK, as a field producer," or off-air reporter, based in the United States, he says. "That was the moment when

I thought, 'This is really exciting. I can do this absolutely every day and find it new and dynamic.' It was my job to figure out what would be interesting across all of North America to a Japanese population as they tried to understand our part of the world," he says. "I was covering the Oklahoma City bombing, a high school for pregnant teens, and gang violence in California's Central Valley. What better thing is there to do in your twenties?"

Everything seemed to be lining up, but Freed didn't see his life as traditionally linear, even then. "This whole notion of career has always been sort of elusive and complicated for me," he says. "I seem to fall into really great jobs and interesting moments and opportunities. I never felt like I had a career." Yet after a couple of years, he asked his bosses if he could become an on-air reporter.

One of Freed's many superpowers is a command of languages. He speaks ten to twelve at any given time and has learned (and forgotten) others. He says of working on air at NHK, "I started doing these taped segments in Japanese where I was stiff as a board, but the company somehow took to them, and I did some interesting segments. After doing that for a while, I started sending out tapes and got job offers in Lubbock, Texas; New Jersey; and a few other places."

At a conference, he met a correspondent at ABC News. Her advice: "Don't take Farmington, New Mexico. It's the smallest TV market in the country, and your first job offer is going to come from there. If you take that job, you're going to end up having to climb five more media markets in ten years than you would if you just hang on and hold out until you can get your first job in a larger market." This is the opposite of what many others would say, and others' experience might differ. But for Freed, it worked. He took a job at News 12 New Jersey, "which was a start-up at the time and literally went on air two weeks before I got there. I launched myself into this career and was so excited, after years of feeling like I'd wandered in the work desert, to feel like I was at a place where I wanted to be.

"Then I looked around and realized the problem was that TV news was imploding. I figured I was going to ride it as long as I could, but it was also very scary," he says. "In that moment, I first made my peace with the idea that a career was possibly a fallacy in our generation; that a career was a notion that belonged to my parents' generation but not to mine."

He adds, "People today who think about a career as a linear, safe progression are going to have a hard time. The people who are most successful today are the ones who realize the rules are in constant flux and that you set them yourself." He worked on air for five years at KNSD, the NBC affiliate in San Diego. And then he kept pitching serious, often hard-to-hear news items. And his news director—whom he still considers a friend—said, "Can you *ever* bring me something with a kitten or puppy in it?"

Adam adds wryly, "He was a prescient guy, because the internet didn't exist yet, so we didn't know how hot cat videos would be, but it was true." In 2001 he rethought his career and applied for and received a journalism fellowship (a yearlong, paid program) at Yale University. But just days after the fellowship started came the terrorist attacks of 9/11.

"I called KNSD in San Diego and told them that I was mere miles from New York and asked what I needed to do. They connected me to the news desk at MSNBC, which sent me up to Boston Logan Airport, where I reported from for three days and had my one and only taste at being a network correspondent," he says. "It was exciting and dynamic, and I was on MSNBC constantly. Afterward the producer called me and said, 'The network really likes you, so why don't you quit this weird-ass program you're in and come work for MSNBC?' I thought to myself, 'Wow, this is the moment.'

"I went back to Yale, quit my program, packed up my apartment, and drove it down to Secaucus, New Jersey. When I got there, the network handed me employment forms for a temp agency. I told them that I was actually an NBC employee on a one-year leave. 'I have NBC benefits, the whole deal,' I told them. 'Just flip the switch, and I'm back on.'

They told me that it didn't work that way and that I'd have to take the temp contract. I asked about health insurance and told them how I speak Soviet border languages and that they were going to send me to Afghanistan. I couldn't accept a temp contract. We went back and forth, and at the end of the day, they told me I was too difficult, rescinded the offer, and sent me home.

"I had a total meltdown after that," Freed says, "and spent a lot of time mumbling in the shower. I went back to Yale, threw myself into my studies, and also made a new demo reel. I had envelopes written out to CNN and ABC, but I never sent them. I really thought about how if this is an industry where they would treat me like this, even as I moved up, then I should really evaluate if it's the right industry for me. However," he adds, "to this day, when people ask me about my dream job, I say I'd like to be a network correspondent." He pauses for effect. "In 1986.

"My pivot into tech was a transition that couldn't have been engineered. I basically emailed all my friends and said, 'Remember me? I'm a reasonably nice guy, I'm pretty smart, and I work really hard. I speak, like, ten languages. Anybody got any ideas?'

"Then I got a call from Sheryl Sandberg, who'd been in my college dorm. She told me how she had just joined this company called Google." Sandberg would go on to become the chief operating officer (COO) of Facebook and author the book *Lean In*. "Sheryl asked whether I knew anything about something called AdWords, which she described as 'an online ad thing.' I said, 'Nope, but I'll learn. Give me five minutes and hum a few bars. I'll figure it out.' AdWords allows advertisers to place paid ads at the top or side of the screen during a Google search.

"I studied my butt off, applied, did twelve to fifteen interviews, and still have no idea why they accepted me. It was 2002 in Silicon Valley, when the bubble had burst, and there were people looking for jobs on every street corner. I was in charge of the international side of this AdWords business, because I spoke all these languages.

"I later found out that the job was really customer service," he says with a laugh. "You can call it whatever you want, but it was customer support, and I thought to myself, 'Oh, my God, I'm a customer support person for French people! How did I get this job?' It was a bit of a comeuppance, but exciting nonetheless."

Freed spent many years at Google, finally leading their six-hundred-person Global Consumer Operations and Policy team. He then went on to become the COO of Etsy, an international online marketplace for crafts, furniture, and goods. It's a tech-heavy company where engineers are constantly upgrading the design, payments, and shipping platforms that make Etsy work. After leaving that company, he joined and spent time with the two sons he's raising with his husband, Ken. But his board work for the for-profit Teachers Pay Teachers evolved into his role as its CEO starting in 2014. "I wanted to take all I had learned in fast-growth companies, all I had learned about community-driven businesses, and my passion for the value of great teachers and for education and use them all," he says. "It seemed a pipe dream that a company could exist that actually brought all of these together. I agreed to become CEO when the founder and team asked. It has been the best job I've ever imagined."

Freed believes deeply in following the path of opportunity; using the arsenal of skills he was gifted with and worked for (including an ability and drive to master many languages) and his willingness to open himself up to his network for new opportunities. Although his network is particularly powerful, he never would have gotten his start in technology and moved into management if he hadn't asked for help in finding a new path.

• • •

Some people walk to the road to change in a more solitary manner, deciding to cut ties with the past and move on, even if people around them think they can't change. One of those individuals is Kristine Danielle, who worked for decades as a prostitute in the Seattle area. She says she turned her first trick when she was twelve. She became a cocaine dealer and user. Later she became a heroin addict. In her forties, well after having a daughter, she decided that her path was leading her toward an ugly, early death. So against what many doctors would advise, she detoxed herself from heroin. (Doing so without medical supervision can be fatal.) Her story speaks to the fact that resilience is not about privilege and does not always express itself in early in life as we'd like.

Willpower is part of the picture. Many scientists believe we can both strengthen and cultivate our will—and also exhaust it. Sometimes we take on too many things at once, like New Year's resolutions, or simply hit what's called "decision fatigue" after having to make a lot of choices in sequence.[2] In his bestselling book *Willpower: Rediscovering the Greatest Human Strength,* written with John Tierney, psychologist Roy Baumeister of Case Western Reserve University goes into the granular components of what strengthens or strips us of willpower—and just how important it is with regard to work. For example, the book states, "A recent study found that workers who were not getting enough sleep were more prone than others to engage in unethical conduct on the job." And setting too many goals undermines our ability to accomplish any one.[3] In earlier research, from 2000, Baumeister and Mark Murvaen described a "limited strength model" of willpower, meaning, in their words, "exertion [of the will] produces short-term fatigue (and hence, subsequent decrements in performance) and that it can lead to improvement or strengthening in the long run."[4] Breaking down this language, it means that, yes, we can hit decision fatigue, but if we learn to manage the process, we can also become stronger at making smart decisions.

For example, in terms of addictions such as Kristine Danielle's, it might mean that each time an addict (alcohol, drugs, even food) exerts will, then cravings can get higher, and relapse is possible. But persistence in building willpower, even if the short-term outcomes aren't always positive, can build up the capacity to make major changes. Many people who exercise willpower in their personal lives still have room for improvement at work—whether that means you're a procrastinator or someone who could be more precise with finances. No matter what kind of behavior you want to change, it's useful to remember that resilience pairs well with persistence. Success often requires failure.

Kristine, who is forty-six and has a grown daughter, had tried quitting drugs many times before. But this time she thought quite clearly about how she was not only living a life she didn't want to live but also that her drug habit would most likely kill her young—and *she had other choices that would prolong and improve her life*. I visited her home just outside of Seattle, where she greeted me warmly, wearing jeans and punctuating her stories with a husky laugh. Her place was cozy and comfortable, the walls filled with recent color photos and black-and-white portraits from previous generations. It was a far cry from her days spent at a sex motel near the city. As we sat on her couch, she described with humor and raw frankness her path to a more stable life.

"In 2006 I had just kind of been drifting," she says. "I had kicked heroin for the first time and didn't want to be back into the lifestyle. I was deciding what to do, and I ended up being offered free training to go to welding school. I'd done some welding before, not professionally, but I liked it."

When Kristine kicked the drugs, she also quit prostitution and made herself unemployed, and she had yet to start job training. "I actually had to take a job as a chambermaid at the two shittiest motels on Aurora," a Seattle-area strip she describes as "right in the heart" of where men go to pay for sex. "Here I am just freshly clean and sober, and I'm cleaning rooms that I've done all kinds of dope in, turned all kinds of tricks in. I've never been offered so much free dope in my life as after I got clean. But I kept my eyes on the prize, so to speak, and just saved up my money from my eight-dollar-an-hour job, and that way I was just able to quit when it was time to go to school."

Turning tricks, Danielle made anywhere from $200 to $800 a day, depending on how often she worked, but being an addict, she spent most of her pay on drugs. As a chambermaid, working maybe ten hours a day, she earned $80. In pipe welding, she could make $200 to $300. With welding, it takes time to build up seniority. Apprentices make less than regular union members.

Getting into a welding training program was not a random choice. It was a return to something she remembered being good at—and the prospect of doing it again boosted her self-confidence and will. "I love metallurgy, and I've always been good at physics and chemistry and the sciences," she says.

Danielle describes her work with obvious relish for the technical details. "I got three months of welding school, then I went straight from there to working at Alaskan Copper. It's like getting thrown into the deep end of the pool, sink or swim. My very first weld at that job, my very first weld as a professional, was with fourteen-gauge stainless steel, which is really, really hard to work with. Stainless steel burns really easily; it's really easy to fuck it up. And I just totally nailed it. So you know, I'll never forget that very first weld I ever did as a professional. I just had an aptitude for it, and so they kept letting me work on more exotic materials. And then they even sent some of us down to Oregon for a three-day seminar at a place that mills zirconium and titanium and niobium, hafnium, tantalum—I mean, crazy reactive metals."

The job is often cold and damp, and Kristine had to get her sea legs to work on the rolling ships. But sometimes she also has to shed some of her warm layers, because her thin, athletic build enables her to squeeze into narrow spaces that a lot of the male welders, who are mainly bulkier, can't. (According to the US Department of Labor, only 3 percent of welders are women, although the American Welding Society has recently made a point of trying to attract more women into the field.)[5] "I usually just wear a lot of layers: long johns, Carhartts, and coveralls if I'm really cold," she explains. "Being that I'm smaller than most of the guys, if there's a tight spot, they say, 'Oh, Kristine, this one's for you.'"

As tough as any of the guys but smaller than most, she is an asset on the job and has been through a lot to claim her space in the profession.

Shortly before we spoke, due to what she describes as a court case involving a violent and abusive ex, she had decided to move—using up money she would have liked to have spent on a new car. The time she spent in court seeking a restraining order made it hard for her to work in welding, as did the lack of a vehicle. When we met, she was working locally, off the books—painting houses, doing welding—but until she scraped up enough money for a new car, her industrial welding career was on a brief hold.

But Kristine wasn't thrown by this. Compared with many other points in her life, the lack of reliable transportation was a small setback. She says of her early days of sobriety and job training, "I just reminded myself that nobody gets to any level of achievement overnight. I would remember that where I'm at now is better than where I was." Although she's contemplating going back to school, she adds, "This whole mentality that you absolutely must go to college—it's a lie. There's plenty of good-paying trade jobs. When I'm working, I'm making a minimum of twenty-five, twenty-six bucks an hour, all the way up to forty-five or fifty. I worked on a couple of the Washington State ferries, and I've worked on tons of stuff for military like the *George H. W. Bush* aircraft carrier. I welded a buttload of the copper nickel that's on there."

She chuckles and says, "I've welded a whole bunch of stuff that we weren't told what it was for. They won't tell you what the name of the ship is. It'll just have, like, a code number on it—it's like super *Secret Squirrel* stuff, and if you weren't born in the United States, you're not allowed to work on it."

Even with all its challenges, Kristine Danielle's life is a lot more stable than in the past. "Years ago, I was a competitive bodybuilder. I did all the 'natural bodybuilding'—without steroids—for seven or eight years in my twenties. But I went from that to, like, straight cocaine addict for a while, in and out of jail. It takes its toll, the ravages of time.

"I had a pretty rough time as a kid. Problems at home and all that, and so I had pretty much been on my own since I was twelve. I did a lot of drugs, as a result of all that." Childhood trauma has insidious effects. It can lead to post-traumatic stress disorder, or PTSD, as well as persistent feelings of unworthiness that can help make drug use seem more attractive. At seventeen, Kristine was hurt badly in an accident, received a large amount of money from a legal settlement, and went to technical college. But she also became attached to a boyfriend who wasn't healthy for her, trafficked cocaine, and did jail time once she began getting high on her own supply.

Kristine sees her return to legal occupations and sobriety as a matter of not just survival but also self-respect. When it comes to her long-term drug use and now her sobriety, Kristine is an example of both resilience and willpower.

"When it comes to changing bad habits or dropping bad habits, especially addictions, you can't do it for anyone else. You can't be doing it for the courts, for your spouse, to please your parents, or to stay out of jail. I mean, none of it. You might have some length of time where you succeed with it because of that, but unless and until you come to a place where you really, really comprehend that 'This is in my best interest,' it's not going to stick. It can't even be because 'I don't want to lose custody of my kids' or 'I don't want to lose my job or end up divorced.' To leave this shit behind, it's a value judgment."

Now Kristine is contemplating taking another step in her career path and going back for a degree. Like many Americans, she's concerned that educational debt could trail her for years as a result. "With a four-year degree in material science and engineering, at least right out of the gate, I wouldn't be making any more money than I'm making at the best of times, welding, you know?" she says. "Physically I'm getting a little bit older. I've got a heavy tool bag, and having to walk on four-inch-wide stiffeners on this boat skeleton, you can get hurt, badly. And somebody my size carrying eighty pounds of equipment and walking on a four-inch-wide piece of steel, one of these times, it's going to end badly." But she doesn't want a desk job. "I tend to get along better with people at the shipyards or in the shop. I like working in the trades better than anything else."

• • •

The four people whose stories you've heard come from very different worlds, but all of them share resilience—the ability to adapt, sometimes with surprising speed, to changes in the workplace and personal challenges. This psychological power is critical when it comes to dealing with the major issues that confront all of us—some seemingly more serious and even more desperate than others, but all of which can seem crushing at the time. The key is to remember that we are in constant motion and constant self-evolution—as is the very way that we find jobs today, the subject we explore next.

6

The *New* New Realities of Job Search

S o YOU NEED a job. Maybe you're unemployed, or you see your company circling the drain, or your entire industry is sinking. Or maybe you want a job. You've got something, but it doesn't feel secure. Or perhaps your job feels secure, but when you imagine spending another five, ten, or twenty years there, you want to run away and join the circus.

Just as America's labor market has changed, so has job search. Twenty-five years ago, there was no online job search. Today there are dozens of sites that enable you to look for opportunity, including Monster, Indeed, and Simply Hired. Often, sites give headhunters and recruiters the opportunity to look for you, as they sort through the millions of profiles on the current big dog of job networking, LinkedIn. Networking—both online and off—is more important than ever. But it's also fraught with questions: How do we gain access to people who can help us if they are busy, powerful, or hard to reach? And how do the biases that exist in everyday life factor into online search?

For example, while I was giving a speech at the University of Texas at Austin, a woman told me she didn't want to put up a LinkedIn profile because she thought her job history and photo would open her up to age discrimination. She asked me if she should lie about her age. I told that her rather than do that, put up a truthful but youthful-looking picture and consider compressing her job history to just the past few years. That's not lying, but it's creative. Others might disagree. In the end, when you walk through the door for an interview, you will have to disclose more about yourself, and you *will* be judged partly on your appearance. But at least you will have gotten through the door and, hopefully, be able to make a clear case why you are valuable at any age (or race, gender, and so on).

Not everything has changed. There are still some very traditional Help Wanted signs in store windows—plus newspaper classifieds, industry conferences where headhunters solicit résumés, and civil service exams. But the rise of the internet has altered job search forever, just as it's changed our world forever. Employment figures are improving at the time I'm completing this book, but there are still roughly twice as many job seekers as there are jobs available. Some jobs that get listed are essentially filled already, because someone has an inside track on the job. No matter how many résumés the company gets, sometimes because it has to list it as a formality, the person hiring already has his or her mind set on an internal or external candidate.

As Matt Youngquist, who runs the job hunting and employment counseling firm Career Horizons, explains, "Especially when talking about professional- or managerial-level positions, networking is a far more common way of landing a job than online job seeking. The reason? Many companies will put out the word to their network about openings first, before investing the time and money to publish them electronically—at which point, in many cases, they then have to deal with literally hundreds of applications. What's more, most companies place a huge premium on candidates who come 'spoken for' through networking, since they figure the endorsement of somebody they trust is far more reliable than taking a chance on a complete stranger who might simply interview well—or have exaggerated their résumé. Make sense? It's essentially the same reason people ask around for referrals when hiring an attorney, accountant, babysitter, or other type of professional. The results are more reliable." But he adds, "That *doesn't* necessarily mean that people shouldn't respond to published openings as well."

Given that listings aren't always what they seem, know that sometimes you can invent jobs—or have a company invent them for you. I'm not talking about entrepreneurship, which is another ball of wax, but about the art of job cocreation. For example, at different points in my career, which has included journalism, stints in technology, and academia, companies have created new opportunities that reflect my skills. I'm not saying that they created the jobs just for me. Companies always create jobs to fit their own needs. But at various times, leaders within companies see potential and harness it.

Creating jobs at the same time that disruptive innovation is creating new industries is alchemy. It requires taking workers who have been trained to do something entirely different and using them in new ways. Think of the example of Adam Freed, who went from television reporting to tech. There are also ways of thinking about how to have a flexible mind-set that makes you more open to pivoting in the workplace. Some business coaches have been turning to the world of improv comedy for inspiration in leadership training—particularly the principle known as "Yes, *and* . . ." The business magazine *Fast Company* describes "Yes, *and* . . ." this way:

Improv is based on soft skills such as listening and communicating. Listening is crucial because you need to be present and in the moment, [improv expert and entrepreneur Charna] Halpern says. "Most people are waiting to speak and not listening in the moment. Instead, they're thinking of what they're going to say," she says. In improv, you must listen to what's been said and pay attention so you can react appropriately. If you're not focused on what's happening around you, you miss an opportunity to build the scene, and the show comes to a screeching halt . . .

In Tina Fey's bestselling book Bossypants, *Fey outlines the rules of improv: Always say "Yes, and . . ." meaning, always agree, and add something to the discussion. For example, in an improvised scene with a partner, never say no. If you're in a boat rowing down the river, you don't say, "No, we're folding laundry." You say, "Yes, and we could really use a paddle instead of my arm." It adds to the scene, humor can develop, and trust is established between scene partners.*[1]

As one example, entrepreneur, author, comedian, and television host Baratunde Thurston, profiled earlier in this book as the RPIT (Cocreator in Chief) archetype, describes his life as based on the "Yes, *and . . .*" principle.

The principle is useful when you are already in a job, particularly as you balance your own perspectives on a task with those of others. It's arguably even more critical to the soft job negotiations, often beginning with an open-ended conversation or informational networking that leads to job cocreation. You might not be a traditional candidate, or someone who's been on a company's radar before, but you are authentic and shine brightly for who you are. You show what you have, the company sees what it needs, and it creates a new job that didn't exist before. In the best of circumstances, it helps both parties (you, as employee, and your employer) grow and evolve. Sometimes things don't work out in these new ventures, just like they don't always work out in positions that have existed for years. The possibility that a cocreated job won't work shouldn't scare you. You can end work relationships gracefully (or not), as we discuss in the next chapter.

The "Yes, *and . . .*" approach in jobs happens under many circumstances, including ones tragic rather than comic. New Orleans construction worker and labor activist Alfred Marshall, profiled as the CHIT (Change Agent) archetype, is someone who took a "Yes, *and . . .*" view of the situation after his son was shot to death. He didn't ignore what had happened (the "Yes"—an acknowledgement of pain and grief) but channeled his energy into community outreach rather than bitterness and retaliation (his "*and . . .*"). His work as a labor and community organizer was an extension of the relationships and skills he'd built in his neighborhood.

In addition to your willingness to network broadly and take a "Yes, *and . . .*" approach to turning contacts into opportunities, leading a successful job search today means being better informed about your options than the next person is. You can boost your odds of finding the right work by knowing how the game is played at all levels. That means keeping track of trends in employment on a national and local level, and knowing who in your circle knows where good jobs are. Achieving satisfaction in a time of disruption and episodic careers is about seeking opportunity and *seeing* opportunity. You can make new choices and create new paths for yourself, but only if you can perceive them first.

Without vision and clarity about your goals and desired workstyle, you might end up landing a job you don't really want. All of us have moments where we dread going in to work. But that shouldn't happen every day, or most days, if we can help it. I acknowledge here: Sometimes you don't have great options. Sometimes your job has to be "good enough for now." Sometimes "now" can feel like or be a very long time. We live in an era of rising inequality and, compared with a couple decades ago, diminished opportunity. But collectively, we are reinventing the world of jobs and careers—upending the very notion of linear careers. That freedom to say "Yes, *and . . .*" can allow you to find work, change paths, and self-define in new ways. And yes: get a job and get paid.

With that in mind:

FIVE TO-DOS *BEFORE* YOU START YOUR JOB SEARCH

1. BEFORE YOU LOOK, LOOK INSIDE

Before you mount a job search, it's critical to examine both your heart and your wallet. How much time can you spend unemployed (if you are unemployed) or unhappily employed (if that's the problem)? If you are looking proactively, not out of need or unhappiness, what are the time costs and financial costs of mounting a search? Will searching damage your work or reputation at your current job?

2. WHAT'S IN YOUR TOOL KIT?

In today's job market, there are several ways to search for a new opportunity:

- use online tools;
- "walk the beat," looking for Help Wanted signs in certain neighborhoods. This can be highly efficient in some places and at certain times (for instance, if you're looking for a seasonal job in a resort town craving workers), but a waste of time in many places;
- through networking; and
- by reaching or being contacted by a headhunter or recruiter, among other ways.

3. FIND YOUR ALLIES . . . AND YOUR "WEAK TIES"

Allies are people who've really "got your back." They are there for you when you really need them, through thick and thin. And they are critical for emotional support and trusted counsel in a job search. But "weak ties"—people who fall outside your circle, but to whom you can gain access—might provide fresher leads on jobs *because* they travel in different circles, something critical to the modern-day job search. Cultivate both. In the words of LinkedIn cofounder Reid Hoffman and coauthor Ben Casnocha from *The Start-up of You: Adapt to the Future, Invest in Your-*

self, and Transform Your Career (referenced in the resource appendix): "[S]ociologist Mark Granovetter asked a random sample of professionals how they had found their new job. It turns out that 82% of them found their position through a contact they saw only occasionally or rarely."

4. CHECK YOUR MARKET VALUE

So, let's say you're on a job hunt because you think you're worth more than you're making. Worth more to whom? It's important to know what similar jobs that you are qualified for are paying before you rush in to ask for a raise. Instead of a raise, you might get the side eye—or the boot. Also, although you might indeed be underpaid at your current job, that alone does not guarantee that you will be able to raise your salary in-house. Nor, in some cases, does a job offer elsewhere ensure higher pay.

For example, for men, receiving a competing offer and bargaining with management seems to be a generally effective strategy. But research, including work by Carnegie Mellon University economist Linda Babcock, coauthor of *Women Don't Ask: Negotiation and the Gender Divide*, indicates that women may be viewed as disloyal when they walk through the door with an offer, whereas a man is just viewed as being rational. As one report coauthored by Babcock summarizes, "Evaluators were disinclined to work with female managers who negotiated for higher pay because they perceived these women to be less nice and more demanding than women who let the opportunity to negotiate pass." Professor Babcock's research indicates that women who make a case for more money fare better if they use an "organizational/relational" approach (meaning, among other things, emphasizing loyalty to the company), as opposed to a market-value-based case focused around a job offer or other comparison. It's not fair, but it's well documented and something for women to keep in mind.

5. FIND YOUR MIC AND BROADCAST YOUR SEARCH

My strategy of contacting three people a day by phone or email and telling them I was looking for a job led me to academia. Yes, I'd had some short-term teaching gigs, but when a professor at NYU said, "There's a great job open, and you have to apply for it in two weeks," I jumped on it. She was someone I had always thought highly of but hadn't stayed in touch with consistently. The fact that I contacted her when I needed help in my search didn't bother her at all, because we had bonded in the past (and have again), and also because we shared a goal of serving students.

Don't be afraid to ask. And don't be afraid to hear "No, I don't know about anything" or "No, I can't help you right now." If you keep widening your circles, you will find new leads. Sometimes—perhaps many times—these will come with complications. Maybe a good lead requires taking a salary cut, or moving, or spending time and money on retraining. But unless you want to remain stuck, you have to do things that take you out of your comfort zone.

ONLINE JOB SEARCH: MYTHS AND REALITIES

Of all the ways to search for jobs, searching online—through LinkedIn or Monster or digital versions of print publications or industry websites—can seem the most appealing. But there are several reasons to be clear on what it can and can't do for you. The annually updated bestselling job search book *What Color Is Your Parachute?* puts the effectiveness at looking for a job online at only 4 percent, compared with 28 percent for hiring a private firm to search for you and 47 percent for knocking on the doors of (generally small, local) companies.[2] Expert Matt Youngquist of Career Horizons names a significantly higher, but still modest, percentage. "In my own experience over twenty years of coaching people through the job-hunting process, and based on most other peers I've collaborated with, we'd put the number at more like fifteen to twenty percent. And unfortunately, while you'll read random statistics all over the web, I don't know of any definitive and/or empirical survey in this regard. In fact," he adds about the multibillion-dollar online job search industry, "it would be hard to conduct such a survey due to all the variables involved. If a friend of yours *steers* you to a suitable job advertisement, and you get hired, does one attribute that hire to networking or online job hunting? Or if a recruiter finds you on LinkedIn, versus you applying for an opening, does that count as well?"

Second, don't mistake browsing for a job for looking for a job. I've been to numerous job centers and public libraries—places where people without offices, or sometimes without broadband internet, often go when they're between jobs. Without invading anyone's privacy, I can see this pattern from across the room:

- Facebook
- Job search
- Solitaire
- Job search
- LOL cat video!
- Job search

If you're not disciplined in your online job search, you can get distracted easily. A screen conveys all sorts of dazzling attractions that are irrelevant to your search for work. It's important to toggle between the "real world" and your screen. Doing so can help your health and your job search. If you're in a public or shared space and you don't want to get up and lose your computer, I get that. But it's important to stretch (in your seat, perhaps, without smacking your neighbor on the head), and break away from the screen and focus on things offscreen. If you don't follow the "rule of twenty" (get up and stretch or walk every twenty minutes) or at least "twenty-twenty-twenty" (look away from your screen every twenty minutes and fix your attention on a spot twenty feet away for at least twenty seconds), you can actually diminish your eyesight (computer vision syndrome) and begin to feel less powerful. Really.

I had the pleasure of giving a speech at a women's leadership conference at Ohio's Kent State University after Amy Cuddy, a professor at Harvard Business School who fought her way through graduate school following a traumatic brain injury suffered in a car accident. She has conducted pioneering research on how our physical stance triggers powerful hormones and affects our minds. In truly dangerous "fight-or-flight" situations, the body releases the stress hormone cortisol for a boost of power and clarity. But if we're always stressed out, it can impair our mental focus, lower immunity (less resistance to colds, flu, and so on), and cause us to gain belly fat. The male sex hormone testosterone (and yes, women have it too) makes us feel more powerful and in control. Cuddy found that standing for two minutes in a victory stance, with your legs wide and arms in a V above your head—like an athlete who's just won a race (or with your hands on your hips and arms wide, like Wonder Woman or Superman) decreases your cortisol level in the bloodstream and raises testosterone. So if you're shaking before a job interview, you can take a quick bathroom break, do two minutes of Superman or Wonder Woman, and emerge from the stall a more confident person. (Where are you going to find Superman's phone booth these days?)

Cuddy's TED Talk about her research has been viewed online more than twenty million times. And in her speech, she revealed that looking at small screens is the reverse of the victory stance. If you spend a lot of time on your laptop or cell phone, that can increase your cortisol and decrease your testosterone, making you feel more stressed out and powerless. That's not a good mentality to have while you're searching for a job—or when your employment requires you to stay on a computer.

Sometimes we (and I include myself, a true computer addict) can stare into the screen as if it were a crystal ball that will give us all our answers. But when it comes to online job searches, sitting and staring—or even sitting and applying—is not the answer. A 2013 study, "Is Internet Job Search Still Ineffective?," by Peter Kuhn and Hani Mansour, says that people who search online find jobs 25 percent faster than those who don't. But, they add, "Internet job search (IJS) appears to be most effective in reducing unemployment durations when used to contact friends and relatives, to send out résumés or fill out applications and also to look at advertisements."[3] In other words, they are talking about using online search and online networking with known contacts, which is different from using it to search alone.

Also, we tend to rely on what we think will work—and then if it doesn't, we expend more effort. But that effort may come too late to help, at least easily.

Unemployed people tend to rely on one or two job search methods at first, the first and most effective of which is contacting employers directly, according to a study by the Federal Reserve Bank of St. Louis. But the chances of getting a job diminish the longer you've been unemployed. Or as the 2014 Kuhn-Mansour study puts it, "The longer an individual is unemployed, the less likely he or she is to find a job. We also found that the longer a person is unemployed, the less it matters which method is used to search for a job: All the finding rates fall and converge with one another."

In other words, if you are unemployed (and not all job searches result from unemployment or even unhappiness), the best time for you to look for a job is right away. Over time, your chances of becoming reemployed in a timely manner diminish. And not only that: the methods that were most effective lose their effectiveness. It's the opposite of the axiom "Everything that rises must converge." Long-term unemployment means that as you're falling out of the workforce, your methods of finding a job converge, but because they're falling in effectiveness.[4]

Economists have a term for this phenomenon: hysteresis. In essence, people who are unemployed become viewed as unemployable. In some cases, people truly do have skill-based challenges, because they have to catch up to a rapidly changing industry. If you lost a job as a logo designer during a transition between paper-based design and computer-based design, and spent two years unemployed, you might be considered out of the loop. Today a better analogy might be a teacher who was downsized during a phase when a school system was putting all its kids on iPads or laptops. There are ways around this, including training yourself. But when you are unemployed, you simply might not have the cash to do so, and simulating a real-world/real-work environment can be hard in the classroom. There's much more on these questions in chapter 8, "Lifelong Learning, Lifelong Earning."

THE IMPACT OF RACE, GENDER, AND RELIGION ON JOB SEARCH

Sociologist Nancy DiTomaso studied how blacks and whites used job networking. As she wrote in the *New York Times* after interviewing 1,463 people:

> *I found that all but a handful used the help of family and friends to find 70 percent of the jobs they held over their lifetimes; they all used personal networks and insider information if it was available to them . . .*
>
> *You don't usually need a strong social network to land a low-wage job at a fast-food restaurant or retail store. But trying to land a coveted position that offers a good salary and benefits is a different story. To gain an edge, job seekers actively work connections with friends and family members in pursuit of these opportunities.*

But even though seven in ten people relied on personal connections to find jobs, they didn't credit that when asked about their careers at large.

When I asked my interviewees what contributed most to their level
of career success, only 14 percent mentioned that they had received
help of any kind from others.[5]

In other words, people rely heavily on their personal networks, even
though they don't see things that way. And like our society, our personal
networks are often separated by race. According to a 2013 study from
the Public Religion Research Institute, 75 percent of white Americans
did not have any black friends in their social network.[6] In addition, researchers at Carnegie Mellon University found that in certain states, the
job profiles of Christians were favored heavily over those of Muslims.[7]

Accordingly, some people have even tried changing their race on
job sites. The site Monster has a question where you can add your race,
if you choose. An unemployed black woman named Yolanda Spivey created a profile with the name Bianca White, saying she was white. She
left up both profiles, with identical résumés, but only "Bianca White"
got the calls, which she documented in a magazine article.[8]

Matt Youngquist of Career Horizons counsels not to dwell on the
question of discrimination but to rely even more on networking. "Common sense (sadly) would suggest that the fact that social media makes a
person's ethnicity/faith more public would correlate with a rise in employers' ability to discriminate." But he adds, "While I've certainly had
many clients express their belief they were being screened out of jobs
due to race, gender, age, or other reasons, they usually can't really prove
it—since employers would obviously never admit they're engaging in
these prejudices and would instead just hide behind euphemisms like
'We had other, more-qualified candidates.'

"As for trying to combat this type of bias? It's hard," he continues,
"but the two things that first come to mind are, one, *really* make sure you
know your stuff, are up to date in your field, and can demonstrate clear
expertise in your occupational niche so that your qualifications hopefully
'trump' possible stereotypes; and, two, try to avoid blaming this factor for

any possible setbacks in your career, since a lot of people seem to believe the only reason they're not being hired is based on discrimination, versus dealing with other potential areas of weakness (for instance, outdated skill sets) that are likely a greater source of the problem.

"Last but not least, place a huge amount of your efforts on networking and pursuing leads through trusted acquaintances who advocate for you and vouch for your abilities. A complete stranger might resort to certain stereotyping—consciously or unconsciously—as they weed through a stack of hundreds of résumés and try to narrow it down to a short list."

WHAT DOES A GOOD (OR BAD) JOB SEARCH LOOK LIKE?

Elaine Chen, profiled as the CPIS (Masterful Realist) archetype, describes herself as "an informal career counselor." I've culled some action items from her journey and the advice she gives to friends.

If You Need a Job Now, Get Real and Set a Timeline

"There are a lot of people who are too stubborn and inflexible about the work they would consider," says Chen. "There's an arc of what it's like to be unemployed." If, say, you have savings or temporary work, "Of course, sure, set six months or eight months and don't compromise. Look for a job in your field that pays X salary. For a period of time that works. But sometimes you're going to see that deadline come and go. Or other people never set a deadline at all! If you're not realistic and don't set a timetable, some horrible things can happen; for example, you could lose your house if you own one and can't pay the mortgage."

Stick to the Timeline; Be Flexible About the Job and Salary

"Being more flexible about the income that you're willing to make, and being flexible on the type of job and on working more than one job—all of these make a huge difference," Chen says. "For example, I got laid off twice in one year. I was making a very good six-figure salary, in my early thirties, in the dot-com space. Instead of sitting around the house for two years, I took a job making literally half of what I had been making, moving over to a new job in advertising."

Master Your Personal Narrative

"I did not want to say how much I had been making," Chen says of the much-lower-paying job she took after her layoff. "But again, I had written an entire narrative that I could tell my employer. I said I enjoyed what I had been doing, but it was so much work. I have a book I'm working on in my spare time, and it would be good for my book for me to be around technology. I convinced them I was a good bargain, and because it was initially a freelance position, they didn't need to worry about how long I was going to stick around. But I made myself useful. I stayed at that job for five years.

"In the course of interviewing, I've learned that you need to have a compelling narrative about yourself, about why you want this particular job—and it has to make sense," she says. "If you can't explain to them why you want this job, they're not going to give it to you. And all this really starts by explaining things to yourself."

Don't Be Afraid to Not Know What You're Doing at First

Chen's first job in journalism was for a highly technical publication that covered semiconductors. "They liked that I had been a lawyer, because they thought that would make me detail oriented," she says. "They were paying so little to get an Ivy League graduate with a graduate degree. They gave me a writing test, and I got hired." At the time, she was in her midtwenties, which Elaine believes was a factor in her being hired. "People will take those risks on you at that salary when you are young," she says. "It gets harder as you get older. They think you won't stick around. And nowadays, there's more competition."

But it wasn't an easy transition. "I still remember this feeling of fear when I started there," she admits. The company said it had hired a reporter experienced in covering the semiconductor industry, but she wasn't due to start for a couple weeks. Chen would have to fill the section until her more experienced coworker arrived.

"At this point, I had never been a reporter before," she says. "I had never interviewed anyone. I'm reading through this publication, I could not understand the articles top to bottom. I thought, 'Well, this is going to be interesting!' But," she adds, "you muddle through. I tell people that nothing I have done before or since has been this hard. Ultimately, at the end of the day, you figure that out."

You Can Make Big Salary Gains Fast If You Show Your Value

"People get freaked out by taking a job that 'pays me less than *X*,'" she says, citing the magic number many of us feel we should be earning. "But sometimes taking a low-paying job can offer a lot of growth if you show your worth. I got a raise from twenty-five thousand dollars to thirty thousand in the first year I was there. Within three years, I was making way more than triple my initial salary. When you start that low, there is a chance to transition. Don't feel like you have to have a grand master plan.

"My salary went up by twenty percent that first year, and I was also freelancing. I didn't match my previous salary, without freelance income, for eight years," she adds. "But because I was willing to work two jobs most of that time, the real salary match was a lot sooner."

• • •

Everyone has to walk a different path to get to the right work. Sometimes the path is circuitous, almost circular. But many people have compared progress to driving up a steep mountain road, where you must spiral ever higher to reach the top. In other words, a series of lay-offs, disappointments, or reversals may end up getting you closer to your goal if you stay focused on what you seek. That has to include a frank assessment of your desired workstyle and the ability to separate your needs, financial and otherwise, from your wants. Otherwise, pro-longing a job search can box you into a financial corner or make you seem less employable. Then there's the question of whether to leave a job you don't like cold; or leave to start a business; or juggle a job search while you are still employed. That requires a frank assessment of what you have versus what you can get—which we address in the next chap-ter, "Hold 'Em or Fold 'Em?"

7

Hold 'Em or Fold 'Em?

When to Stay in a Job, and When to Go

B ARRY JOHNSON HAS led a varied, stimulating, high-powered, and often high-stress career. One thing has kept him on course in good times and bad: he knows and is not afraid to advocate for his worth. That means he has become an expert on knowing when to hold 'em and when to fold 'em—that is, when to stay in or leave a job, as well as how to pursue new opportunities.

He spent his first two years after graduating from Yale University in investment banking, learning quite a lot, but it wasn't his sweet spot. "I don't really fit nicely into anybody's environment," he reflects, going on to admit, "I was not getting certain aspects of what I was supposed to be doing. I didn't ask for help." When he was twenty-two, a supervisor nearly twice his age "said something like 'You'll never amount to anything.'"

Johnson wasn't fired. Despite the bracing criticism, he says, "I did well enough to be there." And through the discomfort of dealing with people who underestimated him, he learned valuable lessons about management, learning that he had to reassure his bosses and not wait for them to mentor him. Much to the surprise of some of the people around him, Johnson was admitted to Harvard Business School. "Many people who where darlings of management were not admitted—young girls and guys whose fathers were in the same country clubs as the firm's management." Looking back, Johnson says, managers "have an ethical responsibility to nurture people or cut them loose. People who run things are not necessarily good people, ethically. They have agendas and may not be supportive."

Johnson didn't come from a country club background. He grew up in segregated Birmingham, Alabama. His mother is a retired longtime educator and social worker with whom Johnson is writing a motivational book. His father worked at the post office and did his own work as a residential and commercial builder. But as a black man in the 1960s, he did not have the freedom to pursue that as a full-time career. Barry's parents were able to get him into a private, overwhelmingly white high school, and from there he went on to the Ivy League, and then into investment banking.

Most importantly, his first job helped him tap into an inner connection to his self-worth, something that's helped with many career transitions. "You don't have to believe what other people tell you," he says. "As a manager, you can tell people, 'This project was done incorrectly.' That's a performance fact. But no one should tell me who I *am*. I had to say, You are free to tell me about my performance. But I will not let you tell me about the *am*-ness of my being."

Much later, Johnson served as a senior economic development advisor, focusing on "inbound investment," or getting international companies to create jobs in the United States, during the first term of President Barack Obama's administration. "I was the only person with an MBA and twenty years in cross-border business development," he says. "The Republicans and Democrats on the Hill liked me; the staff liked me."

But an official in the US Commerce Department, who, he says, was trying to bring in her own favorites, began to attack him. At one point, she began to say, "You are—" With some relish, Johnson recounts that he stopped her midsentence.

"I said, 'You are not a child; I'm not a child. You are free to discuss my performance; you are not free to discuss who I am as a person. Who I am is not up for you to define.'" He redirected the conversation to talk about his position and helped strategize a new role within government so that he could continue his work on a higher level and she could bring in the talent she wanted.

It wasn't the first time that Johnson had to have what he refers to as the "I am" conversation. In 1994 he was at Sony Music in the dual roles of senior director of artist development and marketing, and senior director of interactive media. Artists on his roster included Ozzy Osbourne, Michael Jackson, and Celine Dion. "Michael's History album was coming out. Other executives decided to change his look." He laughs, "To *tell* Michael to change his look." The coworkers who wanted Michael Jackson to change his signature image made sure not to invite Barry to the dinner where they discussed their plans to restyle him. Although that was underhanded, it was a blessing, as Jackson was extremely displeased.

"I got a call from Wayne, his bodyguard, saying, 'Michael wants to come in and see you about the website design,'" Johnson continues. "Well, when Michael comes into the office, there's a big production. The whole building is on Michael Alert. I call down to the president of Epic, one of Sony's labels, and say, 'Michael's here, and apparently he's here to see me.'" Instead of seeing Barry as the man who was able to repair the damage of the misguided dinner, he recounts, "They took it as some betrayal." Johnson left to become the president of a joint venture between Microsoft and Black Entertainment Television (BET), where he did very well.

"I was angry, humiliated, and in disbelief, and I wanted someone to pay. I've grown from it," says Johnson, who has a very strong spiritual practice and is a superconnector among people in business, government, and the arts. "I've learned when people come to shake you, don't be shook. As one of my friends said, 'You were pushed into mud, and you came up dipped in chocolate.'"

Today Johnson is a founding partner at the firm 32 Advisors, where he leads the cross-border trade and investment practice. Knowing your own value, not just monetarily but also emotionally, spiritually, or in terms of self-worth, is key to surviving hostile or indifferent workplaces.

So what do you do if *you* are in a position where people underestimate you or, worse, undermine you on the job? Expert Matt Youngquist of Career Horizons advises, with some caveats, to stick things out while you *think* things out. "You likely shouldn't *quit* a job until you have the next one lined up—unless you're truly in an abusive situation that's leading to depression, hostility, or a severe loss of confidence," he says. "Additionally, of course, if a person is being asked to engage in some highly unethical behavior, that might be a time to immediately cut the cord as well." (We'll discuss ethical dilemmas in chapter 9, "Money and Morality.")

"But in general," Youngquist continues, "I'd encourage a person to 'hold out' as long as possible and just start searching aggressively for something new, on the side, if their current assignment isn't working out—or the company they're with seems to be facing potential challenges."

Below is a list of reasons Youngquist offers for holding out in a less-than-optimal job:

- Many employers today practice "unemployment discrimination" and greatly favor candidates who are currently working elsewhere over those who are "on the street" and unemployed.
- While people might not realize it, their self-confidence is usually a lot higher when they're working somewhere and applying their skills on a daily basis, as opposed to being in the ambiguous limbo that unemployment can represent.

- Things can change fast in organizations these days, so somebody might, for example, be dealing with a bad boss—only to have that boss leave or get replaced in the near future, making things better.
- Last, and most importantly, unless you are independently wealthy and don't have bills to pay, giving up a steady paycheck isn't something to do unless you have almost no alternative.

Youngquist says, "In the new paradigm, people should 'always be looking'—even when they are happily employed—simply because most job tenures now run only two to three years, so it never hurts to be trolling for that next opportunity down the road."

Until my time at New York University, I had never stayed in one job more than four years, something once seen as flighty and unstable but that is now well on the curve of normal experience. Because I switched jobs so often, I became fluent in all the languages of media: digital, print, television, and radio. I can do radio and television hosting and reporting; basic video editing; good but not great audio editing; basic web design and HTML; and both short-form and long-form writing. In media, I am a Swiss army knife rather than a specialist.

That has both good and bad points. I will probably never be as good a writer as the people whose bylines appear in the *New Yorker*, but I can seek opportunities in any media field and also teach in most media disciplines. That versatility is a plus in the shaky journalism job market. But in retrospect, how and when I have chosen to switch jobs demonstrates both the best and the *worst* of strategies for changing paths.

For years, I never quite felt comfortable, no matter what I was doing. At most big companies such as Newsweek and ABC, I felt obligated to champion the underdogs, both on the staff and in stories. At hipster MTV, I was the one arguing we should cover the president's State of the Union address—a relative old-school newshound. When at the start-up Oxygen TV channel, I missed the comparatively bounteous resources (at the time) of network news. And no matter where I was, I always compared what I had to some idea of what *should* be.

When I think of that mind-set, I keep coming back to what Gail Evans, formerly an executive vice president of CNN and author of the bestseller *Play Like a Man, Win Like a Woman*, said to me many years ago: "If you're always unhappy about work, it's probably not really about work." At times, I have been profoundly happy and fulfilled by my work, while at other times, I have felt desperate and trapped. I went to one of the best colleges in the country; have what used to be called a "deep Rolodex" of business contacts; and above all, have close long-term friends and a tight-knit family I can rely on. At moments, I've lived luxuriously. At others, I've failed and flailed, usually when I had a great media-entrepreneurial idea that was either not that great, ahead of its time, or not shored up by the right mix of partners. But I can't complain at all. I've had amazing adventures, including the experiences in the workplace that led me to write this book. Each job you do that you love teaches you more about how to do what you love. Each job you do that you *don't* love should teach you how to navigate unfamiliar systems with grace and humility—or to move on decisively.

Take the story of Vivek Wadhwa, born in New Delhi, India, and educated in Australia and New York. A Silicon Valley RHIS (Empire Builder), Wadhwa specializes in forecasting the nation's labor markets and training entrepreneurial leaders. He brings futurism and more than a touch of self-promotion and showmanship to his quest to make the technology industry more innovative and diverse. He spreads both his personal brand and the brand of the institutions he works for by contributing articles to publications such as *Forbes* and the *Washington Post*, where he has written about the future of jobs, among other topics. Vivek notes that earlier in his life, with a young family to support, he would have fallen into the CPIS (cautious Masterful Realist) archetype. Now, with his children grown, he is an unapologetic risk taker (R) and innovator (I). Wadhwa has built publicly traded software companies, including Seer Technologies; held a half-dozen academic positions; and even produced a Bollywood movie. He's also been shaped by a brutal leadership fight over a company he founded—a fight he won at great cost.

Now he is vice president of academics and innovation at Singularity University, a nontraditional school and think tank for entrepreneurs. He is compelled by high-social-impact (H) ventures that bring together other innovators (I). Both puckish and practical, Vivek has sometimes become a lightning rod for controversy—including that over a book I coauthored with him, *Innovating Women: The Changing Face of Technology,* when he was criticized by some women in technology for speaking extensively about gender diversity in the industry, but not letting women speak for themselves. Others see Wadhwa as a Renaissance man for the high-tech era. He is angry that Silicon Valley remains, in his estimation, biased against gender, race, and age. He's angry that the United States is not doing more to maintain the pipeline of international entrepreneurs who have flocked to this country in the past. In 2012 the Wharton School of the University of Pennsylvania published his book *The Immigrant Exodus: Why America Is Losing the Global Race to Capture Entrepreneurial Talent.*

In order to get to his home base at Singularity University, you turn off Highway 101 and pull up to a security gate. Behind that gate is Moffett Airfield, which includes NASA's Ames Research Center, the institution that masterminded the landing of the Mars rover *Curiosity.* You make a right past the first gate, away from the NASA installation, and drive through the university's open, grassy campus to an innocuous group of buildings. If you walk in at the right moment, you might see a group of twentysomething and thirtysomething students taking a dance break between lectures and demonstrations from top scientists and globe-trotting entrepreneurs. Singularity is very much an un-university built for innovators (I) willing to tolerate risk (R). No degrees are granted. A typical program is ten weeks long. People come from all over the world, at great expense, to attend, learn, and network. Their goal is to form teams and create projects for the common good that will reach a billion people within a decade.

Explaining how he got to where he is today, Wadhwa says, "I founded two companies, Seer Technologies and Relativity Technologies, and then I had a massive heart attack. I realized I was killing myself by working so hard and trying to make money. I was just so fed up with the rat race. The night I was in critical care, and the doctors didn't know if I would make it or not, that's when the venture capitalists decided to steal Relativity Technologies from me."

The year was 2002. Vivek had gone on a cruise with his family and begun experiencing symptoms that he thought were indigestion. Feeling weak, he didn't want to interrupt the family fun, so he didn't make a big deal of it. He should have. Five days later, on the flight home, he had chest pains. By the time he got help, he was immediately put into intensive care.

"I thought I was indestructible," he says. "I hadn't been to a doctor in years. When I got to the hospital, they said within two hours I would have died."

But that wasn't the end of his troubles.

"The next day, while I'm still in the hospital, the VCs call and say, 'We need to renegotiate our financing with you.'"

Previously, the company had overextended itself by refusing to lay off workers during an economic downturn. Instead of firing people, Vivek had used his own personal funds to shore up the business. You'd think that was a good thing, but it put him in a more vulnerable position with his financiers, since they knew how much of his personal fortune was on the line.

"They had me by the balls," Wadhwa says bluntly. "When founders have too much of their own money in the company, the VCs take advantage of it. They know you will tolerate anything because you have so much skin in the game."

While Vivek was still hospitalized, the venture capitalists moved to replace him as CEO, leveraging another mistake that Vivek had made by not filling all the seats on the board to which he was entitled.

All these years later, he says, with a mix of hurt and disgust, "I used to be the rock star CEO with these guys, the poster child for how to do things right. They were such a friendly group that I used to have the board meetings on my porch. I used to think of these people as my friends." The emotional wounds prompted a positive self-exploration, where Wadhwa began to ask himself if the field he was in truly had high social impact just because it was innovative. Even as he geared up to fight for his career, he began reflecting on what he really wanted.

Ultimately, Vivek and his wife gambled what was left of their family money—including their children's college funds (with their blessing)—and fought a successful legal battle to prove that the VCs' move was illegal. They had to wade through thousands of documents—the equivalent of a twenty-foot stack of paper. He and his wife hired a small law firm that agreed to let them act as paralegals, so they did much of the document discovery themselves.

"My wife said, 'You're not going to settle, because if you settle, you'll be miserable for the rest of your life.'"

Vivek won a major settlement. He agreed not to reveal the financial terms, but he would not sign a waiver preventing him from talking about the entire process. Still, it provoked a complete career change.

"I won the battle, but I was so disgusted that I checked out of the tech world entirely," he explains. "I decided to become an academic and get away from it all. Being an academic became a mission to give back to the world."

First, his wife encouraged him to ask a friend at Duke University if he could teach there as an executive in residence. At one point, Vivek held various titles simultaneously at six institutions, including Berkeley, Stanford, and Emory University. His articles made waves in the academic and business communities, and he was sought after as a valued thought leader and brand builder.

"I didn't want another CEO role, because if things got too stressful, then I'd get chest pains again."

And then came along Singularity University, which was founded by a bevy of tech superstars, including Ray Kurzweil, who perfected computer speech recognition and does pioneering work on artificial intelligence, and Dr. Peter Diamandis, the chair of the X Prize Foundation, which organizes multimillion-dollar prizes for people breaking technological barriers. (One team won a $10 million space innovation X Prize, and Google has sponsored a still-active lunar challenge that will reward the winner with $30 million.)

Initially the school offered Vivek the post of president.

"I couldn't do the operational role," he says. "I would have had another heart attack. So we worked out a half-time role, and I run the academics."

His students are already accomplished, often having started their own companies, but they are looking for a larger sense of social purpose. In teams, they work on major projects such as improving access to clean water in developing countries and developing cheap, portable advanced medical diagnostic devices, some of them add-ons to smartphones.

In line with his work at Singularity, Vivek titled one of his columns for the *Washington Post*, "Love of Learning Is the Key to Success in the Jobless Future." In it, he writes of a tech-optimist vision of automation, one that might seem vastly overoptimistic to many but certainly contains wisdom about lifelong learning:

> *Not long ago, schoolchildren chose what they wanted to be when they grew up. . . . Careers lasted lifetimes. Now, by my estimates, the half-life of a career is about 10 years. I expect that it will decrease, within a decade, to five years. Advancing technologies will*

*cause so much disruption to almost every industry that entire pro-
fessions will disappear. And then, in about 15–20 years from now,
we will be facing a jobless future . . . we will gain the freedom to
pursue creative endeavors and do the things that we really like . . .*

*I tell [parents] not to do what our parents did, telling us what
to study and causing us to treat education as a chore; that instead,
they should encourage their children to pursue their passions and
to love learning. It doesn't matter whether they want to be artists,
musicians, or plumbers; the key is for children to understand that
education is a lifelong endeavor and to be ready to constantly reinvent themselves. We will all need to be able to learn new skills,
think critically, master new careers, and take advantage of the best
opportunities that come our way.*[1]

Vivek Wadhwa certainly takes his own advice when it comes to loving learning, reinventing oneself; and being prepared for any changes
that the job market brings. In his case, he knew that "folding 'em"
meant saying good-bye to a workstyle that endangered his health. He is
busier than ever, but in a way that allows him to have more flexibility
with his time, still earn a generous living, and gain both the spotlight
and personal fulfillment from his work.

· · ·

Vivek's story is one of both struggle and triumph.

But what if your career of choice seems to offer few ways out of a
cycle of boom-and-bust opportunity, *and* you love it so much you don't
want to leave? That's what's happened to Deborah Copaken, an award-
winning and *New York Times* bestselling photographer-author of *Shutterbabe*, television producer, and a divorced mother of three. An RHIT
(Promoter of big ideas or causes), Copaken has been taking risks and
making waves since she was in her early twenties.

"I have left careers when I thought what I was doing wasn't helping," Copaken says, reflecting her high-social-impact (H) side. "What I was doing as a producer at NBC—real journalism—was helping. Then I was asked to do a story for another show about tall celebrities. Tall celebrities! I left. It was a stupid, depressing turning point. Every career decision I've made has been to something I thought was meaningful, even though it didn't always work out that way." Reflecting her innovator (I) side, she says, "I like making things. I like initiating."

Early on, Copaken got mixed messages about work, life, and work-style from her parents. "My father was a spectacular artist who did not do his art but became a lawyer instead, at an established white-shoe law firm, Covington & Burling. He said he loved his work, but that was not necessarily true. On the weekends, he was in his art studio all day and then had to go back to his office on Monday. I think he *believed* he liked his job," she says, pausing for a moment. "My choice to do art as a career, to be a photojournalist and write novels and do things I really wanted to be doing every day was very much a result of seeing that. And also seeing my mother.

"Mom didn't work, and the message I got from her was that you go crazy if you don't work. She'd wanted to go to medical school. Her father said he had no money for medical school for girls. So she was a housewife, and she was always depressed."

Copaken has learned something from every job she's had. She describes the lessons from just a few.

"Photography taught me you can do what you want if you want. You can make something out of nothing. I went off on my own at twenty-two." That was in 1989, when she rode along with Afghan fighters who, against all odds, had just beaten down the invading Red Army of the Soviet Union in a war that had lasted nearly ten years. She was the only woman in the group.

Copaken goes on: "A year later, I had an exhibit with major photojournalists in Paris." Her secret weapon? "Being charming. I used my own innocence to my own advantage. You can get anything you want;

you just have to want it badly enough. This was in the age before cell phones, and I didn't know where the hotels were, let alone the rebels. I didn't know how to drive a stick shift. But I figured it out. With enough ingenuity, you can do it."

She writes about her global journeys and the incredible resilience she showed in her bestselling memoir, *Shutterbabe*, which has been sold to television. The book had already been optioned for film, but Copaken thinks the episodic nature of war photography will work better in a TV series than in a film. She admits to not really knowing what photojournalists did when she began covering a real war, but she persevered. "Anytime I have failed tremendously since then, I remember you can start over. So my last book, a novel, *The Red Book*, was a *New York Times* bestseller. Now I can't sell a book," Copaken says, referring to another manuscript that she shopped around but found no buyers. "I started over four weeks ago, working on the same material again with a new tack. And you know what? Rewriting feels better in a new voice."

Despite sometimes tilting at windmills to remain a creative professional, Copaken also has steely insights into why she did and does the work she does. "Being a photojournalist taught me there's the story we tell ourselves and there's the actual story. You have to tell yourself what you do matters, because otherwise—what are you doing with your life? People get mad at me for saying this, but I don't think most of the work a war photographer does changes lives. Every now and then, a lucky photo changes policy. But mainly nobody's going to see it and nobody cares. You have to balance that out with your goals for your career.

"It's important to step back from what you are doing and look at yourself critically," she says intently. "I know part of the attraction of being a war photographer was changing public policy, having a front-row seat to history. Stepping back, this has been an exciting job, and I got to see the world, and that's one reason I loved this job," she continues. But she adds provocatively that people who take on high-social-impact work, including war photographers, "buy our propaganda. A brain surgeon gets off on doing his work." And tapping into that mix of altruism and personal drive or satisfaction is important to recognize, she says, and morally fine.

Copaken has learned plenty from her other career paths as well. She was a producer at NBC, particularly the news program *Dateline NBC*, where she covered Haiti and Princess Diana, among other stories. "I didn't love it," she says bluntly. "Mostly I felt I was helping NBC sell advertising. When I was at ABC News's magazine show *Day One*, I felt I was doing incredible work—stories that really mattered. But it was canceled. When working for a big corporate entity like ABC or NBC, you have to appeal to the lowest common denominator, because that's who is watching. I remember being at NBC during the O. J. Simpson orgy," she says in reference to the endless news stories devoted to the former football star's 1995 murder trial. "Thank God I didn't have to do a lot of that."

Recently, Deborah had a financially and emotionally draining ordeal after signing on to work at a health website, which she described as "a dream job." But things didn't work out as planned. As she explains, "The minute I got there, the company was going public," or moving from being a privately held company to a publicly traded company with stock. "Within the first three weeks, there was a bloodbath. Thirty people were fired. I asked why, and I heard 'We have to fire them to clear the decks for our bottom line,' so the company could seem like it spent very little money and was more profitable. Some of the people being fired were amazing. The whole video production team was fired.

"And then they said, 'By the way, you have no budget.' So I got people to write for free." A well-known actor friend of Deborah's wrote about having skin cancer. "We paid him nothing. I got sick to my stomach getting rich people to write for me. Then," she says, "I *literally* got sick with breast cancer. I told the company, 'It's stage 0'"—the noninvasive stage—"'and I am going to get a lumpectomy. How do I schedule sick time?'

"They said I would have to be working here a year to get FMLA"—

an acronym for the Family and Medical Leave Act. "And they said there is no sick leave. We were supposed to have unlimited vacation, so I said, 'Why don't I take it as vacation?' And they said, 'Well, we know it's breast cancer, so it's not vacation time.' It was incredible." One stupendously good thing did happen: as Copaken went in for surgery, the mass had disappeared. It's rare, but sometimes small tumors are destroyed by the body's own immune defenses and reabsorbed. It should have been a day for celebration, but instead Copaken says this was just another part of the "horrific" experience.

"The day before the scheduled surgery, I'd gotten called in for a pop quiz performance review at six thirty, by my boss and boss's boss. They asked, 'What are your numbers on social media?' and things like that. I told them I would have prepared those numbers if I'd known I was having a performance review. We were doing well," she says, "but it became an inquisition. I looked at them both and said, 'Is this about my job? Are you about to fire me?' It was sounding like a prefiring meeting." They denied it. But three weeks later, they fired her.

"I'm still having a hard time processing what happened," Copaken says. She was eventually able to get three months of severance, but she ended up not only without a job but also without health insurance. A telephone helpline at her COBRA postemployment benefits gave her the wrong payment instructions, and it would not instate her coverage even though she had a reference number to prove with whom she had spoken and why. "I asked to pay quarterly," she explains. "I sent $5,290 to COBRA"—payments of more than $1,700 per month for herself and her children—"and they cashed my check, then canceled my coverage, saying I needed to pay monthly. I owe my doctors thousands of dollars right now." To add insult to injury, the delay in straightening out the decision meant she was too late to get federally mandated insurance via the Affordable Care Act that year.

In a piece for her next employer, a website offering health insurance, Deborah wrote about being rejected in the interim for a job at the

Container Store, which also offered benefits. "I cried for me and my kids, then I cried for everyone else in my same boat, then I cried for everyone in far worse boats," she wrote. "Because seriously, if an Emmy-award-winning, *New York Times* bestselling author and Harvard grad cannot land a job as a greeter at The Container Store—or anywhere else for that matter, hard as I tried—we are all doomed." Fortunately, Copaken has moved on to new freelance work and is awaiting word on whether her book *Shutterbabe* will become a television series. Although it sounds glamorous, there's not much authors can do while TV executives consider possible series—and it's always a long shot what will get made. Deborah is resilient and adaptable, and no matter whether the big dream of a television adaptation of her work pans out or not, she has the skills to continue supporting herself and her family.

Should Copaken and others have moved on from an entire industry, even though they love the work they do? As a reference point, I return to the story of Adam Freed, now CEO of the education company Teachers Pay Teachers. "I think in careers, we all have these moments of transcendence—these 'aha!' moments—that guide us toward the next move. They're moments like when my news directors talked about kitten videos or when I lost the job at MSNBC," he says of his transition into technology and management. "I was standing in the parking lot of Google, which at the time was two buildings and five hundred employees, and I had just spent the day being interviewed. I was exhausted but excited. Everyone in the building was playing Ping-Pong, eating free cereal, and talking in this incredibly optimistic way that I had never heard in the workplace before. It was the first time that I was ever in a place where people were just like 'We're going to reinvent the universe. No problem.'"

· · ·

Balancing your workstyle, your desired salary, and your appetite for risk are just three of the many factors that go into whether to hold 'em or fold 'em at each job. As you see from the stories in this chapter—deliberately chosen to exemplify some of the harder choices—your emotions are a key part of how you do the "math" of job change. We are human and will always be led at least partly by emotion. That's not negative at all. But you also have to learn from the wisdom of your own journey and wise minds who've been through transitions.

Searching for a job when you don't have one is often harder than when you're employed. Burning bridges just leaves you covered in ash, not with long-standing ties and contacts. And even if you are right—for example, if you have grounds for a lawsuit—negotiating a graceful exit might prove to be a better path.

PART FOUR

The Right Work
for America

Part four widens the lens to three issues that affect our work-places, ourselves, and our families: the ever-more-important role of lifelong learning, whether formal or informal; the search for ethically fulfilling work, and what to do when facing moral dilemmas (a key aspect of "right livelihood"); and finally, the redefinition of retirement in the age of episodic careers and changing benefits. This is a chance to learn from work/life masters in the context of major decisions we must make for ourselves and our nation.

8

Lifelong Learning, Lifelong Earning

E NTREPRENEURS ARE ALMOST by nature perpetual learning machines. But Douglas (Doug) Becker has taken things to an extraordinary level. Becker founded several businesses before taking private the publicly traded international education company Laureate Education—which runs universities around the globe and invests in other businesses, such as online education. That means he took a company that was traded on stock exchanges and, with other investors, brought it back under private control in 2007.[1]

Becker's entrepreneurship started well before his eighteenth birthday. In Baltimore, during the 1980s, he and his friend Christopher Hoehn-Saric worked together at the retail chain ComputerLand and dreamed about working in technology. When he was fourteen, Doug switched from a public school to the Gilman School, one of the best private academies in the city.

"The experience of switching from public to private school was really difficult and probably one of the things that made me a bit scrappier," he says. "You know, it's funny: my partners and I sometimes talk about that word *scrappy*. What does it really mean? To me, it's somebody who finds a way to succeed in spite of the obstacles; someone who doesn't give up, who comes back again and again to find a solution to a problem."

Doug had expected to go to college, but life had other plans for him.

"I wanted to be a doctor, so I became a hospital volunteer. But I was also interested in computers—that's where ComputerLand came in. One of the things that amazed me was how I actually had a little bit of an edge over other people because I knew something about PCs when I was just a teen-ager—more, in fact, than almost anyone I knew, including my parents."

Then Doug's two interests converged.

"While I was volunteering at the hospital, I saw how badly the information systems worked. No one had access to their medical records. I could see that people weren't getting the best treatment, and money was being wasted. We would give somebody an X-ray, and then we'd discover that they'd had an X-ray a month earlier and didn't need another one. Or we'd unknowingly give someone two conflicting medications because we had no record of the first."

He and Christopher began working on the idea of automating medical records.

Doug says wryly, "The irony, of course, is that even today there is no universal system for storing medical records. But in 1985 we created something called LifeCard, and if you Google my name and LifeCard, you'll find a wonderful article that came out about it in the *New York Times*. I'll never forget it, because it landed on the front page. No one thought LifeCard was going anywhere, and then I remember my father calling me from the train station just blown away that it had ended up on the front page of the *New York Times*."

Blue Cross Blue Shield agreed to fund the company and produce the data cards to store the patients' records. Blue Cross Blue Shield ultimately spent $1 million (the equivalent of $4.8 million in today's dollars) building the technology.

Meanwhile, all of Doug's friends were preparing for college. He'd been accepted to Harvard, but he deferred for a year so that he could work on the project.

"Then I asked for a second year," he says, "and Harvard agreed but told me that if I wanted to come back, I'd have to reapply. So I never went back."

And so, with just a high school diploma, Doug Becker founded his first company before he could vote. Obviously, this took remarkable talent and intellect, but it also required the emotional intelligence to recognize his true vocation and the foresight to follow his instincts.

Doug's responses to the archetype questionnaire reveal that he considers himself a CHIS, or Sharp-Eyed Analyst. Although his decisions may seem risky (R) on the surface—starting with not going to college—he has a warm, engaging, and confident approach to life and work that is not traditional risk taking but a (seemingly well-founded) assessment that the risks he takes in business will pan out. As he says of the health care technology venture that launched him as an entrepreneur, "For that one minute in history, no one seemed to be exploring how the PC and the health care industries could fit together—which gave me and Christopher, despite our youth, a window of opportunity—and we jumped through it." His desire for blending innovation (I) and high social impact (H) has driven all of his work, from that critical moment forward.

Unfortunately, after Blue Cross Blue Shield bought the company, it faltered. For one thing, its marketing efforts were lackluster—although, frankly, the product might have been ahead of its time for non-tech-savvy individuals. In any event, Blue Cross Blue Shield shut it down.

Doug could have been crushed by the demise of his company or become fixated on another health care venture; instead, he had the maturity to deal with failure and ask himself how he could shape people's lives in another way. That's when he embarked on education.

"I realized that there was actually much less technology being applied to education than there was to health care," he explains. So he bought a small company and turned it into the after-school enrichment program Sylvan Learning. Today Doug runs Laureate International Universities, which serves more than a million students in twenty-eight nations, making it the largest privately held education provider in the world.

"I would say that our number one goal is to increase access to higher education and, therefore, to social mobility in developing countries, which means building the middle classes," Doug asserts.

Then he and his other investors decided to take the company private with $3.8 billion in stock buybacks, giving him more flexibility to pursue the next big thing in education without answering to stockholders. "We went private in August 2007, and I moved with my family to Hong Kong so that I could spearhead the opening of our business in Asia," says Doug. "I could never have done that with a public company, where the investors would have said, 'Look, we make all of our profits in the US and Latin America. Why would you move to Asia?' They would just view it as a very risky, scary thing. Whereas my new investors said, 'You know what? That's the right decision, and, yes, there's some downside to it and some risk, but there are also some huge advantages, so let's do it!'"

Doug has a robust family life. His wife and two children have accompanied him on adventures around the world. In some ways, his desire for work that is both innovative and high social impact puts him in conflict with his desire to spend time with his family. But he has worked hard to create a synergistic environment for work and personal life.

"I was thirty-three when I married Erin. We would joke with each other that we were each other's second spouse even though we'd never been married before," says Doug. "When you're older, you can be a better partner. The mistakes that someone else might make in their first marriage, we had a better chance of avoiding because we just knew ourselves better. Which means that by the time we got married, our lives had reached a reasonable level of stability. The early years of my entrepreneurial ventures, even looking back and seeing how well everything worked out, were very turbulent. There were many, many times when I slept on my office floor, when my partners and I thought we were going to be wiped out. Terrible problems, lawsuits, financial woes—all sorts of challenges that are typical for entrepreneurs."

He continues, "By the time I got married, I had more control over my destiny and my own schedule. Erin is a very, very supportive partner. I have friends with spouses who are very critical when they come home late from work. Erin and the kids know that I'd rather be with them, but they believe in what I'm doing, and they feel it's having a positive impact on people.

"In 2010 I was traveling in China, and I got a phone call from ex-president Bill Clinton's people asking if I would come to Haiti and help him advise the Haitian government on higher education. I'd been away from my family for a couple of weeks and really missed my kids. We were living in Paris at the time, so I just declined. Then I arrived home, walked through the door—my daughter was probably five or so at the time and my little boy was about three—and saw my wife standing there. I told them the story, and I was expecting this big thank-you for coming home instead of doing the cool thing, when suddenly they're staring at me, like 'What were you thinking? You have a chance to help President Clinton in Haiti! Go!'

"And so I literally went with them directly to the pharmacy to get my malaria medication and took the very next flight. I had the chance to be with Bill Clinton and UN Secretary-General Ban Ki-moon before the earthquake hit and had one of the most transformational experiences of my life." The 2010 earthquake in Haiti had a death toll variously estimated between 150,000 and 316,000 people.

Douglas Becker exemplifies how lifelong learning can also lead to an increase in lifetime earning—and perhaps even more important, in satisfaction. Although his formal schooling is less than that of people with a fraction of his net worth, he has trained and challenged himself constantly to learn more about technology, entrepreneurship, how his workstyle would affect his family, and now even philanthropy and diplomacy.

These days, lifelong learning is critical to anyone who wants to remain engaged, employed, and fulfilled. Whether you're talking about formal job or educational retraining or targeted self-learning, today everyone must learn or risk falling behind. That applies to owners of companies with market capitalizations of billions of dollars as well as to neighborhood entrepreneurs.

Auto shop owner Rohan Williams knows his business requires that he and his staff stay up on advances in automotive technology. After immigrating from Jamaica in 1990, he started Brooklyn's Nok Auto Repairs eight years later. He placed his garage in the Prospect Heights neighborhood, where real estate prices have grown so sharply over the past few years that he's going to sell at a tidy profit and relocate. And in order to build that wealth, he's made a commitment to lifelong learning and also to training others.

"I was told by my automotive instructor to train five people," Rohan says. "I'm up to twenty-nine." The men in his shop are generally young and certainly respectful, aware that they are in a business that functions because of customer service as well as automotive engineering. While the principles of good customer service might never change, the automobile has—and continues to.

"I replaced a generation back in the days—carburetor guys," says Rohan. "Now it's fuel injection. But that's going away. We're going into the electronic and hybrid cars. And if I don't keep up, don't go to school and get the new knowledge, then I would be like one of the carburetor guys going out too." Rohan says that his job today includes making sure that the mechanics in his shop learn "the newest technology so I can stay home and sleep," he says with a chuckle—though he invests a lot of time in managing and training his staff. If his business model changes and he goes back into the shop hands-on, he believes he'll have to go back to college to learn the newer technologies.

For Rohan, whose parents in Jamaica let him grow crops on a small plot of land and sell them at the market when he was a child, the most important thing he learned about business was how to manage money. "Money is a tool. You can sleep, and money can work for you. I go out and get renters. I go out and do everything possible to make it keep rolling in instead of me sweating," he says. That leads to his ability, after having raised a family, to live freely. "Every month I go somewhere else—so I'm retired. Retirement means you take a rest from work. I've been doing that for the last ten years after I get the business on a good footing." He envisions running his business for another five to fifteen years. "I could go out now, but I like to teach people," he explains. "If I see them tomorrow, then I'm still on retirement. If they don't come in, then I have to work because I have to pay the bills," he says with a smile.

• • •

No matter your career path, you have to take lifelong learning into account. And most people also have to factor in money as well—not just what you earn or what you spend on education but also how you will amortize the cost of that education over the years. For example, if you are one of the many lawyers who gets a degree but practices for only a few years, how do you value the cost of that education? If you work only five years as a lawyer, do you divide the cost you paid—and interest on debt—by the five years of practice? Or do you believe that even after you have left the field, spending the money on the degree has helped you in your next endeavors? These are hard, if not downright impossible, questions to answer *definitively*. But at some point, as with the discussion on whether to hold 'em or fold 'em, you have to research whether the time and money spent on training and education are worth it to you, given your goals.

The very nature of episodic careers—where you move from one pursuit to the next, drawing on different sets of skills—can make it hard to decide which training and education are best, especially when you also must take into account family concerns, particularly child rearing and caregiving. But episodic careers can also allow you to make soup out of leftovers. Let's say that you are one of the many lawyers who no longer practice, both because you're not interested in a job at a firm and you want more time for other interests. But what if that law degree allows you to be more effective in other sectors of your life? For example, if you're securing care for a parent with health problems, you might be better able to assess contracts with medical providers or be able to help supervise agreements like living wills. If you volunteer at a church or civic association, you might be able to help as an in-house expert—even if you're not formally working as a lawyer—who also reads between the lines for the organization you care about at important times.

But let's get back to hard financials. Formal higher education is more expensive than ever, and the debt load that students take on can throw people into a financial tailspin if their career of choice doesn't have a good roster of available jobs; or if those jobs pay too little relative to debt; or, most of all, if they start a degree but fail to finish—and still must pay the debt. Higher-education loans can't be discharged in a bankruptcy, unlike many other types of debts.

As *Forbes* magazine's Chase Peterson-Withorn wrote in a 2014 article: "Tuition and fees have risen 538% since 1985, outpacing the CPI by over 400%." That's right: higher education costs *five times* as much today as it did just twenty years ago. (CPI, incidentally, stands for Consumer Price Index, one measure of year-to-year costs and inflation.) Furthermore, he adds, "According to the Federal Reserve Bank of New York, the number of student loan borrowers increased 70% from 2004 to 2012. Now more than 70% of students graduate with loans, and outstanding student loan debt totals $1.2 trillion—more than auto and credit card debt."

That's a lot to process, but in essence: college costs are racing ahead of the costs of most goods and services in America; people are taking out more loans; and not surprisingly, many people are having trouble keeping up with payments. Perhaps as a consequence, thirty-year-olds with student debt are less likely to buy a home than ones with no debt.[2]

Economist Austin Goolsbee acknowledges that educational debt can cause financial distress, but he also makes the point that getting a higher-education degree is still a key predictor of who will get and keep a job, even in hard times. "The last thirty years certainly have confirmed that those people who have more skills and better education not only did better during the recession; not only have much lower unemployment rate; not only have higher income; but also have proven far more able to adjust to whatever comes next."

He offers an example from a key US industry: technology. "If you go back to the 1980s, Silicon Valley was a very rich place, and, primarily, what they were doing was making computer hardware"—that is, putting together circuit boards and manufacturing computers. "And now," he continues, "there's virtually no computer hardware made in Silicon Valley whatsoever. It moved away, but unlike Detroit, Silicon Valley didn't become poor as the industry they were doing shifted away. Those people moved on to the next thing, and the reason they were able to do that is they've got a lot of human capital—they're very skilled." Silicon Valley, which was named for the silicon used to manufacture computer chips, is focused now on creating software, mobile apps, social technology platforms, cloud computing, and the like.

"The indicator of the middle class's future in the United States is schooling," Goolsbee says. He notes that the average student debt for people who have it (and, of course, not all college graduates do) is about $24,000. "That's a lot, but the average pay differential for a college graduate compared with a high school graduate is fifteen thousand dollars per year." In other words, a college education for the average debt holder should still pay for itself in two years. Updated figures from the nonprofit research organization Project on Student Debt found that in 2013, 69 percent of graduates from public and nonprofit colleges carried an average educational debt of $28,400.[3] A separate study found that 96 percent of the graduates of for-profit colleges carry debt.[4]

Goolsbee adds, "The US, for many, many years, was number one in the world in the share of its twenty-five-year-olds who had a college degree. We've now fallen behind a lot of other nations. We're not even in the top ten anymore. The reason for that is we still have the highest enrollment—the highest share of twenty-five-year-olds who have ever attended any years of college. But," he adds, "it's just that we have the highest dropout rate from college by far in the whole world." The main reasons include inadequate k–12 education, with people dropping out because they find higher education shockingly difficult after inadequate high school preparation; and also that the price tag for a degree has risen so much, forcing some students to drop out for financial reasons.

In other cases, people complete degrees from unaccredited universities and find later that they are virtually worthless. In a 2013 investigation for the online publication *Salon*, reporter Kai Wright covered the senseless educational debt load carried by a twenty-seven-year-old graphic designer:

> *Last year, Garvin Gittens became a literal poster child . . . For several months, his face was plastered all over the New York City subway system as part of a city-led campaign to warn would-be students about debt scams. When we met last summer, Gittens laid out for me how he racked up more than $57,000 in public and private debt in pursuit of a two-year associate's degree in graphic design at the for-profit Katharine Gibbs School, in Midtown Manhattan. Like subprime mortgages, the debt didn't appear so intimidating at first, but just as balloon payments capsized so many tenuous family finances, a cascading series of loans, a few thousand dollars at a time, eventually caught up with Gittens. In the end, his degree proved as meaningless as it was expensive. When he went to apply for bachelor's programs, no legitimate college would recognize his credits because the school's shoddy performance had finally led the state to sanction it.[5]*

Despite this, Gittens was so determined to get a degree he started the process over again—but tens of thousands of dollars poorer.

Globalization expert Alec Ross believes that a revival of serious vocational education could help build prosperity, particularly for working-class Americans. Sometimes called industrial arts, vocational education was first federally funded in 1917 and, arguably, had its heyday in the late 1940s through the 1950s.[6] Over the years, an industrial arts education took on, for many people, an aura of being second class. But Ross doesn't believe that has to be so. As he puts it:

"Our economy grows increasingly interconnected and increasingly global. Billions of federal dollars flow into vocational education programs today. Those dollar amounts should go up, and the nature of the programs should be fundamentally redesigned. Vocational education is more important today than it's ever been in the past.

"Look," he says, "not everybody has an IQ of 140. Not everybody can get a microbiology degree from Johns Hopkins. So what we have to do is to make sure that everybody has a chance to get a good job. One of the ways we can do that is by making significant investments in vocational education and community colleges. We need to do so not using yesterday's models, but a Singapore-like focus on identifying what tomorrow's skills are and funding the kinds of programs to help ensure that kids coming out of working-class communities have those skills."

The island country of Singapore, which has a robust economy, offers a wide variety of polytechnic diplomas in fields from nursing to engineering to tourism and hospitality. These diplomas take less time to complete than a college degree and are highly focused.

The federally funded CareerOneStop.org provides ways to find federal, state, and local job training and retraining programs, including ones targeted to veterans; to particularly hard-hit local economies; and to different demographic groups, including women. But government-run training is not the only option by far; nor does every program have to be long term. For example, one of the fastest-growing fields is computer science. Private groups such as Hacker School provide short-term training paired with job placement—in one case, teaming up with the online marketplace Etsy (for which I worked briefly) to bring women into the computer-coding job pipeline. There are also online resources such as Codecademy and Khan Academy, which offer non-degree-granting course work; as well as public and private universities offering degree-granting online courses or "low-residency" programs, where students spend a couple of weeks a semester on campus and complete the rest of the work remotely. Pace University, Florida University, and George Washington University are among the schools that offer highly regarded online degree-granting programs; better known universities offer "MOOCs." That's an acronym for "massively open online courses," some taught by esteemed faculty to thousands or even hundreds of thousands of people at once. In other words, you might not have to leave your home in order to further your formal or informal education. And in some cases, the courses are free.

But MOOCs, and many other online education options, also have their downsides. Many people drop out or fail the classes, particularly those who have less previous formal education.[7] This fact, the rising cost of college education, and all of the other challenges of formal study as lifelong learning don't outweigh the need for it. In the era of episodic careers, each person might choose different tools to keep expanding his or her skills and knowledge base, but none of us can afford to stop. However, formal study is only one option for growth.

Sometimes the best way to move forward is to rely on people: yourself, your friends, your colleagues. As Adam Freed, who went from being a reporter to a manager at Google, puts it, "I started reading business books at night, practicing Excel, and doing all the things I hadn't had to do in my prior career. I also got a lot of support from my colleagues." Lifelong learning has always been and will always be self-directed. Who you turn to for help is up to you, and it's wise to do the research to make sure you get the best opportunities at the most reasonable financial cost.

9

Money and Morality

O H, HOW WE love our criminals. From *The Godfather* and *Scarface* to more recent TV fare, including *The Sopranos*, *The Wire*, and *Boardwalk Empire*, America is fascinated by what it takes to get away with living on the wrong side of the law. We're also fascinated by the white-collar criminals depicted in flicks such as *The Wolf of Wall Street*, guys with education and credentials instead of guns. But it's still stick-'em-up time for the little guy. As lead character Gordon Gekko (played by Michael Douglas) says in *Wall Street*:

> *I am not a destroyer of companies. I am a liberator of them!*
>
> *The point is, ladies and gentleman, that greed—for lack of a better word—is good.*
>
> *Greed is right.*
>
> *Greed works.*
>
> *Greed clarifies, cuts through, and captures the essence of the evolutionary spirit.*

Greed, in all of its forms—greed for life, for money, for love,
knowledge—has marked the upward surge of mankind.
*   And greed—you mark my words—will . . . save . . . that . . .*
malfunctioning corporation called the USA.

A bit over the top and corny? Sure. But the movie came out in 1987, the
same year as the massive Wall Street crash known as Black Monday.
Considering how long it takes to get a movie green-lighted, the writers
and filmmakers were prophetic.

Wall Street and movies like it may have obscured the deeper ethical
crisis around work in America. Most people don't have the power to
crash the stock market, let alone the brazenness to make a speech saying "Greed is good."[1] Everyday ethical issues include not only harassment and discrimination (based on age, sex, race, religion, and so on),
but nepotism and other favoritism; and even whether "skimming a little
off the top" is a common practice in the industry.

If we work for a company that is not being fair, in ways big or small,
do we "go with the flow" or do we stand up to power? And if we stand
up, *how* do we do it? Large corporations, and many small ones, have
clearly delineated ethics policies and training on issues such as gender
and discrimination in the workplace, and departments like human resources can provide guidance. Your options, if you feel there is an ethical dilemma at your company, whether it directly involves you or not,
vary widely. Among them:

- Open up directly to your manager.
- Go over your manager's head (particularly if he or she is the problem)
  to a higher-level supervisor. Now, that can definitely nix your long-
  term chances in the workplace if you displease your direct superior
  and he or she turns out to be in the right—or manages to convince
  his or her boss that your complaint is unfounded. But sometimes it
  also successfully outs a person who is flouting the rules.

- Or be diplomatic, raising questions in an open-ended way to see who your allies are for action as a group. But if the corporate culture is riddled with ethical problems, it may be time to move on.

What behaviors are we talking about? There is *illegal* behavior (a managerial or company action or policy that can be pursued with recourse in court), *unethical* behavior (which is sometimes illegal and sometimes not, depending on the statutes and loopholes), and *unfair* behavior (which, just as when you're a kid shouting "That's not fair!" is often left to the eye of the beholder and the discretion of those in power). Sometimes what happens in workplaces is all three, but what's *right*, what's *legal*, and what you can *successfully bargain or sue to get corrected* are very different.

Most career books don't delve too deeply into these issues, but I believe they're important. As a black woman, I've experienced moments of what I consider both racial and gender bias, but I've deliberately chosen never to file a formal grievance. I believe it would have damaged my career. On the other hand, I have also had people specifically mentor me through diversity programs targeted at underrepresented minorities, including ones for black Americans and other racial minorities. Because I was mentored in race-specific programs doesn't balance out my belief that I also faced racial stereotypes—they are simply realities that coexist. I say "my belief" because all of it is old history, and probably disputed history, too. It also doesn't undermine all of the incredible experiences I've had in a complex but fascinating industry.

Early in my career, a white colleague came to me to say that a magazine editor was not considering me for a job, when, in his opinion, I should have been the lead candidate. I've been told outright not to apply for jobs I've been qualified for, and flagged racially inappropriate behavior to management without my statements bringing about any action. Other racial and gender "moments" in my career have been tragicomic. At a corporate cocktail party, the billionaire CEO of a major media company told me his wife worked with black teen mothers on a charitable level—and then asked if *I* had been a teen mother—causing the face of a third person who was part of the conversation to collapse in shame. (The shame, by the way, is not about being a teen parent, as many people do so ably. The shame was that this was the first association that popped into his mind, and a highly unlikely question for him to ask of a white reporter.)

The point here is not to dwell on my experiences but to demonstrate that many people bring their baggage into the workplace, whether it's perceptions about race, gender, and sexual orientation—or a Gordon Gekko–style belief that "Greed is good" and the end justifies the means. Of course, many people bring integrity and fairness into the workplace as well. I have seen them, met them, worked for them, and cherished them. Employees and managers are human—nothing more, nothing less. In other words, if humans are flawed, then workplaces run by humans will be flawed. That can be a nightmare or a simple learning curve, depending on how we approach things.

We can always learn from and evolve in our behavior. We always have the choice to champion ourselves and others. A spirit of generosity and learning rather than fear and greed will go a long way toward making our workplaces happier and, frankly, our economy stronger. (See the discussion in chapter 1 on how stress diminishes productivity, or Alec Ross's words on how gender equality can raise our national fortunes.) I was touched by a blog post by author and business guru Seth Godin titled "But Not People Like You." It says simply:

We're hiring, but not people like you.
    I'm looking for a doctor, but of course, not someone like you.
    We're putting together a study group, but we won't be able to include people like you.

He then goes on to add:

When we say, "I don't work with people like you, I won't consider supporting someone like you, I can't invest in someone like you," we've just eliminated value, wasted an opportunity, and stripped away not just someone else's dignity, but our own.

What have you done? What do you know? Where are you going? Those are a great place to start, to choose people because of what they've chosen, not where they started. Not because this will always tell us what someone is capable of (too many people don't have the head start they deserve) but because it is demonstrably more useful than the crude, expensive, fear-based shortcuts we're using far too often.

In a society where it's easier than ever to see "you," we can't help but benefit when we become anti-racist, pro-feminist, in favor of equal opportunity and focused (even obsessed) on maximizing the opportunity everyone gets, early and often.[2]

It's a critical time in American history, one where many people are afraid about the economy and feel aggrieved. And it's critical that we each take responsibility for making sure we do our part to create fair and just workplaces.

I think of the example of my grandmother. She began working at Social Security after having six children, and after being one of the top students in her school but not being able to afford college. She took some classes later but never got a bachelor's degree. Yet she managed to work her way to a level where she had her own secretary and plenty of managerial responsibilities. Nevertheless, her career stalled for several years. Why? She found out that when applicants were given an entry-level test, all of the white applicants were offered jobs, regardless of their scores, before any of the black applicants. She became an internal whistle-blower, and was told repeatedly by colleagues of all races to drop it—that a middle-aged woman like herself had no future if she made a fuss. Later, a change in management rewarded her for the same behavior others had punished her for. She received a Commissioner's Citation, a recognition that she had brought her ethical values to bear on her workplace, and was willing to endure years of anxiety and repercussions to do what was right.

Many people in my family, including my mother, have set various examples for doing what is right even if it's not easy. But let's turn to a legal angle on what happens if, like my now gone but never forgotten grandmother, you are being discriminated against or retaliated against for speaking out.

• • •

Dominique Day is a human rights lawyer who has worked around the globe and in the United States for private firms and nonprofits as well as clerking in US District Court. She obtained her law degree from Stanford University. Her view of how the law treats employment bias is nuanced and frank.

"The law is getting worse and worse," says Day. "So while the policy arena improves—for example, management inaction postreport of discrimination or harassment is recognized as a basis for employer liability—every time the Supreme Court touches the issue, they make it worse. For example, management discrimination now needs to be by someone with direct supervisory authority and the ability to fire or sanction, according to the recent case *Vance v. Ball State University et al.* Plenty of firms will settle to avoid the enormous cost of litigation and the fact they are technically in the wrong. But even if you have the money to proceed through a multiyear lawsuit, it is really difficult to litigate these cases without very substantial—even flagrant—evidence of misconduct."

She continues, "So, outside the context of impact litigation, filing a lawsuit is typically a plan to get a financial or declaratory settlement—for example, positive references, severance and benefits, a 'cleaned-up' personnel file—and really a last resort." In other words, filing a lawsuit should be what you do when you have no other options, not plan A. "Judges want to see meaningful attempts to resolve these issues before approaching the courts, and many companies will recognize written communications contesting reviews, or the like, as prelitigation documents that are more cheaply and simply resolved internally, particularly where there are well-founded concerns raised by the employee. With respect to human resources action," she says of these internal options, where you approach your company management directly, "I've been involved in plenty of cases where people have done it. But it is usually when you are about to be fired or received an unfair bad review. So the potential benefits typically outweigh the risk only after an actual sanction that is career threatening. The exception to that is sexual harassment, where the strategy of women, especially white women, shifting the burden to the employer is a bit more successful."

Finally, she says, "In my experience, discrimination cases are getting harder and harder to win in the courts, particularly as cases go up on appeal. But not every employer wants to be in court defending inappropriate corporate behavior, and many will do the right thing based on the foreseeability of litigation." If you write a formal letter to management, it might signal that you are willing to go to court, and the company might then settle or take other action to resolve the issues. "But," she concludes, "you need to have good, documented evidence that you were doing high-quality work, and that the sanctions are likely arbitrary and subjective, in order to even mount this defense."

This points out the need to document your own work and also to read reviews to make sure they are appropriate. Once, after receiving a review that I thought was unfair—not based on race or gender but other performance questions—I wrote a rebuttal and made sure it was included in my file. I believe my documentation was a smart decision, but having moved on to other employment many years ago, I doubt anyone in the known universe really cares about that performance review.

As I conducted the survey research that helped me build the archetype system in this book, I also asked many other questions, including about experiences of discrimination. One question asked: "Have you ever experienced employment discrimination based on age, gender, race, or sexual orientation?" Obviously, this is self-reporting, meaning that each person decided what he or she did or did not experience. Almost one in three (31 percent) responded yes; slightly more than half (55 percent) said no; and roughly one in eight (13 percent) said they were not sure.

Then I asked a follow-up question: "Did you report the employment discrimination to either an internal (HR or EEO within the organization where you worked) or an external party (government entity, journalist, etc)?" Of those responding, 22 percent chose "No. I was afraid of what would happen on my job or to my reputation if I did"; 58 percent answered "No. I had other reasons I chose not to report it"; 6 percent chose "Yes, and I feel I got a positive outcome from reporting it"; and 13 percent answered "Yes, and I feel I had a negative outcome from reporting it."

So based on this nationally weighted survey of more than two thousand men and women (that's larger than many presidential election polls), nearly a third of workers feel they have experienced bias, but the vast majority do not report it. And of those who do report, twice as many are dissatisfied with the outcome than satisfied. Again, these are individuals describing their own experiences. But it demonstrates that most people who feel they face bias do not choose to go through official channels to resolve the question, and those who report are twice as likely to feel the outcome was not satisfactory.

These are just my findings on perceptions of employment bias. And there are many ways in which employees must choose how to manage their reputations. In the era of episodic careers, when people switch jobs more often than in the past, it's still critically important to document your work, highlight your successes, and challenge what you believe to be unfair evaluations. But it's also much more likely that you will be judged on the recommendations you can get from former co-workers (fair or unfair) and, if applicable, a body of work you can show that was yours. Let's say that you do a specialty in home renovation, and sometimes you get your own contracts and work solo, but sometimes you're hired to work as part of a larger team. If you end up working with different teams on a case-by-case basis, document what you do as you go. In the case of a cabinetmaker, for example, that might mean taking photographs of your work as well as getting testimonials from the people who'd hired you. (Do this soon after the project is finished, before people forget.) It's a business reality that you have to document the work you do, especially if you don't always work for the same clients or companies.

Where does this intersect with ethics? Some people coast along by relying on other people to do much of their work but claiming all the credit; while others contribute greatly but are never given their due. That could happen in a grade school (say, with teachers and classroom aides), a law firm, a janitorial crew, or a Fortune 500 company. Claiming credit for what you do, and what you are due, is critical: thus the need to document your work and, if you can, obtain recommendations or testimonials. I also make sure to help people who've worked well on teams with me seek new employment if we've worked on a project together that's ending. That's not strictly an ethical question, but championing good employees as they move and transition in our chaotic labor environment is important to me.

I go out of my way to try to make matches between good employers and good employees, and people I know do the same for me. It's a virtuous circle that takes advantage of the value of networking without exploiting it. I never recommend anyone for a job who I don't think can do the job. On the other hand, a referral- and recommendation-based employment world can also lead to "social replication," or people hiring only those like them. On Twitter, @kemullholand argued, "It took me way too long to realize that 'We only hire on referrals' is what corporate racism looks like nowadays." Whether or not you agree with that specific diagnosis, it's a reminder that referral-based systems can screen out a wide variety of qualified candidates as well as unqualified ones.

Finding "the right work" includes blending your skills, desires, financial goals, and ethical goals. More than ever, America needs people who bring an ethical spirit to the work they do, and who actively engage in ways of making sure that workplaces are emotionally functional and equitable. Deborah Copaken, whom we met in chapter 7, admires her father for drawing a moral line in the sand. "He was given a tobacco company case to represent," she says. "And he said to his firm, 'If I have to represent a cigarette company, I'm going to quit.' So they gave him a pro bono case, representing people on Culebra." The US Navy was bombing that Puerto Rican island, a US territory, as a munitions test site, even though it had several hundred residents. "My father said, 'There are people there!' He worked on the case for years and finally won, in 1975. I learned from him that you don't engage in business practices that damage others." Her father, Richard Copaken, later wrote the story of the case—in which the 743 residents eventually won the right not to have their island bombed—in the book *Target Culebra: How 743 Islanders Took On the US Navy and Won*. He passed away in 2008.

Other people find themselves working within or affiliated with companies that are ethically troubled. Let's take a look back at the 2001 fraud and bankruptcy of energy giant Enron Corporation. The Houston-based company once employed twenty thousand people and was repeatedly named "America's Most Innovative Company" by *Fortune* magazine. In 2000 it claimed revenues of $111 billion. By 2001, it had totally and completely folded, after it was exposed as actually losing money—and much more importantly, hiding that fact through a series of lies and accounting schemes that benefited Chief Financial Officer Andrew Fastow and other top executives. In essence, when Enron failed, it destroyed the retirement accounts of thousands of its employees (who'd been urged to invest in company stock) and precipitated a wave of other corporate bankruptcies and devastating personal losses, including suicides. When the scams were revealed and the stock price fell from $90 to less than $1, it didn't just hurt "corporate America," it hurt people.[3]

Ten years after the company's collapse, the Associated Press interviewed former Enron plant manager George Maddox, who was seventy-eight at the time.[4] As a result of losing most of his $1.3 million in stock-related retirement savings, he and his wife lost their home. They both had to go back to work after moving into a rural farmhouse to save money. She died; he continued to work mowing pastures while raising their fourteen-year-old grandson. That's just one example of the devastation that unvarnished greed wrought.

A man who had an inside view of the ethical dilemmas, and whose reputation was damaged—though he continues to live a very comfortable life—is the globally minded New Yorker Frank Savage. In ways that many others involved with Enron did not, he has reflected publicly on the company, his role as a board member, and the era of excess in which Enron flourished. Today Savage is a business leader, investor, father of six, and author of the memoir *The Savage Way: Successfully Navigating the Waves of Business and Life*. His book explores how he came from a working-class DC family, went to Howard University, conquered corporate America—and then had an Icarus-like fall as one of the board members of Enron. Board members have a "fiduciary duty" to the company, meaning they are charged with making decisions in the company's interest. When Enron collapsed, Savage also lost his seats on other high-powered corporate boards that were concerned with taint by association, whether or not Savage could have foreseen what the company's executives were doing.

When we spoke, Savage told me, "What happened at Enron was the bad apple syndrome. If you don't trust management, you should never join a board. Later people said, 'Didn't you know Andy Fastow was a crook?' I said, 'No!' It was the eighties and nineties. People thought the boom would continue. You become optimistic. But I was not less diligent. I never took my eye off the ball. I just never expected a team member to be the criminal among us."

Fastow and Enron CEO Jeffrey Skilling have been identified as the key players in the scheme. But Kirk Hanson, executive director of the Markkula Center for Applied Ethics at Santa Clara University, also placed some blame on the board in an analysis the year after the bankruptcy. "The board of directors was not attentive to the nature of the off-books entities created by Enron, nor to their own obligations to monitor those entities once they were approved," he said. "The board did not pay attention to the employees because most directors in the United States do not consider this their responsibility. They consider themselves representatives of the shareholders only, and not of the employees. However, in this case, they did not even represent the shareholders well—and particularly not the employees who were shareholders."[5]

For Frank Savage, being on the board of Enron—once a prize—became a devastating reversal in a long and lauded career. "My record has always been exemplary," he says. "But I was there, so I had to take the pain. Being a leader, that's part of being part of the business world." He adds, "Trust and integrity are everything. When you agree to serve on the board of a company, a public company, you have to assess the company and yourself to decide, 'Can I make a contribution?' "

Today Savage is a principal in a very different kind of company, one that seeks to match college students with work in call centers. Many of these types of jobs have been offshored, meaning taken to other countries. It's not glamorous work, but it can provide people with a solid income as they seek an education. The company is called Jobs America Inc. Says Savage, "College costs bother me. I have six children, and none of them had debt from college." That, of course, was because Savage was able to contribute to their educations as needed. "We shouldn't have a country where only people who can pay for college with family savings can go. We can help kids avoid taking on so much educational debt," he says. And while many of Jobs America Inc.'s employees are students, who are allowed to work a maximum of twenty hours a week, so they can focus on their studies, some workers are, of course, full-time employees—many of whom have not been able to access the economic recovery. Savage says that the jobs crisis "is hitting lower-income families in America big-time. It's a threat to the American way. Most of people who work for us are not from affluent families."

Savage himself did not grow up in a financially affluent family, but one that taught him rich lessons about work. Today, by the way, he considers himself an RPIT archetype (the Cocreator in Chief, a classic entrepreneurial model), although earlier in his career, he would have been a RHIT (the Promoter, someone who promotes ideas). Savage's childhood taught him to promote the idea that anyone can do any-thing—a contested idea in a time of wealth inequality, but he believes that with vision, training, and effort, all things are possible.

"Everything I learned about work came from my family," he says, "especially my mother, Grace," a well-known Washington, DC, beautician and entrepreneur. "Her business name was Madame La Savage. Everything I learned about business came from seeds she planted in me as a young man. She started her business in my bedroom. She'd take her clients up to my room and do their hair. I had to wait downstairs until she was done before I could go to sleep. My grandfather would come down and tell me it was okay to go upstairs. That was sacrifice." She later went on to run a thriving business near Howard University.

Today, says Savage, "I'm concerned about the widening economic gap between people in America. If everything is based on money, and people think 'I got mine, and I don't care about them'—well, that's something we do not want to happen in America." He adds, "In a lot of the developing countries, you have a huge wealth gap. That's why they don't grow. This kind of wealth and class divide has led to the downfall of many civilizations—including Greece and Rome."

• • •

Frank Savage, with his long and distinguished career, has to live with the fact that he was also part of the board of a company that cost people their savings and their futures. A different perspective on corporate ethics comes from the whistle-blowers who speak out against illegal or unethical business practices, and often pay a price. Many of these whistle-blowers find their careers destroyed or dead-ended. But the story of Tony Menendez illustrates two important points: yes, some companies punish rather than reward employees who point out ethical failings; but also, speaking up doesn't need to mean the end of your career.

Menendez graduated from the University of Houston in 1995. He married his college girlfriend after she became pregnant, and switched his major to accounting, which he genuinely enjoyed, as a way to steer toward financial security.

"It was the go-go nineties," he says of the fast-paced business environment to which he graduated. But over the next decade, he saw a dramatic shift in how people viewed corporate accounting. "In 2001, with the Enron scandal and the implosion of WorldCom, there was a real implosion of public trust." WorldCom, a telecommunications company, filed the largest bankruptcy to date in 2002, after accounting scandals. Menendez takes seriously the word *public* in the title of certified public accountant, or CPA, and it worried him to see the integrity of his field erode. As a result, in 2002 Congress passed and President George W. Bush signed into law the Sarbanes-Oxley Act, designed to reform corporate and auditing accountability.

With corporate scandals and federal legal changes as the backdrop, Menendez was contacted by a headhunter and asked to interview for a position at Halliburton, a multibillion-dollar global energy company headquartered in Houston. By that time he had divorced, spent some time as a single father, and had a family with his second wife, Cindy. He started there in 2005, a year after the company settled an investigation with the Securities and Exchange Commission (SEC), a federal regulatory agency sometimes called "the watchdog of Wall Street," over failures to disclose changes in its accounting practices. (The company also paid $7.5 million in fines.) "When I started at Halliburton, not only were people coping with the new regulations, but Halliburton was coping with a lot of bad press," Menendez says, adding that he had some initial reservations about being recruited by the company.

His fears were allayed when he met with his future boss. "He sold me on how critical my job was. He said he wanted me to be 'Smokey the Bear'"—meaning to send warning signals of any accounting troubles—"and my job was to keep him out of the *Wall Street Journal*." Several people Menendez had worked with at the huge accounting firm Ernst & Young had also gone to work at Halliburton.

But despite his supervisor's words, says Menendez, "It didn't take too long to realize there were some real problems in the company. I don't think it was for any nefarious reasons, but the company almost went bankrupt for a couple of years. Accounting went by the wayside for a while and really got sloppy.

"At first there was a wide recognition: 'We'll fix these things.' My job was almost like a risk management role at the end of the day." But he says, "After finding a few thing that were wrong with Halliburton's accounting system, the welcome mat for finding things wrong started to wear thin." This was only three or four months after he'd started work. After finding accounting discrepancies in the range of $5 million to $10 million— which he describes as "smaller ones," given the size of the company—he discovered, in his words, "the entire company's revenue recognition model was wrong." Among other things, Halliburton was counting lucrative equipment sales as revenue before it had finished work for its clients.

But if a customer left the contract, that meant that the "revenue" would never actually be a part of the company's real bottom line—and at the time, equipment sales added up to billions of dollars.

Menendez's wife believed he could become a fall guy for the company, so at her urging, he decided to audiotape his supervisor, who told him that a memo he'd sent out was accurate but that he needed to be "politically sensitive" and not put things in email. The supervisor said on tapes that Menendez later provided to the SEC that he wasn't asking Menendez "to compromise your ethics, and I'm not asking you to compromise the position that you feel strongly about."

Audiotaping seemed extreme to Menendez. "I was incredibly nervous and uncomfortable with it. It was not something I wanted to do. I'm not proud of it. I wish it hadn't had to happen, but I'm glad it did," he says, given the company's reaction. "In the backdrop was WorldCom and Enron people going to jail. I was worried about going to jail" for not reporting the violations.

After seeming as if the company would make a change in accounting practices, Halliburton decided to stick by its existing record keeping. And then the company sent out a memo to employees saying that the SEC was investigating complaints filed by Menendez, and began to take away his responsibilities at work and shut him out of meetings. He also found himself persona non grata with a lot of his coworkers. "It's not like evil minions," he says. "These are people I worked with on a daily basis, I thought we were friends." Two of his coworkers did stand by him, though one made a point of making sure that Menendez was listed under a nickname on his phone contacts, so that if his phone rang in a meeting, no one would know they were still close.

"You really start to see how the power of the groupthink mentality really is," he observes. "No one wants to think of themselves as being a bad person. But the problem is so many people are involved, they all want to pass it off on someone else."

Menendez's wife, Cindy, helped keep him going. "I absolutely couldn't have done any of this without her support," he says. "But what really kept me going was how much I believed this was true."

The SEC declined to pursue a case against Halliburton in 2006, and after that Menendez decided to file a whistle-blower claim under the Sarbanes-Oxley Act, alleging the company had retaliated against him. But even though he provided evidence that Halliburton had written a memo about a meeting with him that had never taken place, he lost this case. Over the course of several more years, Menendez worked as a consultant to pay the bills *and* represented himself in an appeal of the verdict. (His second lawyer had declined to pursue further appeals.) "I was so optimistic and naive in the ways of big corporations," says Menendez. "But I read a lot, I studied, I did a lot of homework. That's why, compared with my very first attorney, I knew what to do more than he did."

In 2014, after a series of appeals and counterappeals, Menendez won his case against Halliburton. The judge awarded him $30,000—*more* than he'd asked for but, arguably, less than he could have gotten if he'd pushed for a larger financial award.

The question remained: What would lie ahead for Menendez's career after the years he'd spent fighting for his reputation? While he was fighting the legal battles, he also studied how to be an investigative accountant, or what's called a forensic accountant. "I took classes on how to interview and go through depositions. I worked with lawyers on depositions of lawyers and auditors," he says. Through a contact, he landed an interview with Nick Cypress, the comptroller and chief accounting officer for General Motors. The giant auto manufacturer was facing bankruptcy, and in Menendez's words, Cypress "was not your typical executive. He was in the twilight of his career, focused on protecting his reputation, getting GM right, and making sure there were clean books." Cypress, impressed rather than intimidated by Menendez's devotion to getting accounting rules right, hired him.

"I don't want to give people a false sense of hope that you can be a whistle-blower and get a job right away. It's still very hard," Menendez says. "Hopefully, people will learn something from what I do. Many people are going to be touched by a whistle-blower: a friend, family member, or coworker. People need to have a better awareness of why we do this. There's no way anyone could go back in time and convince me not to do it. I believed this was so wrong that someone had to pay attention."

Not many of us, thankfully, will face ethical dilemmas as stark as Menendez's. But questions of ethics and fairness come in many forms. Knowing what you stand for, what you will and will not put up with, and what behavior you choose to model and encourage in your workplace is better assessed before issues arise than in a moment of confusion or conflict.

10

Retirement, Remixed

N OCTOBER 2014 I sat in an auditorium in Tempe, Arizona, watching the most extraordinary group of people take the stage to be honored. A truly stylish and sexy-at-any-age Kate Williams walked onstage guided by her daughter. After losing her eyesight to a degenerative disease, the businesswoman forged a new career doing job placement for visually impaired and blind people. Her placement rate is 40 percent—for people who are often considered unemployable. Compare that with the rates for online job search for all people, estimates which range from 4 percent to 20 percent.

Child psychiatrist Dr. Pam Cantor is the founder of Turnaround for Children, an organization that partners with public schools to address the obstacles to teaching and learning that stem from the impact of poverty-related stress on the developing brains and bodies of children.

And the Reverend Richard Joyner of Conetoe, North Carolina, talked about how he begged God to send him a new revelation. After seeing members of his rural, lower-income community dying too young from diseases such as diabetes, largely because they did not have fresh food, he had a vision that the spirit was calling him to farm. Why was he upset at that? He had been a child sharecropper, pushed beyond the limits of what anyone should endure, far too young, to reap harvests—with the profits going largely to other people. Despite his reservations, he heeded the call. Today, his church-based agricultural and mentorship program takes teens into the fields, has them grow crops and receive intensive leadership mentoring, and then those crops are sold to community members. As a result of having access to fresh food, emergency room visits in his congregation are down 40 percent, and premature deaths as well. And as a result of the teen mentoring, college and job placement rates have risen dramatically.

All these individuals, and several more, were winners of the Purpose Prize, an award created by Encore.org (with financial benefits as well as recognition), given to adults over the age of sixty who have used life experience and skills from their previous careers to forge new paths and ways of helping others. Some people view the Encore movement as unrealistic, what with many individuals stretched already by the demands of saving for their own retirement. I found it inspiring. Not everyone has to start a new organization, but the idea that the area from midlife to senior citizenship needs to be and is being redefined as a period of growth rather than of folding inward is critical. The baby boom generation is too engaged with the world to settle for being sidelined as time marches on. And many generations—including those both before and after the currently retiring baby boomers—have come to embrace retirement as a period of life where you do what you choose rather than what you have to do.

The waters of that beautiful vision are deeply troubled by the financial crises in America. The mortgage crisis and the Great Recession cut the knees out from under the retirement planning of many Americans. You can't talk about formal retirement if you don't have the means to stop working. And just because you have left, or been laid off from, a job in your sixties or seventies does not mean that you have the money to live well now, let alone into your eighties, nineties, or beyond, if you should be so lucky.

So, as we end this book, looking at retirement—both proactively, for people far from their retirement years; and head-on, for people who have two or three decades to build up (or lose) savings—I want to be both hopeful and realistic. Just as the reality of episodic careers is redefining the world of work, America is also redefining the notion of retirement. Social Security, a both lauded and maligned program that upon inception ended the worst of elder poverty, is in the midst of gradually raising its retirement age. Also, the reality of what Social Security offers is based on your lifetime earnings history. It's capped, but the more you earn over time, the more you get as a benefit. If you are a widow or widower, you also receive additional benefits. And obviously, the cheaper the place in which you live (and there is a robust and growing community of retiree expats who move to cheaper countries, where a check goes farther), the farther Social Security stretches.

But most people, including those who *are* living totally on Social Security, want more money coming in—from work; from pensions; from insurance; from savings. I'm currently forty-six. Since your Social Security benefits are based, in part, on your earnings over the years (though the range is capped), I've done as well as I can in that arena. I have a retirement benefit from AFTRA, the American Federation of Radio and Television Artists, which I belonged to for many years of doing television and radio full-time. And I also have personal retirement savings. I don't feel insecure, but I also don't believe I am coasting toward retirement. I don't own a home, for example. I've lived a (mainly New York) renter's life. I'd like to save more. Who wouldn't? But I'm also aware that I have many options. Hopefully, with good health, I will have many more years in the workplace and of adding retirement savings ahead of me. I work in two professions—academia and writing—

that are fairly open toward older workers and less likely to push aging members out of the fold. I'm adaptable. And I'm also willing to retire someplace cheaper than the United States if need be—certainly someplace cheaper than New York.

There is also a different concept of retirement: the "miniretirement" or sabbaticals or vacations that you can take throughout your life, rather than waiting for a moment when you stop running and just exhale. Although I've worked for most of my life, I've also taken weeks and sometimes months at a time to travel, do academic fellowships, and write independently. I wouldn't say I was just goofing off, but I certainly wasn't saving toward my retirement. And while that may negatively affect my current net worth, it has greatly enriched my life. Books such as *The 4-Hour Work Week: Escape the 9–5, Live Anywhere and Join the New Rich*, the 2007 bestseller by Timothy Ferriss, urge people to break the habit of working nine to five. Instead of waiting until you are older to relax and travel, he advises people to take several miniretirements throughout their lifetime. Although the idea of a four-hour workweek is more concept than reality (Ferriss, who runs a whole business empire now, certainly works more than that), the idea of miniretirements is gaining hold among younger workers who have portable skills such as nursing and computer coding.

And then there are people like my friends Doreen and Marc Gounard. When they met in Washington, DC, in the 1980s, Marc—who was born and raised in France—was an experienced commercial sea captain. Once they fell in love and got married, and decided to have children, he assured her that one day his sailor's heart would want to take the family out to sea. So when their daughter was thirteen and their son was seven, they boarded a sailboat they had built themselves from an architectural plan and set out on a four-year circumnavigation of the globe. Their children are now grown, but Marc and Doreen still live on the houseboat today. Marc makes, and made, jewelry from precious stones and beach shells, which he sold to bring in cash, as they would dock for up to three months at a time at global ports. Doreen homeschooled—or, rather, boatschooled—the children. Everyone, including the kids, contributed to the maintenance and navigation of the boat. During an interview, the Gounards told me about being chased by Somali pirates (who, luckily, had an engine failure before they could catch them). But the scariest moments of their journey, says Doreen, were when they'd been on long hauls on open ocean, for weeks at a time, and a storm would whip up, and they'd be tossed and battered with no one to rely on but themselves. But they talk about how meaningful it was to take this journey with their family when they were young enough to endure its hardships—and also to expose their children to an extraordinary, vivid way of life. Was their four-year journey a "retirement"? Not in the traditional sense. But a four-year adventure outside of the traditional world of work is certainly more than a pause.

The Gounards now live in Sausalito, California, on their boat, in a houseboat community that Doreen manages. The Marin County area is stunning, idyllic, and increasingly pricey. The houseboat community includes people whose boats couldn't make it across the San Francisco Bay and are docked purely to live on, as well as sleek motor-driven boats and ones, like theirs, that can be sailed on ocean voyages or lived on. Their house—that is, their boat—is filled with love; and both have other intellectual and money-earning pursuits now that they don't sail full-time.

Retirement is also about reenvisioning daily life—including possible downsizing or relocation. Sharon and Roque Gerald of Washington, DC, are relative newlyweds yet simultaneously planning retirement. She's fifty-six, he's sixty-one, and they met after having each raised children from other marriages. Both are warm and engaging, Sharon and I bonded over a shared background in the Baltimore area, and Roque and I spoke about his Afro-Panamanian family, whose older generations had intersected with global black luminaries including Kwame Nkrumah, who later became the first president of Ghana. Although

Roque was born in Panama, he has lived in America most of his life. Yet the couple—and Sharon is white and born and raised in America—are likely planning to retire to Panama in a few years. I asked Roque to tell me more about their decision-making process.

"We anticipate moving at the end of 2016 or beginning of 2017," he says. "Our decision to retire in Panama was motivated by a number of factors: cost of living, pensioner benefits—including lack of taxation on pension income by Panama—stability of government and stability and strength of local economy, climate and topographical diversity in Panama (mountains, beaches on Pacific and Caribbean, large city, and major airports and transportation systems), natural beauty, friendliness of Panamanians, English and Spanish as languages, comfort as an interracial couple, the existence of a global expat community, racial and ethnic diverse native population, and proximity to the US for visits with friends and family." (Clearly, they have thought this out!) Roque adds that as a dual Panamanian-US citizen, this is a "return to homeland" for him—one that would not exist even in other places that many US expats go, such as Costa Rica. It's a place where he has ties and can guide Sharon as she settles in.

Financially, the couple have a mix of pension, 401(k) retirement savings, and stock; as they reach their midsixties, they will get Social Security as well, which can be received anyplace in the world. Postretirement, they are planning to let life settle organically into a new pattern. "We are relatively recently married," Roque says, "and have, separately and together, experienced several major challenges: cancer and the loss of a child among them. Our initial plans are to be unstructured in our lifestyle and to take the time to really enjoy our time together, without schedules and obligations. We feel that we will find something purposeful as we move into retirement and are interested in letting that unfold naturally and don't want, at this moment, to plan what direction we will take."

While Sharon and Roque seem like very careful planners who have taken into account their life cycles and finances and cultural wishes, they see a lot of their circle struggling with the idea and reality of retirement. "For the most part, our friends have expressed that they are not prepared for retirement," he says. "This seems to be mostly because of financial concerns: insufficient retirement savings, we assume, combined with the current cost of living in the Baltimore-Washington metro area. Few will receive a pension during retirement—pensions are increasingly being eliminated or, at best, replaced with savings plans subject to the fluctuations of the stock market." Roque adds that many of the couple's friends have drained their own finances to pay for their children's educations, sometimes signing on to help with student debt. And unlike Roque and Sharon, many of their friends are not willing or able to move away from the communities where they've spent most of their lives, either because of family obligations or a desire to be around parents or children—or just to stay where they're already familiar with things. Retiring in a major US city (or an equally pricey global one) is sometimes a shock even to those who believe they have planned well.

Economist Austan Goolsbee and personal finance expert Carmen Rita Wong put the questions of contemporary retirement in a larger context. Says Goolsbee, "You've got to, even at a young age, in your thirties, be thinking 'I want to establish a retirement account,' and thinking realistically about how much you are going to need when you're retired or semiretired. Usually the amount you're going to need is well in excess of what anybody anticipates. In the world of the future, if it involves more freelance and job switching, there are a series of things that, in the past, were taken care of by your employer, where now the onus gets put on the individual to take care of it themselves. And you've got to be smart about it" in a way that people didn't have to be before. "Personal savings for education, for having a family, for buying a house and health insurance—all of that stuff is going to involve more planning than it did in the old days. The world where 'I don't have to think about it' is for sure gone.

"And if you want to avoid a mad scramble from age fifty-eight to sixty-five, where you say, 'Oh my God, what was I thinking? I didn't save any money, I have no compounding interest from long-accrued savings'—well, you've got to be proactive about that," he continues. Goolsbee also points out that health care crises for uninsured or underinsured Americans are the leading cause of personal bankruptcy. A seemingly well-designed retirement plan that doesn't include disability insurance or adequate health care may fail. Goolsbee hopes that the Affordable Care Act passed during the first Obama administration, in which he served, will help people with these challenges.

In general, says, Goolsbee, Americans must take charge of their own fortunes in a way that many assume (wrongly) they do not have to. "Retirement is one category of life expense. Saving for a house, saving for a family, buying a car—all of those things are going to involve accumulating some assets. People that had capital [that is, financial savings, in cash, stock, real estate, and so on] accumulating have done very well for themselves." Prosperity requires "getting in a mind-set that 'I'm not just going to spend every dollar I have. I'm going to save some away.'"

Personal finance expert Carmen Rita Wong sends a similar message. "I don't think it's dismal, but I do think the days of assuming that you can retire when you want to is probably gone," she says. "And I don't necessarily think that's a bad thing, because coming from immigrant parents, I never understood the assumption that retirement was a given. I always assumed that I would just figure it out and keep working as long as I physically could." She points out that less than 20 percent of major companies today offer pensions, whereas the majority of such companies did in the 1950s and 1960s. "You can't assume retirement, period," she says bluntly. "The majority of companies now don't offer matching even on 401(k)s." My employer, New York University, still does offer a dollar-for-dollar match to retirement savings, up to a maximum percentage. And this is truly unusual. It even puts 5 percent of your salary into a retirement fund after the first year, even if you *don't* match. "You think freelancers have Roths and IRAs and all that business? Not really," Wong says of the retirement accounts that self-employed individuals (among others) can create. In a survey I ran in August 2015, 16 percent of respondents had these types of accounts, while more than half had an employer-created retirement account from a current or previous job. But the survey also shows huge amounts of doubt and uncertainty among people as they look toward retirement. When asked to respond to the assertion "I believe I will have enough income (from savings, pension, or other sources) to live on comfortably during retirement," 37 percent said yes; 34 percent said no; and 30 percent responded that they weren't sure.

Wong says, "There's no doubt the retirement age is not a given and we have to work more. And if there's ageism in the middle-class and upper-middle-class workplace, what does a working retirement look like? It probably means downsizing and moving," she adds, in line with the way Roque and Sharon Gerald have structured their plans. "I don't want to say 'unfortunately,' because I don't see that as the end of the world." In fact, under the right circumstances, downsizing and moving can be a great adventure. I know couples and singles of retirement age who have sold homes, moved into apartments (sometimes in retirement or assisted living communities, sometimes not), reduced their fixed costs, taken on more travel and more time with grandkids (if they have them), and generally had a lot more fun.

"What I see as the end of the world is not being able to work at all, meaning your health being compromised," Carmen continues. "Odds are that forty percent of Americans will have diabetes in their lifetime, for example. It's ridiculous. A side effect of living long enough to have chronic diseases is that a third of working Americans end up on disability at some point in their lives. For women, it's more so, of course, because of childbirth," which usually just involves taking temporary leave. "My biggest fear is for my health and not being able to work at all," she says. "My fear is *not* working in retirement. So what are we going to do about the fact that there are a lot of people living longer, and they're going to get sick? That's what I'm concerned about."

Let's take a look at what a real worst-case scenario looks like. Author and education reporter Stacey Patton penned an article with the grim headline "Suicide Is My Retirement Plan." It's a quote from one of several adjunct college teachers she interviewed for the *Chronicle of Higher Education* who were nearing retirement age without much to show for what can be an intellectually rewarding but financially injurious career.

The woman who made the statement is Debra Leigh Scott, an artist and adjunct professor at Temple University. While she says she does not actually want to kill herself, she can't imagine another "dignified" exit. And while most of those interviewed by Patton were not quite as dramatic, all were deeply worried. As the article states:

> *[Scott is] a member of the first generation of a relatively new breed of adjunct: the teacher who wanted to become a full-time professor but never got the opportunity. A divorced mother of two grown children, she has now been teaching for over 25 years, cobbling together different types of jobs to scrape by. She got beaten down by the recession, lost several jobs and her home, and she's used what little savings she had to stay afloat.*
>
> *Though she knows how to "bend a nickel in five directions," Scott hasn't been able to put any money aside for retirement. Her decision to pursue an academic career has required that she live as simply and frugally as possible, without the ability to help launch her children into their adult lives.*
>
> *"I couldn't help them with tuition. My son has chosen to leave college and is working full-time, and my daughter has a six-figure debt that she'll be paying in her 40s," Scott says. "So you could say that they've already paid for my life choices." . . .*
>
> *. . . professors who serve on a temporary or at-will basis can spend a lifetime working with no upward mobility and no ability*

to amass savings. The retirement-planning structure that benefits tenured professors doesn't work for adjuncts, they say, and their colleges often leave them on their own when it comes to their post-teaching security.[1]

There's no question that at least for the near term, many Americans will have to do more with less. Statistics from the Federal Reserve reveal that family income, adjusted for inflation, dropped for all but the top 10 percent of Americans between 2010 and 2013. (Remember that the Great Recession was in 2007–09.) Now we are in a period of low and slow economic growth, but it's far from evenly distributed. Overall, American incomes went down by 5 percent in that 2010–13 period. But the incomes of the top 10 percent rose. Yes, the figure was only 2 percent, but obviously the top earners will not feel the squeeze that middle-class and lower-wage workers feel, both because they're earning more and because their basic material needs should be met. In a *New York Times* op-ed, Wall Street executive Steven Rattner, who led the Obama administration's task force on the auto industry in 2009, lays out a series of statistics showing that the United States has lower taxes *and* much lower services—like education—than other developed countries. When taking taxation into account, he argues that America is the most wealth-unequal country in the nation.[2]

Going back to my original survey research from 2014, among the sobering findings of my national study were that 35 percent of respondents said they had spent retirement-plan funds or personal savings earmarked for retirement to supplement their wages. Specifically, 20 percent relied only on earmarked personal savings; 4 percent, on retirement-plan savings, such as an early withdrawal from an IRA or 401(k); and 11 percent spent both. I asked the question again in my August 2015 survey and found similar numbers, with a total of 37 percent of respondents answering that they had withdrawn savings targeted for retirement to pay bills. According to an analysis of data from the Federal

Reserve and the US Census Bureau by the firm HelloWallet, in 2010 one in four Americans withdrew money from their retirement accounts. And the Transamerica Center for Retirement Studies found that a third of unemployed or underemployed workers made early withdrawals.

But as much as there are people who have chosen or been forced to undermine their retirement prospects, there are those like Chicago's Kenneth Addison who have learned to embrace constant change and profit from that skill. Addison says he's chosen "to go with the tide, rather than against it." His life and career path have taken him from working with troubled urban youth to becoming a (now retired) social science professor, businessman, and real estate investor.

Addison embraces this definition of retirement, emailing me a passage of writing by clinical psychologist Dr. Jack D. Williams:

> *On the practical level, retirement is the career change you make when you are no longer required to work full time and you have some freedom to choose the life that you want to live. Retirement is a career change because it has all the practical hallmarks of a career change, such as the need for planning, the need to learn about your own strengths and priorities, the need for networking, the change in income, the need to try out new things, and the choice of a new direction. To have a thriving retirement, you need to be doing something that you believe in and that feels important to you.*
>
> *On an emotional level, retirement is a process of letting go, followed by renewal—just like a career change . . . And the more you know about making the transitional trip and the more you know about the new country, the better off you are.*

Addison says, "I had a simple plan for my retirement: I got a state university tenure track teaching position in a state where the retirement obligations are protected by the [Illinois] state constitution." That's not the case in many other states. "I got tenured so that I had freedom to consult and have a private practice to augment my reasonable salary, and saved some money. I viewed my retirement like an investment bond that would pay dividends during retirement so I could pick and choose consulting jobs. I retired with eighty-five percent of my top four years of income without a requirement to pay state income taxes, so I earn as much in retirement as I made on average as a full professor."

Professor Addison continues, "I enjoy being retired because things at the university were becoming stressful with budget cutbacks. I was getting tired of administrating. I loved teaching but hated the grading and logistics, since we had no teaching assistance. Now I consult a bit and follow what the day brings. I have had some major health issues, so I'm glad to be retired. I have three wonderful kids, three grandchildren, and two great-grandchildren whom I try to see as often as I can. With the economy, I find myself having to help two of my children financially, which, thankfully, I have been able to do so far."

The professor is also quite informed and analytical about the big picture. He refers me to an article in the *Harvard Business Review* by Robert C. Merton, "The Crisis in Retirement Planning," which goes into the transition from defined-benefit (DB) retirement plans, such as pensions, to defined-contribution (DC) plans, which include 401(k)s and IRAs. Merton argues that "putting relatively complex investment decisions in the hands of individuals with little or no financial expertise is problematic. Research demonstrates that decision making is pervaded with behavioral biases. (To some extent, biases can be compensated for by appropriately framing choices. For example, making enrollment in a 401(k) plan the default option—employees must opt out rather than opt in—has materially increased the rate of enrollment in the plans.)"[3]

Professor Addison says, "Working people who made their retirement plans based on the belief that their pension rights were secure and backed by legislation, and the idea that a contract was a contract are no longer protected." In fact, he retired a bit earlier than he intended to avoid a potential change in the law affecting his benefits.

All of this is a lot to take in. But the key is to retain a sense of pragmatism *and* optimism—to realize that you have to be informed about your options.

One of the people inspired by the way that Americans are remixing retirement is Marci Alboher, a vice president at the nonprofit organization Encore.org. The organization is reshaping the idea of the bridge between work and retirement, and their awards ceremony was referenced at the beginning of the chapter. Although Marci, at forty-eight, has a couple of decades left before the typical retirement age, she says that one of the perks of her job is seeing new patterns emerge that will shape her own choices. "I'm part of something that if we succeed will shape the future. I'm working with a lot of people twenty years older than me, and it's affecting my experience of what it means to age in many different ways."

Alboher has already been a pioneer in writing about careers and living an adventurous one of her own. After attending a top-notch college (University of Pennsylvania) and law school (American University), she became a corporate lawyer. But, she says, "I was really happy in my legal education. But as a practicing lawyer, it was never a good fit. I was an advertising lawyer—an unusual, specialized field of law." She adds firmly, "The only reason someone needs an advertising lawyer is because they're doing something underhanded. The consumer protection laws are very straightforward."

Marci describes having a "crisis of conscience" because she believed she was not acting in the public interest. So she left the field, which radically changed how much she earned—and her entire way of life. "I am still not making anywhere near what I was making when I abandoned corporate law in 1999," she says. "I left the field and a marriage to someone making a lot of money. We were in this earning trajectory that I thought would continue. In that marriage, I had two homes: an apartment in the city and a weekend house. We traveled around the world, often first class." She now lives in what she calls a "modest but really comfortable home" with her second husband, an entrepreneur who runs an art and event space devoted to the history of baseball. Her corporate life allowed her to buy a home outright, giving her more flexibility to take a lower nonprofit-industry salary.

But there was and is a whole other career in between corporate law and working for Encore.org. Marci cultivated a life writing books and columns on careers, particularly developing the notion of a "slash career," where you do two or more things at once. Her book *One Person/Multiple Careers: A New Model for Work/Life Success* is cited in the resource guide as a text that helps offer new ways of looking at careers. "What inspired me to write it in 2007 was that in that period I was finding there was a new way that the virtual world, technology, and the more expansive view of work was letting people express many sides of themselves professionally." She republished the book under her own imprint in 2012. Marci also wrote a career column and blog for the *New York Times*. "It felt like good work," she says, adding bluntly, "and it was summarily ended."

Feeling "cast adrift" when the column ended, Marci had already committed to going to the Encore.org conference. Marc Freedman, the group's founder, whom she'd interviewed, offered to cover her expenses, since it was no longer a conflict of interest with journalistic work. That became the start of his recruiting her into the organization to help him work on marketing and communications. He's based at one of the company's two headquarters, in San Francisco, while Marci is in New York in a coworking space (a shared workspace often used by tech start-ups). "I'm now living the very stuff I used to write about," she says with satisfaction. "I have created a work life that allows me to be who I am in a 24/7 way." And as she looks ahead, the work she does, and the lessons she's learning from people a couple of decades older will influence how she sees the concept of "retirement," its financial realities, and the possibility of crafting a full life at any age.

Final Thoughts

Reflections on Happiness, on the Job and Off

F YOU REMEMBER from my introduction, I was considering taking a bicoastal job. I decided not to, in order to focus on creating a balanced and healthy lifestyle for myself. The workstyle of being bicoastal was a dream for me earlier in life, but dreams and desires change, and pursuing old dreams leads to new problems. I've taken on other media and consulting tasks in New York in addition to teaching, which presents new challenges in how I balance my time, my personal passions, and my money. Having met and spoken with so many people, and researched where we are headed economically, has given me more perspective on making informed decisions in my own life, as well as respect for the grit and determination with which so many American workers approach their own choices. None of us completely controls our own life and fortune. But we've each been given the gift to seek our true path.

Wishing you the best in your choices and your journey,
Farai

Acknowledgments

FIRST OF ALL, I offer thanks to everyone who agreed to be interviewed for the book. I asked a lot of very personal questions, and I appreciate your openness.

Deepest of thank-yous to my editor at Atria, Leslie Meredith, for her craft and guidance, and to the multitalented Malaika Adero for acquiring the book.

Appreciation goes to the team at SurveyMonkey for helping me navigate putting together a national survey for the book, and through which I connected with CEO Dave Goldberg, who was deeply beloved by so many. My thoughts are with his friends and family. Many thanks to researchers including Susan Wilson, Josiane Georges, Samantha Shankman, and Kristen Van Nest, plus all the transcriptionists who worked on this book, most of them public radio producers; and to Kathleen Anderson. Deep thanks to New York University's Arthur L. Carter Journalism Institute.

Of course, I have to offer massive amounts of love and gratitude to all my friends and family, who have supported me this time and every time over the past twenty years I have neared the finish line of writing a book and then *really* freaked out. (You know who you are. Thanks for listening.)

Pointers and Resources

Because of the vast number of resources available online, I'm going to suggest a few ways of searching for information and offer a tightly curated list of resources organic to my writing of the book.

SEARCHING FOR INFORMATION

All my techie friends tell me that doing a natural language search for information (sometimes known as Googling) is better than trying to type sentences you think a machine wants to hear. Try being specific about items like location and time. A search for "Job fairs in the Houston area in July 2016" might show more relevant results than "Houston employment opportunities." Precisely because many good job suggestions come from your networks—friends, family, and local resources—it's important to customize the resources you tap in the ways that suit you best. Based on what we learned about online-only job search (just hunting for listings) versus networked job search (using your contacts to find out about jobs before they are listed, or even find out about companies' willingness to create positions), you will want to be sure to present yourself to employers and potential employers proactively.

With that in mind, here are some of the national online platforms for job search, networking, and job listings:

LinkedIn (www.linkedin.com)

The current crossroads of job-search and deep career-building tools, including an embedded social media stream. Paid upgrades get you features including the ability to see what a computer algorithm considers your rank among people who'd apply for the job you're seeking.

CareerBuilder (www.careerbuilder.com), Monster (www.monster .com), Indeed (www.indeed.com), Simply Hired (www.simplyhired .com)

Each of these sites, and many others, indexes job listings from across the country and makes them searchable by location and industry.

Career One Stop (www.careeronestop.org)

Sponsored by the federal government, this site lists apprenticeship opportunities for skilled trade jobs, as well as adult basic education and college opportunities and funding. It also offers career self-assessment tools and pointers to local job agencies.

BOOKS ABOUT CAREERS AND JOB SEARCH

Reid Hoffman and Ben Casnocha, *The Start-Up of You: Adapt to the Future, Invest in Yourself, and Transform Your Career* (Crown Business, 2012, with resources available online at www.thestartupofyou .com)

This guide to the era of networked job search is coauthored by LinkedIn cofounder Reid Hoffman, the current leader in networked job search and career-building business genre. Full of practical tips about how to brand yourself online and off, it's a great resource for understanding career trends.

Richard N. Bolles, *What Color Is Your Parachute? A Practical Manual for Job-Hunters and Career-Changers* (Ten Speed Press, 2013)

This annually updated bestseller offers both practical job search tips and detailed exercises designed to help you reflect on internal desires (everything from salary to whether you want to work in an office or outdoors). It also includes a long index of professional career coaches nationwide.

Marci Alboher, *One Person/Multiple Careers: A New Model for Work/Life Success* (2012 updated and self-published edition available on HeyMarci.com and through online retailers; 2007 edition from Warner Books)

Alboher covers "slash careers"—the rise of people who do two or more careers at once, including profiling a management consultant/cartoonist. Her book offers a guide to successfully blending different pursuits at the same time for fun and profit.

Nicholas Lore, *The Pathfinder: How to Choose or Change Your Career for a Lifetime of Satisfaction and Success* (Touchstone, 2012)

This book focuses on stories and exercises about tailoring your career to your personality, and your creative and ethical values.

Roman Krznaric, *How to Find Fulfilling Work* (Macmillan, 2012)

This small book packs a lot into its pages, taking the reader on a journey of understanding what makes work right for you—whether that's financial goals, creative, or world-changing—and why work is, for most people, a critical part of modern satisfaction.

CAREER COUNSELING

If you want to find group or individualized career counseling, you can find someone to work with locally—or work with someone by phone or remotely—by looking at resources such as the website of the National Career Development Association (www.ncda.org/aws/NCDA/

pt/sp/consumer_find); the index of *What Color Is Your Parachute?*; or by doing a search for your "area career counselor association." Most major metropolitan areas have their own or more than one.

The expert I spoke with in *The Episodic Career* is Matt Youngquist, Career Horizons, www.career-horizons.com.

Data Dig

A Closer Look at the Archetypes

Whichever Work/Life Matrix archetype you fall into, be assured that it's a good one—it's yours! There's as little point in me wishing I were a different archetype as there is in me wanting to be six feet tall. (I'm five foot five and a half, by the way.)

There are differences among the archetypes, ones borne out by data as well as storytelling. As I go through the data here, it's simply a way for you to connect more deeply to how different kinds of workers function. It might help you better understand not only yourself but also your coworkers—and even your family.

WORK/LIFE MATRIX ARCHETYPES

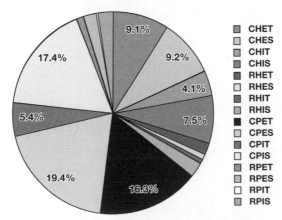

267

C	cautious
R	risk taking
H	high social impact
P	passive social impact
I	innovator
E	executor
S	solo decision maker
T	team decision maker

PERCENTAGE OF THOSE WITH MATCHED CATEGORIES

CHET	9.05 Percent
CHES	9.19 Percent
CHIT	4.10 Percent
CHIS	7.50 Percent
RHET	1.98 Percent
RHES	0.85 Percent
RHIT	0.71 Percent
RHIS	2.40 Percent
CPET	16.27 Percent
CPES	19.38 Percent
CPIT	5.37 Percent
CPIS	17.40 Percent
RPET	1.13 Percent
RPES	2.26 Percent
RPIT	0.14 Percent
RPIS	2.26 Percent

Not surprisingly, more people surveyed consider themselves cautious careerists than risk takers. Here are additional findings based on self-employment, gender, race, and optimism about the economy.

PEOPLE WHO OWN THEIR OWN BUSINESSES

- Business owners are more likely to be risk takers (32.35 percent of Rs own their own business, compared with 13.54 percent of the overall group).
- 67 percent of people who own their own business are the sole employees of said business. This points out how many people who own their own business are running them as a true sole enterprise or a side job to working for another employer.
- A majority of the people who made over $500,000 per year owned their own business.
- People who own their own business are more likely to make risky choices.
- People who own their own business are more likely to be working for enjoyment and/or creativity.
- People who own their own business are more likely to believe that America's economy won't be stronger a generation from now.

GENDER

- Women are more likely to be interested in jobs with a high social impact; 63.67 percent of Hs were female.
- Women are less likely to think their income is sufficient to meet their material desires.
- Women are more likely to report experiencing some form of employment discrimination; 35 percent of women report experiencing discrimination compared with 27 percent of men.

RACE

- White Americans are more likely to work for enjoyment and/or creativity.

- White Americans are more likely to disagree that they will have better job opportunities in five years (38 percent compared with 26 percent of other races).

- Nonwhite and Hispanic Americans were more likely to have borrowed money from friends or family in 2013 to pay bills (28 percent compared with 18 percent of white Americans).

- White Americans are more likely to think they have enough income to meet their needs (66 percent compared with 55 percent of other races).

- Nonwhite and Hispanic Americans are more likely to think America's economy will be stronger a generation from now than it is today (38 percent compared with 30 percent for white Americans).

- Nonwhite and Hispanic Americans were more likely to have had a negative outcome from reporting workplace discrimination (18 percent compared with 12 percent of white Americans) and also more likely to report discrimination (26 percent compared with 16 percent).

- White Americans are somewhat more likely to believe their workplace is fair (64 percent compared with 54 percent of other races).

- Nonwhite and Hispanic Americans are more likely to believe that nepotism plays a role in their workplace (56 percent compared with 48 percent of white Americans).

OPTIMISTS

The findings about optimists show a mix of indicators, including that optimists are less likely to do high-social-impact work (perhaps linked to the stress of that work), and more likely to make team-based decisions. But while they are more likely to think they will have enough income for retirement, they are also more likely to have borrowed money from family in 2013 to pay bills. Other findings include:

- Optimists are more likely to be employed full-time.
- Optimists are more likely than average to indicate that the reasons they work are to pay the bills, to save for their future, and to provide money for other people.
- Optimists are more likely to believe that America's economy will be stronger a generation from now than it is today.
- Optimists were most likely to be ages eighteen to twenty-nine.

Notes

Chapter 1: Work and the Pursuit of Happiness

1. Brigid Schulte, "5 Reasons Why You Shouldn't Work Too Hard," *She the People* (blog), *Washington Post*, February 21, 2014, www.washingtonpost.com/blogs/she-the-people/wp/2014/02/21/5-things-you-get-from-working-too-hard.
2. Gretchen Reynolds, "How Walking in Nature Changes the Brain," *The New York Times*. 22 July 2015. Web. 26 Aug 2015.
3. Claudia Dreifus, "Finding Clues to Aging in the Fraying Tips of Chromosomes," *The New York Times*, 3 July 2007. Web. 26 Aug 2015
4. Paul B. Brown, "A Simple Solution to the Lawyer Glut," *Forbes*, October 30, 2013, www.forbes.com/sites/actiontrumpseverything/2013/10/30/a-simple-solution-to-the-lawyer-glut.
5. Jeff Jacoby, "US Legal Bubble Can't Pop Soon Enough," *Boston Globe*, May 9, 2014, https://www.bostonglobe.com/opinion/2014/05/09/the-lawyer-bubble-pops-not-moment-too-soon/qAYzQ823qpfi4GQl2OiPZM/story.html.
6. Teresa Amabile and Steven Kramer, "Do Happier People Work Harder?," *New York Times*, September 3, 2011, http://www.nytimes.com/2011/09/04/opinion/sunday/do-happier-people-work-harder.html.
7. Catherine Taibi, "Jeff Bezos Makes Big Cuts to *Washington Post* Benefits," *Huffington Post*, September 24, 2014.
8. Susie Poppick, "The Money-Happiness Connection," *Time*, June 9, 2014, http://time.com/money/2802147/does-money-buy-happiness.

Chapter 2: The *New* New Realities of Work

1. Mariya Pylayev, "Surprising Stats About Fast Food Workers," AOL Jobs, August 13, 2013, http://jobs.aol.com/articles/2013/08/13/fourth-adult-fast-food-workers-are-parents.
2. Table Ba50-63, "Female Workforce Participation Rate, by Age and Race: 1800 to 1900." Source: Susan B. Carter, Scott Sigmund Gartner, Michael R. Haines, Alan L. Olmstead, Richard Sutch, and Gavin Wright, eds. *Historical Statistics of the United States, Millennial Edition*, vol. 5, *Work and Welfare* (Cambridge: Cambridge University Press, 2006).

3. *Labor Force Characteristics by Race and Ethnicity, 2013* (Washington, DC: US Bureau of Labor Statistics, August 2014), www.bls.gov/cps/cpsrace2013.pdf.

4. *Statistical Overview of Women in the Workplace*, Catalyst Knowledge Center, March 3, 2014, www.catalyst.org/knowledge/statistical-overview-women-workplace.

5. "In Your State," Lambda Legal, accessed August 26, 2015, www.lambdalegal.org/states-regions.

6. Simon Maloy, "Boehner Messes Up Paul Ryan's Image Rehab: Attacks Unemployed as Lazy and Unmotivated," *Salon*. September 19, 2014, www.salon.com/2014/09/19/boehner_messes_up_paul_ryans_image_rehab_attacks_unemployed_as_lazy_and_unmotivated.

7. Heidi Shierholz, "Hires and Quits Were Flat in April, While Job Openings Rose," Economic Policy Institute, June 10, 2014, www.epi.org/publication/hires-quits-flat-april-job-openings-rose.

8. "Average (Mean) Duration of Unemployment," Federal Reserve Bank of St. Louis, last modified August 7, 2015, https://research.stlouisfed.org/fred2/series/UEMPMEAN.

9. Aamer Madhani, "Once a Sure Bet, Taxi Medallions Becoming Unsellable," *USA Today*, May 18, 2015, http://www.usatoday.com/story/news/2015/05/17/taxi-medallion-values-decline-uber-rideshare/27314735.

10. Josh Mitchell, "Job Market Looks Ripe for Liftoff," *Wall Street Journal*, February 6, 2015, www.wsj.com/articles/jobs-report-u-s-adds-257-000-jobs-unemployment-ticks-up-to-5-7-1423229564.

11. Jodi Kantor and David Streitfeld, "Inside Amazon: Wrestling Big Ideas in a Bruising Workplace," *The New York Times*, August 15, 2015. http://www.nytimes.com/2015/08/16/technology/inside-amazon-wrestling-big-ideas-in-a-bruising-workplace.html.

12. David Streitfeld and Jodi Kantor, "Jeff Bezos and Amazon Employees Join Debate Over Its Culture," *The New York Times*, August 17, 2015. http://www.nytimes.com/2015/08/18/technology/amazon-bezos-workplace-management-practices.html.

13. Sonja Blum and Daniel Erler, "Germany Country Note," in *International Review of Leave Policies and Research*, ed. P. Moss (April 2015), www.leavenetwork.org/fileadmin/Leavenetwork/Country_notes/2015/Germany.pm.pdf.

14. Susie Steiner, "Top Five Regrets of the Dying," *Guardian* (Manchester, UK), February 1, 2012, http://www.theguardian.com/lifeandstyle/2012/feb/01/top-five-regrets-of-the-dying.

15. Federal Reserve Bank of St. Louis, "Gross Domestic Product (2015:Q2)," 30 July 2015. Web. 26 Aug 2015. https://research.stlouisfed.org/fred2/series/GDP/.

16. Hilary Wething, "Job Growth in the Great Recession Has Not Been Equal Between Men and Women," *Working Economic Blog*, Economic Policy Institute, August 26, 2014, www.epi.org/blog/job-growth-great-recession-equal-men-women.

17. Judy Goldberg Dey and Catherine Hill, *Behind the Pay Gap* (Washington, DC: American Association of University Women Educational Foundation (April 2007), www.aauw.org/files/2013/02/Behind-the-Pay-Gap.pdf.

18. Adam Grant and Sheryl Sandberg, "Speaking While Female," *New York Times*, January 12, 2015, http://www.nytimes.com/2015/01/11/opinion/sunday/speaking-while-female.html?_r=0.

19. Maria Konnikova, "Lean Out: The Dangers for Women Who Negotiate," *New Yorker*, June 10, 2014, www.newyorker.com/science/maria-konnikova/lean-out-the-dangers-for-women-who-negotiate?utm_source=tny&utm_campaign=generalsocial&utm_medium=facebook&mbid=social_facebook&mobify=0.

Chapter 3: The Economic Long View

1. *Stress in the Workplace* (Washington, DC: American Psychological Association and Harris Interactive, March 2011), https://www.apa.org/news/press/releases/phwa-survey-summary.pdf.

2. Karen Higginbottom, "Workplace Stress Leads to Less Productive Employees," *Forbes*, September 11, 2014, http://www.forbes.com/sites/karenhigginbottom/2014/09/11/workplace-stress-leads-to-less-productive-employees.

3. Reid Hoffman, Ben Casnocha, and Chris Yeh, "Tours of Duty: The New Employer-Employee Compact," *Harvard Business Review*, June 2013, https://hbsp.harvard.edu/cbmp/product/R1306B-PDF-ENG.

4. US Bureau of Labor Statistics, "Number of Jobs Held, Labor Market Activity, and Earnings Growth Among the Youngest Baby Boomers," news release, July 25, 2012, www.bls.gov/news.release/pdf/nlsoy.pdf.

5. Derek Thompson, "A World Without Work," *Atlantic*, July/August 2015, www.theatlantic.com/magazine/archive/2015/07/world-without-work/395294.

6. Julie Hirschfeld Davis, "U.S. Acts to Curb Firms' Moves Overseas to Avoid Taxes," *New York Times*, September 22, 2014.

7. Raj Chetty, Nathaniel Hendren, Patrick Kline, and Emmanuel Saez, "Where Is the Land of Opportunity? The Geography of Intergenerational Mobility in the U.S, (Executive Summary)," Equality of Opportunity Project, Harvard University, January 2014, http://obs.rc.fas.harvard.edu/chetty/website/v2/Geography Executive Summary and Memo January 2014.pdf.

8. Organisation for Economic Co-operation and Development (OECD), *Divided We Stand: Why Inequality Keeps Rising* (Paris: OECD Publishing, December 2011), http://www.oecd.org/els/soc/dividedwestandwhyinequalitykeepsrising.htm

9. Annie Lowrey, "Household Incomes Remain Flat Despite Improving Economy," *New York Times*, September 17, 2013, www.nytimes.com/2013/09/18/us/median-income-and-poverty-rate-hold-steady-census-bureau-finds.html.

10. US Bureau of Labor Statistics, "Employment Projections: 2012–2022 Summary," news release, December 19, 2013, www.bls.gov/news.release/ecopro.nr0.htm.

11. Victoria Stillwell, "Almsot 97% of the Good Jobs Created Since 2010 Have Gone to College Grads," *BloombergBusiness*. 17 Aug 2015. Web. August 26, 2015.

12. Oganisation for Economic Co-operation and Development (OECD), "Average Annual Hours Actually Worked Per Worker," accessed August 26, 2015, https://stats.oecd.org/Index.aspx?DataSetCode=ANHRS.

Chapter 4: Mastering the Work/Life Matrix

1. Rick Brooks and Ruth Simon, "Subprime Debacle Traps Even Very Credit-Worthy," *Wall Street Journal*, December 3, 2007, www.wsj.com/articles/SB11966 2974358911035.
2. "Frequently Asked Questions and Answers About Section 3 of the Housing & Urban Development Act of 1968," U.S. Department of Housing and Urban Development, accessed February 17, 2015, www.hud.gov/offices/fheo/section3/FAQ08.pdf.

Chapter 5: Resilience Is Everything

1. Diane Coutu, "How Resilience Works," *Harvard Business Review*, May 2002, https://hbr.org/2002/05/how-resilience-works.
2. John Tierney, "Do You Suffer From Decision Fatigue?," *New York Times Magazine*, August 17, 2011, www.nytimes.com/2011/08/21/magazine/do-you-suffer-from-decision-fatigue.html?_r=0.
3. Roy F. Baumeister and John Tierney, *Willpower* (New York: Penguin, 2011), 60, 86–107.
4. Mark Muraven and Roy F. Baumeister, "Self-Regulation and Depletion of Limited Resources: Does Self-Control Resemble a Muscle?," *Psychological Bulletin* 126, no. 2 (March 2000): 247–59, http://bama.ua.edu/~sprentic/672%20Muraven%20 %26%20Baumeister%202000.pdf.
5. Heesun Wee, "Hey Women, Want a Hot Career? Become a Welder," CNBC.com. February 11, 2014, www.nbcnews.com/business/careers/hey-women-want-hot-career-become-welder-n26426.

Chapter 6: The *New* New Realities of Job Search

1. Lindsay Lavine, "Yes, and . . . Improv Techniques to Make You a Better Boss," *Fast Company*, January 9, 2014, www.fastcompany.com/3024535/leadership-now/yes-and-improv-techniques-to-make-you-a-better-boss.
2. Richard N. Bolles, *What Color Is Your Parachute? 2014 Edition: A Practical Manual for Job-Hunters and Career-Changers* (Berkeley, CA: Ten Speed Press, 2013), 104–6.
3. Peter Kuhn and Hani Mansour, "Is Internet Job Search Still Ineffective?" Forschungsinstitut zur Zukunft der Arbeit (IZA)/Institute for the Study of Labor, September 2011, http://ftp.iza.org/dp5955.pdf.
4. James D. Eubanks and David G. Wiczer, "Job Searching: Some Methods Yield Better Results than Others," *St. Louis Fed on the Economy* (blog), Federal Reserve Bank of St. Louis, March 20, 2014, https://www.stlouisfed.org/On-The-Economy/2014/March/Job-Searching-Some-Methods-Yield-Better-Results-than-Others.
5. Nancy DiTomaso, "How Social Networks Drive Black Unemployment," *New*

York Times, May 5, 2013, http://opinionator.blogs.nytimes.com/2013/05/05/how-social-networks-drive-black-unemployment/?_r=0.

6. "Analysis: Race and Americans' Social Networks," Public Religion Research Institute, August 28, 2014, http://publicreligion.org/research/2014/08/analysis-social-network/#.VcddlcrbI5s.

7. Alessandro Acquisti and Christina M. Fong, "An Experiment in Hiring Discrimination Via Online Social Networks" (unpublished paper, Carnegie Mellon University, Pittsburgh, PA, October 26, 2014), available on Social Science Research Network (SSRN), http://ssrn.com/abstract=2031979.

8. Celeste Little, "Equal Opportunity Employers—Right?" The Root, November 22, 2012, http://www.theroot.com/articles/culture/2012/11/does_race_matter_when_youre_applying_for_a_job.html.

Chapter 7: Hold 'Em or Fold 'Em?

1. Vivek Wadhwa, "Love of Learning Is the Key to Success in the Jobless Future," *Washington Post*, July 27, 2015, www.washingtonpost.com/news/innovations/wp/2015/07/27/a-love-of-learning-will-guarantee-todays-students-succeed-in-the-jobless-future.

Chapter 8: Lifelong Learning, Lifelong Earning

1. Jonathan Liss, "Laureate Education to Go Private in Management-Led Buyout," Seeking Alpha, January 29, 2007, http://seekingalpha.com/article/25370-laureate-education-to-go-private-in-management-led-buyout.

2. Chase Peterson-Withorn, "How Today's Student Loan Debt Is Failing Future Generations," *Forbes*, July 30, 2014, www.forbes.com/sites/chasewithorn/2014/07/30/how-todays-student-loan-debt-is-failing-future-generations.

3. Matthew Reed and Debbie Cochrane, *Student Debt and the Class of 2013* (Oakland, CA: Project on Student Debt, Institute for College Access & Success, November 2014), http://ticas.org/sites/default/files/legacy/fckfiles/pub/classof2013.pdf.

4. Kai Wright, "Young, Black and Buried in Debt: How For-Profit Colleges Prey on African-American Ambition," *Salon*, June 9, 2013, www.salon.com/2013/06/09/young_black_and_buried_in_debt_how_for_profit_colleges_prey_on_african_american_ambition.

5. Kai Wright, "Young, black and buried in debt: How for-profit colleges prey on African-American ambition," *Salon*, June 9, 2013, http://www.salon.com/2013/06/09/young_black_and_buried_in_debt_how_for_profit_colleges_prey_on_african_american_ambition/.

6. Patrick N. Foster, "Lessons from History: Industrial Arts/Technology Education as a Case," *Journal of Vocational and Technical Education* 13, no. 2 (Spring 1997), http://files.eric.ed.gov/fulltext/EJ543959.pdf.

7. Maria Konnikova, "Will MOOCs Be Flukes?," *New Yorker*, November 7, 2014, www.newyorker.com/science/maria-konnikova/moocs-failure-solutions.

Chapter 9: Money and Morality

1. Chris MacDonald, "Wall Street (1987)—'Greed Is Good,'" *Business Ethics Blog*, October 12, 2010, http://businessethicsblog.com/2010/10/12/wall-street-1987-greed-is-good.
2. Seth Godin, "But Not People Like You," Seth Godin's Blog, November 2, 2014, http://sethgodin.typepad.com/seths_blog/2014/11/but-not-people-like-you.html.
3. "Enron Fast Facts," CNN Library, last modified April 26, 2015, www.cnn.com /2013/07/02/us/enron-fast-facts.
4. Associated Press, "10 Years Later: What Happened to the Former Employees of Enron?," *Business Insider*, December 1, 2011, www.businessinsider.com/10-years-later-what-happened-to-the-former-employees-of-enron-2011-12.
5. Atsushi Nakayama, "Lessons from the Enron Scandal," Markkula Center for Applied Ethics, Santa Clara University, accessed February 19, 2015, www.scu.edu/ethics/publications/ethicalperspectives/enronlessons.html.

Chapter 10: Retirement, Remixed

1. Stacey Patton, "'Suicide Is My Retirement Plan,'" Vitae, November 25, 2014, https://chroniclevitae.com/news/818-suicide-is-my-retirement-plan.
2. Steven Rattner, "Inequality, Unbelievably, Gets Worse," *New York Times*, November 16, 2014, www.nytimes.com/2014/11/17/opinion/inequality-unbelievably -gets-worse.html?_r=0.
3. Robert Merton, "The Crisis in Retirement Planning," *Harvard Business Review*, July/August 2014, https://hbr.org/2014/07/the-crisis-in-retirement-planning.

Index

About the Author

Farai has combined media, technology, and socio-political analysis during her twenty-five-year career as an award-winning author, journalist, professor, and lecturer. She is a Distinguished Writer in Residence at New York University's Arthur L. Carter Journalism Institute. She was previously a spring 2012 fellow at Harvard's Institute of Politics. A regular contributor to FiveThirtyEight, the data and politics outlet founded by Nate Silver, she appears frequently on cable television and public radio, speaking about current affairs, race, and culture.

She was born and raised in Baltimore, Maryland, and graduated with a BA from Harvard University magna cum laude in 1990. Find out more at Farai.com.